INTERSECTIONS OF IDENTITY AND SEXUAL VIOLENCE ON CAMPUS

INTERSECTIONS OF IDENTITY AND SEXUAL VIOLENCE ON CAMPUS

Centering Minoritized Students' Experiences

EDITED BY

Jessica C. Harris and Chris Linder

FOREWORD BY

Wagatwe Wanjuki

STERLING, VIRGINIA

Published by Stylus Publishing, LLC.
22883 Quicksilver Drive
Sterling, Virginia 20166-2102

Library of Congress Cataloging-in-Publication Data
Names: Harris, Jessica C., editor. |
Linder, Chris, 1976- editor.
Title: Intersections of identity and sexual violence on campus :
centering minoritized students experiences /
edited by Jessica C. Harris and Chris Linder.
Description: First edition. |
Sterling, Virginia : Stylus Publishing, [2017] |
Includes bibliographical references and index.
Identifiers: LCCN 2016024650 (print) |
LCCN 2016042670 (ebook) |
ISBN 9781620363874 (cloth : acid free paper) |
ISBN 9781620363881 (pbk. : acid free paper) |
ISBN 9781620363898 (library networkable e-edition) |
ISBN 9781620363904 (consumer e-edition)
Subjects: LCSH: Rape in universities and colleges--United States. |
Rape in universities and colleges--United States--Prevention. |
Sexual minorities--Crimes against--United States. |
Minority college students--Crimes against--United States. |
Women college students--Crimes against--United States. |
College students with disabilities--Crimes against--United States. |
Classification: LCC LB2345.3.R37 I67 2017 (print) |
LCC LB2345.3.R37 (ebook) |
DDC 371.7/82--dc23
LC record available at https://lccn.loc.gov/2016024650

13-digit ISBN: 978-1-62036-387-4 (cloth)
13-digit ISBN: 978-1-62036-388-1 (paperback)
13-digit ISBN: 978-1-62036-389-8 (library networkable e-edition)
13-digit ISBN: 978-1-62036-390-4 (consumer e-edition)

Printed in the United States of America

All first editions printed on acid-free paper
that meets the American National Standards Institute
Z39-48 Standard.

Bulk Purchases

Quantity discounts are available for use in workshops and for
staff development.
Call 1-800-232-0223

First Edition, 2017

CONTENTS

FOREWORD

On the morning of Monday, August 8, 2016, I made one of the riskiest decisions in my professional career to date: I climbed to my friends' Philadelphia rooftop, doused my 12-year-old Tufts University sweatshirt in lighter fluid, and lit it on fire as people from across the country watched on Facebook Live. During the live broadcast, I explained the changing relationship I had with the worn-in sweatshirt. Wearing it was a symbol of pride for me; I bought it the second semester of my senior year of high school in celebration of my acceptance into Tufts. I loved wearing the sweatshirt because it meant I was finally part of the community I desperately wanted to join after learning about Tufts' self-declared values of human rights and active citizenship. Unfortunately, three years after my acceptance into Tufts I learned that the school wasn't willing to walk the walk with their espoused values when I reported that another student raped and assaulted me. Instead of providing assistance after I mustered the courage to report the sexual, physical, and emotional violence I endured, the school refused to help me. One year after I reported it, I was expelled from Tufts.

This burning was clearly overdue.

As the sweatshirt went up in flames, I looked into my cell phone's camera and spoke directly to the administrators at Tufts:

> I am tired of your pretending that I don't exist and I am now demanding an apology for your institutional apathy and betrayal. If the university stays silent and refuses to apologize, I will continue to burn different items until I run out of items to burn.

Unsurprisingly, Tufts (and Harvard University, the other target of the campaign) has remained silent despite widespread media coverage. As I write this foreword three weeks after I lit my Tufts sweatshirt on fire, I am preparing for another burning: a pile of bills for my private student loans that I was unable to pay back after my expulsion from Tufts.

I share this narrative because reading *Intersections of Identity and Sexual Violence on Campus* made me realize that it is high time that we activists stop doing business as usual. The decisions to burn Tufts items, to demand an apology, and to create a new antirape organization were all started after

I read, and was inspired by, the contents of this book. The book chapters that follow offer the validation that the most minoritized survivor-activists in the movement have sought, but didn't know they could receive. Many of us, survivor-activists, were attracted to the idea of the law being on our side for once, but a depressing reality quickly set in: The avenues to justice that we were promised failed to give us the solutions we so sorely needed. I went through this emotional rollercoaster myself as I slowly realized that my Blackness is a barrier to the justice I long heralded. When I first spoke publicly about my experience at Tufts in 2009, I was empowered by knowing that I had the law—specifically Title IX—on my side. But that empowerment quickly faded. I soon became frustrated and disappointed when I realized that the laws—both criminal and civil—weren't made for people like me.

After my expulsion, I filed a Title IX complaint with the Department of Education in late 2009. I had to convince the department that I should have my injustice investigated. When I tried to explain over the phone with an Office of Civil Rights investigator that I didn't file my complaint immediately because I didn't even know I had rights under the law, I was quickly interrupted by the investigator—"It doesn't matter whether you knew Title IX existed or not." And that's when I knew, despite the Office of Civil Rights name, the government was not concerned with doing the right thing. It was yet another bureaucratic institution that only allegedly cared about enforcing rules—rules made by people who probably never had a student like me in mind: Black, female, first-generation American, a survivor. But even throughout my spring 2016 speaking tour, I continued to tout the use of Title IX as the main avenue for justice. I felt that it was the only option I had. To my relief, it is not.

This book shows that students, survivor-activist, and educators don't have to settle for ineffective bureaucratic methods. The chapters in this book hold the information that the campus anti-sexual violence movement needs to achieve its goals of a rape-free education. If we members of the movement truly want change, we cannot continue business as usual; in short, playing nice with powerful academic institutions and the government as they function now will not lead to the transformative change needed on our college campuses.

For far too long, student-activists (including myself) have felt the pressure to conform to the norms and expectations of the same institutions that allowed us to be raped and betrayed in the first place. When I first went public with my story as a survivor of both abuse and institutional betrayal, I was hyperconscious of the racist stereotypes that worked against me. I knew that, as a Black woman, I had the burden of fighting the stereotypes of being an angry, hypersexual, vindictive woman; in the eyes of the overwhelmingly white university administration I was virtually unrapeable. I tried my best to conform to the respectability politics that police the behaviors of survivors and Black women in hopes that the people in charge will believe us. But I will no longer do that; I now know that there are paths to justice and safer campuses outside the dominant narrative of legislating our way to equity. As noted by Palacios and Aguilar in chapter 10 of this book, institutions must offer empowerment-based practices to create a campus community that is adequately equipped and prepared to prevent and respond to gender-based violence. Using laws to proverbially twist the arm of reluctant universities to change bits of their sexual misconduct policies will not result in meaningful or tangible change. Administrators must commit to do the work of properly understanding gender-based violence alongside understanding power, privilege, and domination. While I still work with well-known antirape organizations such as Know Your IX and SurvJustice, which focus on campus sexual violence, I know that the foci of these organizations cannot be the be-all and end-all solution. The work of these organizations must be complemented by efforts that actively operate from the idea that we can live in a world free of sexual violence, and that starts by centering the needs of the most minoritized survivors.

As I read *Intersections of Identity and Sexual Violence on Campus,* I couldn't help but think about the Tufts administrators I turned to after I was raped. My heart ached as I thought how different my experience on campus would have been had they read and absorbed even a fraction of the content in this book. Academic administrators have an incredible amount of control over the life paths of their students. This book provides much-needed insight and solutions for any administrator who interacts with survivors and offers a blueprint for how to compassionately and properly support survivors with intersecting and minoritized identities. Once administrators stop addressing sexual violence as yet another item on a checklist for compliance and start approaching sexual violence with a genuine desire to do the right thing, we will be able to take unprecedented strides in reducing campus sexual violence.

I am amazed and humbled by the opportunity to introduce the contents of this book. It may sound like hyperbole when I say, "It changed my life," but I honestly cannot think of a better way to describe its impact on my belief in organizing to eradicate sexual violence—on campuses and off. As a "veteran" of the campus movement, I have gone through many waves and shifts in opinion as to why I thought Tufts' treatment was wrong. Now, I believe I have found my home. This book outlines what I've needed as a survivor during my times as a student and activist; this book should be mandatory reading for every individual who works with the issue of campus gender-based violence. Journalists, activists, and administrators alike stand to gain the knowledge needed to spur the transformative work of a power-conscious, history-informed, and intersectional understanding of the dynamics of sexual violence.

Wagatwe Wanjuki
Feminist writer and activist

PREFACE

Jessica C. Harris and Chris Linder

Why This Work and Why Now?

Rates of sexual violence on campus have remained steadily high over the past 60 years; the statistic that one in five women will experience sexual violence during college remains consistent (Adams-Curtis & Forbes, 2004; Black et al., 2011). In the last few years, the work of student and community activists pushed the reality of sexual violence to the forefront of issues affecting higher education. In fall 2012, an Amherst student's editorial about her negative experiences reporting sexual violence to administrators captured national attention. Almost simultaneously, students from the University of North Carolina at Chapel Hill filed a Title IX complaint with the Office of Civil Rights (OCR) challenging the ways administrators handled their sexual violence complaints (Schnoebelen, 2013). Title IX of the Education Amendments (1972) is a federal law that prohibits discrimination on the basis of sex by federally funded institutions, in this case, U.S. colleges and universities. By April 2016, 178 institutions of higher education were under investigation by the OCR for mishandling sexual violence cases (Mangan, 2016).

Student activism and the fastidious growth of schools under investigation for Title IX violations ignited a media storm that instantaneously positioned sexual violence as one of the most challenging and critical issues for educational leaders to address on college campuses. An inundation of popular press articles depicting sexual violence in higher education (including pieces in *TIME*, *Cosmopolitan*, and the *New York Times*) contributed to significant momentum on the issue. President Barack Obama's administration developed the White House Task Force to Protect Students from Sexual Assault (White House Council on Women and Girls, 2014), signaling the significance of sexual violence on campus at the federal level. In the winter of 2015 a feature-length documentary, *The Hunting Ground* (Ziering & Dick, 2015), examined the experiences of several students who were sexually assaulted while attending four-year colleges and universities. Social media made it easier for survivors to share stories, stay up-to-date on the latest issues and activism, and pressure campus administrators to take action (Linder, Myers, Riggle, & Lacy, in press). Hashtags such as #RapeCultureIsWhen,

#SurvivorPrivilege, and #TheEmptyChair produced ongoing public discussion of sexual violence in society and higher education.

Higher education leaders found themselves under intense public scrutiny for failing to keep campuses safe and supportive for students. Some institutions and organizations responded swiftly to this concern. In 2014 the University of Virginia (UVA) instituted a zero-tolerance policy for perpetrators of sexual violence on campus. The policy, however, was "unclear" in its parameters, sanctions, and goals for sexual violence at UVA (Bidwell, 2014). During the summer of 2015, a fraternity alumni group at the University of Missouri proposed to ban women from fraternity houses on weekends to avoid rape (Griffin, 2015). Professional associations, including ACPA: College Student Educators International and the National Collegiate Athletic Association, established task forces to address sexual violence on campuses. Many campus administrators formed offices, wrote and received governmental grants, and implemented climate assessments that focused explicitly on sexual violence on campus.

Into the 2016 school year, reports of sexual violence continued to increase across campuses (which may be attributed to increased activism surrounding the issue and not necessarily an increase in sexual violence). Administrators, policymakers, and the general public acknowledged that "sexual violence on campus has reached epidemic levels" (Carey, Durney, Shepardson, & Carey, 2015, p. 678). However, many researchers and educators have not yet explored fully effective and useful strategies for addressing sexual violence on college campuses (White House Council on Women and Girls, 2014). This may be because the vast majority of this work continues to approach sexual violence from an identity-neutral and power-evasive perspective, resulting in several ineffective strategies to address and prevent sexual violence. By drawing attention to the complexities of sexual violence and addressing the intersections of sexual violence and other forms of systemic oppression, such as racism, homophobia, and transphobia, we aim to contribute to a more nuanced conversation related to sexual violence, informing better, more intentional strategies for prevention.

Identifying and addressing what is missing from higher education and societal conversations concerning sexual violence on college campuses is what brought us to this book. We believe the conversation on sexual violence must expand to include perspectives, identities, and histories that are rarely if ever explored in the discourses on sexual violence. Furthermore, this discourse must acknowledge and center power, privilege, and oppression. Failing to broaden the conversation will result in sexual violence remaining an "epidemic" (Carey et al., 2015, p. 678) on college campuses and society writ large.

What Brings Us to This Work?

I, Jessica, began to critically think about the voices that were erased, hidden, or missing from the conversation concerning sexual violence in the middle of a Title IX investigation at Occidental College, my undergraduate alma mater. While rewatching the 2013 press conference that detailed the suit filed against Occidental, I was intrigued by whom I understood, through perception and alumni connections, to be involved in the case. The majority of the students, faculty, and lawyers involved, or at least those the press decided to show, all appeared to be white cisgender women. What was unsettling about this observation was that during my four years at Occidental, I saw, heard, and felt how sexual violence affected and silenced men, women of color, and gender-nonconforming students, none of whom were seemingly portrayed in this public lawsuit. In no way do I wish to negate the narratives of the women from Occidental who appeared in the media, but I can no longer stand by as other individuals' narratives and identities are perpetually silenced. I continue to witness the exclusion of minoritized communities in the master narrative of sexual violence in higher education and am further troubled that this dominant story is often reflected in higher education literature and practice. Research on sexual violence often ignores the complexities and histories of race, gender, ability, class, and other social identities. These experiences and observations led me to believe that sexual violence on college campuses will not be eradicated if research and practice continue to gloss over a systemic analysis of the issue. We, as a field, must ground this issue in history, account for *all* identities and institutional types, and explore the influence of interlocking systems of domination in sexual violence across college campuses.

At the same time, I, Chris, began a new role as a tenure-track faculty member after having worked as the director of a campus-based women's center for seven years. I observed a shift in momentum in addressing campus sexual violence and wondered what contributed to that shift, so I organized a research team and began collecting data about the strategies of campus sexual violence activists. During this time, I noticed that activists featured most prominently in mainstream media sources attended elite colleges and universities. Further, survivors featured in the media tended to be stereotypically pretty, apparently white, cisgender, heterosexual women assaulted by men. I also noted that the media often focused on Black male athletes as perpetrators of sexual violence, despite the reality that they are not the only perpetrators of sexual violence. I believe that misrepresentation, coupled with a long history of racism in the criminal justice system and cultural beliefs that white women are more worthy of protection from sexual violence than women of color, leads to high rates of violence. As a society and as educators, we fail to understand the complexities of power, privilege, and entitlement related to sexual violence. Relying on stereotypes about race, gender, and sexual orientation allows the dominant perpetrator—an economically privileged, straight, cisgender white man—to continue to commit sexual violence because we do not see them as perpetrators.

These personal understandings informed our proposal for this edited volume. The gaps identified earlier were originally anecdotal; they stemmed from our lived experiences in education; however, as we dove into the higher education literature about sexual violence, our personal observations were confirmed: Scholars approach sexual violence from an identity-neutral, power-evasive perspective, reporting findings in an objectivist manner, resulting in the numerical majority's experiences as being uncritically centered. For instance, some authors remove responses from respondents belonging to minoritized populations, such as in the following: "Because the frequency of nonheterosexually identifying individuals in the sample was very low ($n = 3$), those individuals were removed" (Jozkowski & Peterson, 2013, p. 518). This renders many students' experiences invisible, resulting in an incomplete picture of the effectiveness of sexual violence prevention and response efforts. In this volume, we identify and begin to address several gaps in educational research that support the invisibility of minoritized populations in the discourse of sexual violence on college campuses. By centering the experiences of students relegated to the margins, we aim to provide readers with a more nuanced understanding of sexual violence on college campuses.

References

Adams-Curtis, L. E., & Forbes, G. B. (2004). College women's experiences of sexual coercion: A review of cultural, perpetrator, victim, and situational violence. *Trauma, Violence, & Abuse, 5*(2), 91–122.

Bidwell, A. (2014, November 25). UVA board supports zero tolerance sexual assault policy. *U.S. News & World Report.* Retrieved from www.usnews.com/news/articles/2014/11/25/university-of-virginia-board-commits-to-zero-tolerance-policy-on-sexual-assault

Black, M. C., Basile, K. C., Breiding, M. J., Smith, S. G., Walters, M. L., Merrick, M. T., . . . Stevens, M. R. (2011). *The National Intimate Partner and Sexual Violence Survey.* Retrieved from www.cdc.gov/violenceprevention/pdf/nisvs_executive_summary-a.pdf

Carey, K. B., Durney, S. E., Shepardson, R. L., & Carey, M. P. (2015). Incapacitated and forcible rape of college women: Prevalence across the first year. *Journal of Adolescent Health, 56,* 678–680.

Griffin, R. (2015). *University of Missouri considers banning women from fraternity houses during party hours.* Retrieved from www.huffingtonpost.com/2015/06/09/mizzou-frat-proposal-banning-women_n_7544100.html

Jozkowski, K. N., & Peterson, Z. D. (2013). College students and sexual consent: Unique insights. *Journal of Sex Research, 50,* 517–523.

Linder, C., Myers, J. S., Riggle, C., & Lacy, M. (in press). From margins to mainstream: Social media as a tool for campus sexual violence activism. *Journal of Diversity in Higher Education.*

Mangan, K. (2016, April 21). Lawsuit takes aim at education dept.'s Title IX guidance. *The Chronicle of Higher Education.* Retrieved from chronicle.com/article/An-Accused-Student-s-Lawsuit/236190

Schnoebelen, A. (2013, March 5). Push to improve campus policies on sexual violence gains momentum. *The Chronicle of Higher Education.* Retrieved from chronicle.com/article/Push-to-Improve-Campus/137689

Title IX of the Education Amendments, 20 U.S.C. §1681 et seq. (1972).

White House Council on Women and Girls. (2014). *Rape and sexual assault: A renewed call to action.* Retrieved from iaclea.org/visitors/about/documents/WhiteHouseCouncil_sexual_assault_report_1-21-14.pdf

Ziering, A. (Producer), & Dick, K. (Director). (2015). *The hunting ground.* United States: Weinstein Company.

INTRODUCTION

Jessica C. Harris and Chris Linder

In this introduction we explore how previous and current researchers often approach sexual violence on college campuses in identity-neutral, power-evasive, and ahistoric manners. This approach often results in ineffective strategies to address and prevent sexual violence. Furthermore, a lack of focus on identities, power and domination, and history (re)constructs and maintains systems of domination that lead to violence. To contextualize this book, we examined literature about campus sexual violence in the United States and exposed large gaps in research and practice, specifically related to historically minoritized students. Our search criteria included articles focusing on college students, sexual violence, and U.S. institutions of higher education. In our search for literature, we included peer-reviewed articles published after 2000, although we included a few articles prior to 2000 if they were frequently referred to in the later literature. In reviewing approximately 100 articles, we identified five major themes related to sexual violence on college campuses: prevention, alcohol, gender, minimizing and reporting sexual violence, and policy. Although scholars' focus on one or several of these five major themes is relevant, this often unilateral research does not provide a complete picture of the problem of sexual violence on college campuses.

In an attempt to explore exactly how existing literature obscures the nuances of sexual violence on college campuses, we synthesized the themes of prevention, alcohol, gender, minimizing and reporting sexual violence, and policy and explore them in more depth in this introduction. We conclude by detailing how each subsequent chapter in this book fills gaps in the knowledge base and builds a foundation for systemic understanding of sexual violence on college campuses.

Prevention

Sexual violence prevention pervades research about sexual violence on college campuses. Research on sexual violence prevention can be explored under four major categories: bystander intervention (Exner & Cummings, 2011; S. McMahon, Postmus, & Koenick, 2011), risk reduction (Brecklin, 2004;

A. Turchik, Probst, Chau, Nigoff, & Gidycz, 2007), evaluation of prevention and social norming programs (Katz & DuBois, 2013; Stein, 2007), and rape myth acceptance (Hayes, Abbott, & Cook, 2016).

Bystander Intervention

Bystander intervention programs rely on community norms and practices to interrupt a climate that allows sexual violence to thrive (Banyard, Plante, & Moynihan, 2004). For example, some research describes programs designed to train men to intervene in situations where they observe signs of potential sexual violence (Barone, Wolgemuth, & Linder, 2007). Scholars believe assessing community readiness for change and encouraging prosocial bystander behavior may contribute to a decrease in sexual violence in specific communities, including college campuses (Banyard et al., 2004). Bystander intervention studies (see S. McMahon et al., 2011; S. McMahon et al., 2014) often use the Bystander Attitude Scale or the Bystander Behavior Scale that are frequently paired with the Rape Myth Acceptance Scale to determine whether bystander programs have an impact on participants' understanding of rape myths (Bannon, Brosi, & Foubert, 2013). Findings suggest that prevention programs result in decreased rape myth acceptance scores and increased bystander attitudes and behavior scores immediately after the prevention program (Bannon et al., 2013; S. McMahon et al., 2011; Potter, 2012). However, no research on bystander intervention has resulted in an actual decrease in the number of sexual assaults that occur on a college campus (Adams-Curtis & Forbes, 2004).

Risk Reduction

The literature on risk reduction explored characteristics that made people more susceptible to sexual violence as a method for attempting to protect people from sexual violence. Several studies explored the predictive factors associated with women's experiences of sexual violence (Brecklin, 2004; Hertzog & Yeilding, 2009; Kalof, 2000; A. Turchik et al., 2007); no studies explored predictive factors associated with men's or trans* students' experiences with sexual violence. First-year women students report higher occurrences of sexual violence than other women students (Gross, Winslett, Roberts, & Gohm, 2006). Additionally, prior victimization (Gidycz, Orchowski, King, & Rich, 2008) and childhood sexual violence (Brecklin, 2004; Walsh, Blaustein, Knight, Spinazzola, & van der Kolk, 2007) are the most common predictors of sexual violence for women in college. One study indicated that women were most susceptible to sexual violence after having experienced an act of sexual violence (Daigle, Fisher, & Cullen, 2008). Some scholars argue for the use of self-defense (Brecklin, 2004) and confidence and self-advocacy training (A. Turchik et al., 2007) for college women with prior victimization because these characteristics are correlated with increased use of verbal and physical resistance strategies (A. Turchik et al., 2007).

Much of the literature in the risk reduction category contributes to victim blaming, as highlighted by a study exploring "sexual victimization and health-risk behaviors" (Gidycz et al., 2008, p. 744). In some studies, the very framing of the questions contributes significantly to victim blaming, even in research designed to address sexual violence from a risk reduction perspective (e.g., Kalof, 2000). For example, Hertzog and Yeilding's (2009) Risk Behavior Scale includes items such as "I consume alcohol beverages on the first date" and "I leave my drink unattended at a social gathering to go dance or use the restroom" (p. 68). Authors also reinforced the idea that women who chose to engage in sexual intercourse at a young age were more likely to experience sexual victimization later in life (Gidycz et al., 2008).

Evaluation of Prevention and Social Norming Programs

Scholars frequently publish evaluations of individual prevention programs on college campuses immediately after a program takes place. These assessments often use convenience samples with no control group, resulting in little comprehensive information about the effectiveness or longevity of the effects of onetime programming (e.g., Potter, 2012; Rothman & Silverman, 2007). Evaluations of prevention and social norming programs generally demonstrate an immediate reduction in rape myth acceptance scores and an increase in bystander attitudes and efficacy scores, but little else (Kress et al., 2006; Potter, Moynihan, Stapleton, & Banyard, 2009). Some programs even resulted in no change in rape myth acceptance scores and an increase in harmful beliefs related to consent (Milhausen, McBride, & Jun, 2006). Finally, faculty are beginning to integrate information on sexual violence in their courses, often resulting in a change in rape myth acceptance scores and a self-reported deeper understanding of sexual violence (Franiuk, 2007; Katz & DuBouis, 2013).

Rape Myth Acceptance

The Rape Myth Acceptance Scale was developed in 1980 (Burt, 1980) and updated by Payne, Lonsway, and Fitzgerald (1999). High rape myth acceptance scores have been linked with increased propensity to commit sexual violence among college men (Truman, Tokar, & Fisher, 1996). The majority of studies examining sexual violence prevention on college campuses use one of the Rape Myth Acceptance Scales as a measure of change and a measure of students' understanding of sexual violence on campuses (Yeater & O'Donohue, 1999). Research consistently indicates male students have a higher rape myth acceptance than female students (S. McMahon, 2010). Additionally, males involved in all-male groups such as fraternities and athletic teams have higher rape myth acceptance scores than males not involved in these organizations (S. McMahon, 2010). Scholars debate whether this is correlation or causation: Do men who already subscribe to rape myths participate in these organizations, or do these organizations perpetuate rape myth acceptance? (Murnen & Kohlman, 2007). The Rape Myth Acceptance Scales perpetuate the problem of addressing sexual violence from an individual rather than a societal perspective. By focusing on ways individuals accept or do not accept rape myths, educators and scholars fail to examine larger societal and cultural values contributing to the overwhelming acceptance of rape myths (Hayes et al., 2016).

Alcohol

After prevention, alcohol and sexual violence garnered the most attention from higher education researchers and scholars (Abbey, Ross, McDuffie, & McAuslan, 1996; Benson, Gohm, & Gross, 2007; Davis et al., 2012; Harrington & Leitenberg, 1994; Lawyer, Resnick, Bakanic, Burkett, & Kilpatrick, 2010). According to college sexual violence studies focusing on alcohol, students believe alcohol disinhibits sexual behavior and increases sexual risk-taking (Pumphrey-Gordon & Gross, 2007). Alcohol consumption also places one at a higher risk of sexual victimization (Abbey, 2002; Benson et al., 2007; Krebs, Lindquist, Warner, Fisher, & Martin, 2009; Mouilso, Fischer, & Calhoun, 2012; Novik, Howard, & Boekeloo, 2011) and intensifies dangerous behavior among male college students, specifically sexual aggression (Abbey, 2002; Abbey & McAuslan, 2004; Tuliao & McChargue, 2014). Furthermore, women students who consume alcohol at high levels "experienced more severe victimization" (Benson et al., 2007, p. 349). For instance, when compared to attempted rape, completed rapes are more likely to involve the consumption of alcohol (Abbey, Clinton, McAuslan, Zawacki, & Buck, 2002; Harrington & Leitenberg, 1994).

When alcohol is consumed prior to sexual violence, victim blaming and rape myth ideologies are often employed (Armstrong, Hamilton, & Sweeney, 2006; Cowley, 2014; Harned, 2005; Untied, Orchowski, Mastroleo, & Gidycz, 2012). When a victim of sexual violence is under the influence of alcohol, and the perpetrator is sober, students are more likely to assign responsibility for the violence to the victim and not the perpetrator (Untied et al., 2012). Furthermore, victims are less likely to report their assault when alcohol was involved in the encounter (Fisher, Daigle, Cullen, & Turner, 2003; Sabina & Ho, 2014; Sudderth, Leisring, & Bronson, 2010).

Students who have experienced sexual violence also use alcohol as a coping mechanism (Gilmore, Stappenbeck, Lewis, Granato, & Kaysen, 2015; Snipes, Green, Javier, Perrin, & Benotsch, 2014; Stappenbeck, Hassija, Zimmerman, & Kaysen, 2015). In other words, heavy drinking increases one's risk of sexual violence on college campuses, and sexual violence leads to heavy drinking. Although a high volume of scholarship is dedicated to alcohol and sexual violence on the college campus, this research not only negates systems of oppression that influence sexual violence but also masks and maintains these systems. Researchers and educators have placed a heavy focus on addressing alcohol consumption rather than power, privilege, and domination. While alcohol, an individual and microlevel issue that at most is a surface influence of sexual violence, gains increased attention and awareness, systems of domination continue as usual on the college campus.

Gender

Gender is a highly complex piece of the research related to sexual violence. Although the vast majority of research includes demographic information related to gender, few studies address the power associated with gender through sexism and genderism (assuming that gender is only binary and that every person identifies as either a man or a woman). Virtually no research explored the experiences of trans* students with sexual violence, and because the majority of research is conducted using quantitative methodology, most studies did not include an option for participants to identify as a gender other than woman or man. Further, although the terms *woman* and *man* (gender identity) have different meanings from *female* and *male* (sex), most scholars did not define how they were using the terms. In this literature review, we use the terms employed by researchers in their studies, most frequently male and female.

Male Students

While research is inconclusive and often competing, some scholars have found that more than 26% of college males will perpetrate at least one act of sexual violence during college (Abbey & McAuslan, 2004; Abbey, McAuslan, & Ross, 1998). Several variables and characteristics predict male students' likeliness for committing assault. Male students are more likely to engage in sexual aggression if they believe in traditional gender roles and hold hostile or rape-supportive attitudes toward women (Abbey et al., 1998; Abbey & McAuslan, 2004; Bouffard, 2010; Burgess, 2007); consume alcohol in sexual situations (Abbey, 2002; Abbey & McAuslan, 2004; Tuliao & McChargue, 2014); engage in risky behavior, such as high-risk drinking and drug use; have antisocial traits; or have experienced childhood adversity (Zinzow & Thompson, 2015a). Male students who have a history of sexual aggression are also more likely to engage in forced sexual acts in college than those who have no such history (Jackson, Gilliland, & Veneziano, 2006; Zinzow & Thompson, 2015b). Finally, higher rates of sexual violence perpetration have been linked to male students' membership in a fraternity or on an athletic team (Franklin, Bouffard, & Pratt, 2012; Humphrey & Kahn, 2000; Murnen & Kohlman, 2007). Some scholars argue it is likely the patriarchal systems and beliefs that are fostered and maintained in athletics and fraternities that contribute to a culture of sexual violence rather than the predisposition of males who belong to these groups (Jackson et al., 2006).

Although a plethora of research examines male students as perpetrators of sexual violence, minimal research has focused on male students as survivors of sexual violence. The small amount of extant literature that centers on sexual violence for male students focuses on the negative outcomes of violence. For instance, several scholars have linked sexual victimization to increased alcohol and drug use, sexual risk-taking, and inhibited sexual functioning for male college students (Larimer, Lydum, Anderson, & Turner, 1999; Palmer, McMahon, Rounsaville, & Ball, 2010; J. A. Turchik, 2012). The focus on negative outcomes and on male students as perpetrators leaves the field severely underinformed about male students as survivors of sexual violence.

Female Students

While the majority of literature on male students and sexual violence focuses on these students as perpetrators, the majority of literature on female students and sexual violence focuses on these students as victims. This focus may be because an alarmingly high percentage (reports range from 20% to 30%) of female students report experiencing some form of sexual violence during college (Gross et al., 2006; Krebs et al., 2009; Lawyer et al., 2010). Female students assaulted in childhood are more likely to encounter sexual violence in college (Brecklin, 2004; Walsh et al., 2007) and have lower college grade point averages than females who were not assaulted prior to college (Jordan, Combs, & Smith, 2014). Female students who are assaulted during college may experience a decline in their academic performance (Benson et al., 2007; Jordan et al., 2014).

Few scholars address issues concerning women of color and sexual violence; moreover, the little that is known is inconclusive. For instance, one study found that African American female students (36%) report experiences with sexual violence at higher rates than white female students (26.3%; Gross et al., 2006). Another study found that 13.7% of female students who attended a predominantly white institution and 9.7% of female students attending a historically Black college or university reported experiences with sexual violence (Krebs, Lindquest, & Barrick, 2011). Although these results are inconclusive, they suggest that Black women students' experience with sexual violence differs from that of white women students. Racism, sexism, stereotypes, and other social injustices also lead Black women to respond differently than their white peers to being sexually violated (Henry, 2009; Littleton & Dodd, 2016). Moreover, sexual violence often results in post-traumatic stress disorder, depressive symptoms (Lindquist et al., 2013), and other psychological issues (Henry, 2009) for Black women. Finally, the literature, or lack thereof, also points to the dearth of knowledge concerning sexual violence for women of color who do not identify as (only) Black.

Gender Differences

A handful of studies have reinforced the gender binary by focusing on differences and similarities between men and women students and their differing perceptions of and experiences with sexual violence. One such theme in this literature is the matter of consent to sex, which "is a highly gendered issue" (Jozkowski, Sanders, Peterson, Dennis, & Reece, 2014, p. 446). For example, women tend to be more passive when giving consent, whereas men often use consent tactics that border on pressuring, aggression, or deception (Jozkowski & Peterson, 2013, 2014; Jozkowski, Peterson, Sanders, Dennis, & Reece, 2014; Jozkowski, Sanders et al., 2014). These methods of consent follow traditional gender roles that construct men as initiators of sex and women as passive receivers of sex (Jozkowski, Peterson et al., 2014; Jozkowski, Sanders et al., 2014). Another theme in the literature comparing male and female college students focuses on rape myths and victim blaming. College females reject victim-blaming rape myths at a higher rate than college males (Bannon et al., 2013; White & Kurpius, 2002), whereas college males place the blame on male victims more than female victims (White & Kurpius, 2002).

Female students are more willing than college males to intervene in potential situations that could lead to sexual violence (Bannon et al., 2013). College women also believe that significant barriers exist on campus for men to seek help or report sexual violence, whereas men do not report as high a perception of these barriers (Allen, Ridgeway, & Swan, 2015). Reasons for not reporting also differ by gender (Sable, Danis, Mauzy, & Gallagher, 2006). Males may be hesitant to report because they are afraid their masculinity will be questioned, and females may be hesitant to report for fear of retaliation from the perpetrator (Sable et al., 2006).

Minimizing and Reporting Sexual Violence

College students underreport their experiences with sexual violence (Fisher et al., 2003). Men are less likely than women to report or seek support after unwanted sexual encounters (Banyard et al., 2007), and the majority of college women who are sexually assaulted fail to acknowledge or report the incident (Cleere & Lynn, 2013; Orchowski, Untied, & Gidycz, 2013). Women students who do not acknowledge their sexual assaults often blame themselves or minimize the situations because their experiences do not align with a traditional rape script or rape myth (Cleere & Lynn, 2013; Edwards et al., 2014; Orchowski et al., 2013; A. Turchik, Probst, Irvin, Chau, & Gidycz, 2009). For instance, women who were sexually assaulted by an acquaintance are more likely to minimize their sexual assault than those assaulted by a stranger (Cleere & Lynn, 2013; Kahn, Jackson, Kully, Badger, & Halvorsen, 2003; Orchowski et al., 2013; Sabina & Ho, 2014) and are less likely to report these interactions (Orchowski & Gidycz, 2013). Research suggests that these rape scripts are further nuanced by the intersection of race and gender, as Black women believe victims of sexual violence respond to this violation with self-blame, but white students believe victims respond with feelings of isolation (Littleton & Dodd, 2016).

Similarly, students are more likely to report sexual violence when the perpetrator is a stranger or of a different race (Fisher et al., 2003). Women also report that boyfriends and friends are more likely to perpetrate sexual violence, resulting in a low number of reported sexual assaults (Gross et al., 2006). Precollege factors such as prior victimization (Sabina & Ho, 2014; Sudderth et al., 2010) and college factors such as living on campus and being a junior or senior (Sudderth et al., 2010) increase the likelihood that students will report their experiences with sexual violence. Students are more likely to report their assault to a friend (Orchowski, Meyer, & Gidycz, 2009) or on a survey (Orchowski et al., 2009) than they are to tell a campus official. Unfortunately, and not surprisingly given the OCR's growing list, college and university administrators underreport the number of crimes committed on their campuses (Yung, 2015).

Policy

Several federal laws provide guidance and requirements related to sexual violence policy on campus. Specifically, Title IX, the Clery Act, and Campus SaVE attempt to provide federal guidelines for addressing sexual violence on campus (Cantalupo, 2009; Duncan, 2014), although these laws largely function from a response rather than a prevention approach (Silbaugh, 2015).

While lawmakers and some advocates claim that responding to sexual violence effectively will result in lower numbers of sexual violence overall, this has yet to occur. Most campuses spend exorbitantly more resources responding to sexual violence after it happens rather than attempting to change the climate in which it happens (Silbaugh, 2015).

Scholarship on campus policy related to sexual violence frequently focuses on the confusion campus administrators feel related to effectively integrating requirements of each of these federal laws (Cantalupo, 2009; Koss, Wilgus, & Williamsen 2014; Yung, 2015). The U.S. Department of Education issued the Dear Colleague letter in 2011. The letter reminded higher education institutions receiving federal funds of their responsibility to comply with Title IX, which attempts to address and prohibit sexual harassment and sex discrimination. To attempt to provide additional guidance for colleges and universities struggling to adhere to Title IX, the National Institute for Justice provided a model policy for the prevention of and response to sexual violence (P. P. McMahon, 2008). However, administrators continue to express frustration at attempting to understand and comply with multiple and competing federal guidelines. For example, the standard of evidence to be used for campus judicial processes remains unclear. Some campuses use a "preponderance of evidence" standard as recommended by the Department of Education; however, other campuses use a more criminal-like standard for their proceedings (Duncan, 2014). Although Title IX has been in existence since 1972, it has strictly been employed to address sexual harassment and violence only recently. Finally, although sexual violence advocates have historically opposed mediation and restorative justice as a mechanism for addressing sexual violence on campus, some scholars argue that restorative justice is not a form of mediation and should be considered as a potential tool for addressing sexual violence on campus (Koss et al., 2014).

The Danger of a Single Narrative

The literature mentioned here creates a narrow story about sexual violence on college campuses. In its simplest form, according to the story, sexual violence occurs when a male student assaults a female student. Alcohol is most likely a factor in the violence, influencing the victim's minimization of and failure to report the act. The story renders invisible three very important and necessary factors in addressing and redressing sexual violence on college campuses: identity, history, and an acknowledgment of power and interlocking systems of domination.

First, in regard to identity, as it stands, white, straight cisgender women are raped by straight cisgender men. What about trans* and male survivors;

lesbian, gay, bisexual, and queer survivors; survivors with disabilities; survivors of color; and perpetrators who are not straight cisgender men? These populations often experience sexual violence at higher rates than nonmarginalized populations (Edwards et al., 2015; Gross et al., 2006), yet they are continually ignored and silenced.

Second, the current research approaches sexual violence on college campuses from an ahistoric lens that negates the reality that sexual violence continues to be used as a tool to confer power and privilege on white men, while subordinating and terrorizing, mentally and physically, minoritized populations (Smith, 2005). Ahistoricism also contributes to a restrictive view of equality (Crenshaw, 1988), which focuses on equality as a process and not an outcome. This allows educators to implement one catchall policy that addresses sexual violence on college campuses, but in actuality only caters to the needs of one dominant population or one identity. These catchall policies not only negate students' intersectional identities and multiple systems of domination but also obscure how a history colinization, terrorization, and domination continue to influence sexual violence in higher education. Third, current literature lacks a critique of the role power, privilege, and dominance play in sexual violence. Power, privilege, and dominance influence sexual violence, not alcohol, fraternity affiliation, or being an athlete.

An identity-neutral, power-evasive, ahistoric perspective informs higher education research and practice, resulting in a narrow view and surface-level approach to addressing sexual violence on college campuses. For instance, the proposal to ban women from fraternity houses at the University of Missouri negates the root causes of sexual violence. This policy places the responsibility to avoid rape on women students; if they stay out of specific spaces they will be safe from sexual violence. Yet by placing the onus on women and not the privileged and dominating environments of fraternities, this policy overlooks the history and embeddedness of patriarchy, power, and male privilege that contribute to sexual violence in this particular setting. In negating the complexities of identity, sociohistorical factors, and power and privilege, scholars and educators remain limited in their understandings of sexual violence, survivors' needs, and prevention and practices that systemically address and eliminate sexual violence on campus.

Overview of This Book

In this book, we place sexual violence in a historical context and highlight the influence of racism, classism, homophobia, transphobia, and other forms of oppression in current sexual violence prevention and response strategies.

Readers are exposed to the complexities of sexual violence on college campuses to gain a better understanding of how this act of dominance and control has an impact on all students, institutions, scholars, and practitioners. This critical approach focuses on the power, privilege, and oppression implicit in sexual violence, allowing a more systemic understanding and deconstruction of the issues across college campuses. Through this book, we encourage readers to move from theoretical understandings to action steps that are inclusive of multiple student populations and identities. Ultimately, this book is not and cannot be all things to all people. We aim to fill a small gap in a wide chasm in the sexual violence literature. This book is a necessary beginning, a foundation for others to build future research and practice that critically addresses the complexities of sexual violence.

In the first part of the book, we take a historical approach to sexual violence on college campuses. Although the issue has come to the forefront of higher education and society in the last few years, sexual violence has always been a prevalent, yet often unaddressed, issue on college campuses. Therefore, to understand sexual violence on today's college campuses, the act and issue must be grounded in history.

In Chapter 1 Luoluo Hong reviews historical legislation and policy related to sexual violence on college campuses and highlights four unsupported dominant narratives perpetuated by sexual violence policy and legislation. Hong concludes her chapter by providing a social justice framework that challenges educators and administrators to move away from traditional frameworks for addressing sexual violence and move toward employing power-conscious strategies for addressing this issue on contemporary college campuses.

Reaching farther into history, Jessica C. Harris in Chapter 2 uses a critical race theory and critical race feminism perspective to root out the white supremacist and patriarchal systems embedded in the colonial history of the United States and the colonial college system. She explores the historical implications and lasting impacts of colonization, terrorism, and dominance over women of color's bodies in society and the way this continues to inform sexual violence on college campuses today.

In Chapter 3 Chris Linder also reaches deep into the history of the United States to provide a context of the current state of sexual violence on college campuses. Although many scholars and activists credit feminist consciousness-raising groups of the 1970s as the beginning of the sexual violence movement in the United States, Linder argues that the 1970s were a continuation of a century of sexual violence organizing by Black women. However, Black women's history is consistently ignored by mainstream white feminists in sexual violence organizing. Linder concludes by examining what the history of silence within activism means for today's campus activist.

The second part of this volume moves from a historical perspective to a contemporary perspective. Specifically, the chapters in this section address the intersections of multiple forms of systemic oppression, including racism, homophobia, transphobia, and ableism, that have an impact on student survivors of sexual violence on college campuses. Each chapter centers the realities of gender-based violence outside the traditional paradigm (cisgender white women at predominantly white institutions) often featured in the media and higher education research and practice.

In Chapter 4, Susan B. Marine examines the ways trans* survivors of college sexual violence are ignored through campus-based prevention and response services. She discusses the ways health care and counseling services have historically failed trans* survivors and provides recommendations for more compassionate skilled care for trans* survivors of sexual violence on college campuses. Marine also discusses the resilience of trans* survivors of sexual violence.

Through interviews with cisgender and transgender men who survived sexual violence in college, Daniel Tillapaugh in Chapter 5 sheds light on the ways current response and prevention programs ignore or minimize men survivors of sexual violence. Tillapaugh presents the stories of four men survivors of sexual violence and the common themes in their stories, including negotiating fear and shame, problematizing sexual violence responses on campus, and examining masculinity and sexual violence.

Chapter 6 builds on Chapter 2 and explores the contemporary experiences of women of color and sexual violence on college campuses. Ciera V. Scott, Anneliese A. Singh, and Jessica C. Harris describe common challenges students who are women of color experience on college campuses, including racism and sexism, as barriers to reporting and healing from sexual violence. The contributors approach this chapter from a psychological standpoint, focusing on the ways women of color college students resist and are resilient to multiple oppressions and nurture their own liberation and healing.

LaVerne McQuiller Williams adds to this book by reviewing the very limited literature that concerns sexual victimization among Deaf and hard-of-hearing college students in Chapter 7. She focuses specifically on the intersectionality of sexual orientation and auditory status, as well as Deaf and hard-of-hearing male victims of sexual violence. LaVerne concludes the chapter with a proposed research agenda based on existing information and provides suggestions for supporting college students who are Deaf and hard of hearing and sexually assaulted.

In Chapter 8 Jason C. Garvey, Jessi Hitchins, and Elizabeth McDonald synthesize the limited literature about queer-spectrum students' experiences with sexual violence and provide implications for research, practice, and policy related to queer-spectrum students and sexual violence on college campuses. The contributors provide an in-depth explanation of the significance of language when working with queer-spectrum students and specific examples of appropriate resources for queer-spectrum survivors on college campuses. Further, Garvey, Hitchins, and McDonald identify gaps in the research about sexual violence and offer recommendations for researchers interested in this topic.

The third part of this book presents the voices of historically minoritized populations while simultaneously calling for coalition building between these socially constructed identity groups. Informed by historical and contemporary understandings of sexual violence in higher education, this final section provides action-oriented steps and recommendations for addressing sexual violence at several institutional types and accounts for students' intersecting identities.

Chris Linder and Jess S. Myers examine the strategies of campus sexual violence activists in Chapter 9. Through an online ethnography, including interviews with 23 activists, they examine how activists negotiate power and privilege associated with social identities in their activism. Further, Linder and Myers discuss the role of social media in contemporary activism and emphasize the need for intersectional coalition building to effectively address sexual violence on college campuses.

In Chapter 10 Naddia Cherre Palacios and Karla L. Aguilar push campus administrators and policymakers to implement prevention and implementation strategies that involve best practices based on ongoing evaluations, systemic approaches, and student empowerment and leadership. In this chapter, the contributors stress the importance of empowerment-based sexual violence prevention and intervention across college campuses. This empowerment-based approach encompasses comprehensive strategies using key components, including student leadership, creativity, and passion for building healthier relationships and community across campus.

Aligning with Chapter 1, Susan V. Iverson in Chapter 11 details findings from a policy discourse analysis of sexual violence policies to uncover embedded assumptions and predominant meanings constructed through the policies. Iverson discusses how understandings of sexual violence (against women) are dominated by an overreliance on one-dimensional analyses of the problem of sexual violence. She argues that an intersectional approach can illuminate how identity differences (i.e., race, gender, sexuality), too often seen as separate spheres of experience, are systems that overlap and interlock to create complex intersections where two or more dimensions of identity converge and determine social, economic, and political dynamics of oppression.

Finally, in Chapter 12, Chris Linder and Jessica C. Harris synthesize the strategies for recommendations provided by the contributors to this volume and challenge educators, activists, and policymakers to move away from traditional approaches to sexual violence prevention and response. In this chapter, Linder and Harris advocate for historically grounded and power-conscious approaches to addressing sexual violence with the goal of eradicating, rather than simply preventing, sexual violence on college campuses. This final chapter details how the other chapters work together to generate new ideas, practices, policies, and other action steps that critique, expose, and address the systems and realities of sexual violence on college campuses.

References

Abbey, A. (2002). Alcohol-related sexual assault: A common problem among college students. *Journal of Studies on Alcohol and Drugs, 14*, 118–128.

Abbey, A., Clinton, A. M., McAuslan, P., Zawacki, T., & Buck, P. O. (2002). Alcohol-involved rapes: Are they more violent? *Psychology of Women Quarterly, 26*, 99–109.

Abbey, A., & McAuslan, P. (2004). A longitudinal examination of male college students' perceptions of sexual assault. *Journal of Counseling and Clinical Psychology, 72*, 747–756.

Abbey, A., McAuslan, P., & Ross, L. T. (1998). Sexual assault perpetration by college men: The role of alcohol, misperception of sexual intent, and sexual beliefs and experiences. *Journal of Social and Clinical Psychology, 17*, 167–195.

Abbey, A., Ross, L. T., McDuffie, D., & McAuslan, P. (1996). Alcohol and dating risk factors for sexual assault among college women. *Psychology of Women Quarterly, 20*, 147–169.

Adams-Curtis, L. E., & Forbes, G. B. (2004). College women's experiences of sexual coercion: A review of cultural, perpetrator, victim, and situational violence. *Trauma, Violence, & Abuse, 5*, 91–122.

Allen, C. T., Ridgeway, R., & Swan, S. C. (2015). College students' beliefs regarding help seeking for male and female sexual assault survivors: Even less support for male survivors. *Journal of Aggression, Maltreatment & Trauma, 24*, 103–115.

Armstrong, E. A., Hamilton, L., & Sweeney, B. (2006). Sexual assault on campus: A multilevel, integrative approach to party rape. *Social Problems, 53*, 483–499.

Bannon, R. S., Brosi, M. W., & Foubert, J. D. (2013). Sorority women's and fraternity men's rape myth acceptance and bystander intervention attitudes. *Journal of Student Affairs Research and Praxis, 50*(1), 72–87.

Banyard, V. L., Plante, E. G., & Moynihan, M. M. (2004). Bystander education: Bringing a broader community perspective to sexual violence prevention. *Journal of Community Psychology, 32*(1), 61–79.

Banyard, V. L., Ward, S., Cohn, E. S., Plante, E. G., Moorhead, C., & Walsh, W. (2007). Unwanted sexual contact on campus: A comparison of women's and men's experiences. *Violence and Victims, 22*, 52–70.

Barone, R. P., Wolgemuth, J. R., & Linder, C. (2007). Preventing sexual assault through engaging college men. *Journal of College Student Development, 48*, 585–594.

Benson, B. J., Gohm, C. L., & Gross, A. M. (2007). College women and sexual assault: The role of sex-related alcohol expectancies. *Journal of Family Violence, 22*, 341–351.

Bouffard, L. A. (2010). Exploring the utility of entitlement in understanding sexual aggression. *Journal of Criminal Justice, 38*, 870–879.

Brecklin, L. R. (2004). Self-defense/assertiveness training, women's victimization history, and psychological characteristics. *Violence Against Women, 10*, 479–497.

Burgess, H. (2007). Assessment of rape-supportive attitudes and beliefs in college men: Development, reliability, and validity of the Rape Attitudes and Beliefs Scale. *Journal of Interpersonal Violence, 22*, 973–993.

Burt, M. R. (1980). Cultural myths and supports for rape. *Journal of Personality and Social Psychology, 38*, 217–230.

Cantalupo, N. C. (2009). Campus violence: Understanding the extraordinary through the ordinary. *Journal of College and University Law, 35*, 613–690.

Cleere, C., & Lynn, S. J. (2013). Acknowledged versus unacknowledged sexual assault among college women. *Journal of Interpersonal Violence, 28*, 2593–2611.

Cowley, A. D. (2014). "Let's get drunk and have sex": The complex relationship of alcohol, gender, and sexual victimization. *Journal of Interpersonal Violence, 29*, 1258–1278.

Crenshaw, K. (1988). Race, reform, and retrenchment: Transformation and legitimation in antidiscrimination law. *Harvard Law Review, 101*, 1331–1387.

Daigle, L. E., Fisher, B. S., & Cullen, F. T. (2008). The violent and sexual victimization of college women: Is repeat victimization a problem? *Journal of Interpersonal Violence, 23*, 1296–1313.

Davis, K. C., Kiekel, P. A., Schraufnagel, T. J., Norris, J., George, W. H., & Kajumulo, K. F. (2012). Men's alcohol intoxication and condom use during sexual assault perpetration. *Journal of Interpersonal Violence, 27*, 2790–2806.

Duncan, S. H. (2014). The devil is in the details: Will the campus SaVE act provide more or less protection to victims of campus assaults? *Journal of College and University Law, 40*, 443–466.

Edwards, K. M., Probst, D. R., Tansill, E. C., Dixon, K. J., Bennett, S., & Gidcyz, C. A. (2014). In their own words: A content-analytic study of college women's resistance to sexual assault. *Journal of Interpersonal Violence, 29*, 2527–2547.

Edwards, K. M., Sylaska, K. M., Barry, J. E., Moynihan, M. M., Banyard, V. L., Cohn, E. S., . . . Ward, S. K. (2015). Physical dating violence, sexual violence, and unwanted pursuit victimization: A comparison of incidence rates among sexual-minority and heterosexual college students. *Journal of Interpersonal Violence, 30*, 580–600.

Exner, D., & Cummings, N. (2011). Implications for sexual assault prevention: College students as prosocial bystanders. *Journal of American College Health, 59*, 655–657.

Fisher, B. S., Daigle, L. E., Cullen, F. T., & Turner, M. G. (2003). Reporting sexual victimization to the police and others: Results from a national-level study of college women. *Criminal Justice and Behavior, 30*(1), 6–38.

Franiuk, R. (2007). Discussing and defining sexual assault: A classroom activity. *College Teaching, 55*, 104–107.

Franklin, C. A., Bouffard, L. A., & Pratt, T. C. (2012). Sexual assault on the college campus: Fraternity affiliation, male peer support, and low self-control. *Criminal Justice and Behavior, 39*, 1457–1480.

Gidycz, C. A., Orchowski, L. M., King, C. R., & Rich, C. L. (2008). Sexual victimization and health-risk behaviors: A prospective analysis of college women. *Journal of Interpersonal Violence, 23*, 744–763.

Gilmore, A. K., Stappenbeck, C. A., Lewis, M. A., Granato, H. F., & Kaysen, D. (2015). Sexual assault history and its association with the use of drinking protective behavioral strategies among college women. *Journal of Studies on Alcohol and Drugs, 76*, 459–464.

Gross, A. M., Winslett, A., Roberts, M., & Gohm, C. L. (2006). An examination of sexual violence against college women. *Violence Against Women, 12*, 288–300.

Harned, M. S. (2005). Understanding women's labeling of unwanted sexual experiences with dating partners: A qualitative analysis. *Violence Against Women, 11*, 374–413.

Harrington, N. T., & Leitenberg, H. (1994). Relationship between alcohol consumption and victim behaviors immediately preceding sexual aggression by an acquaintance. *Violence and Victims, 9*, 315–324.

Hayes, R. M., Abbott, R. L., & Cook, S. (2016). It's her fault: Student acceptance of rape myths on two college campuses. *Violence Against Women*. Advance online publication. doi:10.1177/1077801216630147

Henry, W. J. (2009). The effects of sexual assault on the identity development of Black college women. *Michigan Journal of Counseling, 36*(2), 17–23.

Hertzog, J., & Yeilding, R. (2009). College women's rape awareness and use of commonly advocated risk reduction strategies. *College Student Journal, 43*(1), 59–73.

Humphrey, S. E., & Kahn, A. S. (2000). Fraternities, athletic teams, and rape. *Journal of Interpersonal Violence, 15*, 1313–1322.

Hunter, M. L. (2005). *Race, gender, and the politics of skin tone*. New York, NY: Routledge.

Jackson, A., Gilliland, K., & Veneziano, L. (2006). Routine activity theory and sexual deviance among male college students. *Journal of Family Violence, 21*, 449–460.

Jordan, C. E., Combs, J. L., & Smith, G. T. (2014). An exploration of sexual victimization and academic performance among college women. *Trauma, Violence, & Abuse, 15*, 191–200.

Jozkowski, K. N., & Peterson, Z. D. (2013). College students and sexual consent: Unique insights. *Journal of Sex Research, 50*, 517–523.

Jozkowski, K. N., & Peterson, Z. D. (2014). Assessing the validity and reliability of the perceptions of the consent to sex scale. *Journal of Sex Research, 51*, 632–645.

Jozkowski, K. N., Peterson, Z. D., Sanders, S., Dennis, B., & Reece, M. (2014). Gender differences in heterosexual college students' conceptualizations and indicators of sexual consent: Implications for contemporary sexual assault prevention education. *Journal of Sex Research, 51*, 904–916.

Jozkowski, K. N., Sanders, S., Peterson, Z. D., Dennis, B., & Reece, M. (2014). Consenting to sexual activity: The development and psychometric assessment of dual measures of consent. *Archives of Sexual Behavior, 43*, 437–450.

Kahn, A. S., Jackson, J., Kully, C., Badger, K., & Halvorsen, J. (2003). Calling it rape: Differences in experiences of women who do or do not label their sexual assault as rape. *Psychology of Women Quarterly, 27*, 233–242.

Kalof, L. (2000). Vulnerability to sexual coercion among college women: A longitudinal study. *Gender Issues, 18*(4), 47–58.

Katz, J., & DuBois, M. (2013). The sexual assault teach-in program: Building constructive campus-wide discussions to inspire change. *Journal of College Student Development, 54*, 654–657.

Koss, M. P., Wilgus, J. K., & Williamsen, K. M. (2014). Campus sexual misconduct: Restorative justice approaches to enhance compliance with Title IX guidance. *Trauma, Violence, & Abuse, 15*, 242–257.

Krebs, C. P., Lindquist, C. H., Warner, T. D., Fisher, B. S., & Martin, S. L. (2009). College women's experiences with physically forced, alcohol- or other drug-enabled, and drug-facilitated sexual assault before and since entering college. *Journal of American College Health, 57*, 639–647.

Krebs, C. P., Lindquest, C. H., & Barrick, K. (2011). The sexual assault of undergraduate women at historically black colleges and universities (HBCUs). *Journal of Interpersonal Violence, 26*(18), 3640–3666.

Kress, V. E., Shepherd, B., Anderson, R. I., Petuch, A. J., Nolan, J. M., & Thiemeke, D. (2006). Evaluation of the impact of a coeducational sexual assault prevention program on college students' rape myth attitudes. *Journal of College Counseling, 9*, 148–157.

Larimer, M. E., Lydum, A. R., Anderson, B. K., & Turner, A. P. (1999). Male and female recipients of unwanted sexual contact in a college student sample: Prevalence rates, alcohol use, and depression symptoms. *Sex Roles, 40*, 295–308.

Lawyer, S., Resnick, H., Bakanic, V., Burkett, T., & Kilpatrick, D. (2010). Forcible, drug-facilitated, and incapacitated rape and sexual assault among undergraduate women. *Journal of American College Health, 58*, 453–460.

Lindquist, C. H., Barrick, K., Krebs, C., Crosby, C. M., Lockard, A. J., & Sanders-Philips, K. (2013). The context and consequences of sexual assault among undergraduate women at historically Black colleges and universities (HBCUs). *Journal of Interpersonal Violence, 28*, 2437–2461.

Littleton, H. L., & Dodd, J. C. (2016). Violent attacks and damaged victims: An exploration of the rape scripts of European Americans and African American U.S. college women. *Violence Against Women*. Advance online publication. doi: 10.1177/1077801216631438

McMahon, P. P. (2008). Sexual violence on the college campus: A template for compliance with federal policy. *Journal of American College Health, 57*, 361–365.

McMahon, S. (2010). Rape myth beliefs and bystander attitudes among incoming college students. *Journal of American College Health, 59*(1), 3–11.

McMahon, S., Allen, C. T., Postmus, J. L., McMahon, S. M., Peterson, N. A., & Hoffman, M. L. (2014). Measuring bystander attitudes and behavior to prevent sexual violence. *Journal of American College Health, 62*(1), 58–66.

McMahon, S., Postmus, J. L., & Koenick, R. A. (2011). Conceptualizing the engaging bystander approach to sexual violence prevention on college campuses. *Journal of College Student Development, 52*, 115–130.

Milhausen, R. R., McBride, K. R., & Jun, M. K. (2006). Evaluating a peer-led, theatrical sexual assault prevention program: How do we measure success? *College Student Journal, 40*, 316–328.

Mouilso, E. R., Fischer, S., & Calhoun, K. S. (2012). A prospective study of sexual assault and alcohol use among first-year college women. *Violence and Victims, 27*, 78–94.

Murnen, S. K., & Kohlman, M. H. (2007). Athletic participation, fraternity membership, and sexual aggression among college men: A meta-analytic review. *Sex Roles, 57*, 145–157.

Novik, M. G., Howard, D. E., & Boekeloo, B. O. (2011). Drinking motivations and experiences of unwanted sexual advances among undergraduate students. *Journal of Interpersonal Violence, 26*, 34–49.

Orchowski, L. M., & Gidycz, C. A. (2013). To whom do college women confide following sexual assault? A prospective study of predictors of sexual assault disclosure and social reactions. *Violence Against Women, 18*, 264–288.

Orchowski, L. M., Meyer, D. H., & Gidycz, C. A. (2009). College women's likelihood to report unwanted sexual experiences to campus agencies: Trends and correlates. *Journal of Aggression, Maltreatment, & Trauma, 18*, 839–858.

Orchowski, L. M., Untied, A. S., & Gidycz, C. A. (2013). Factors associated with college women's labeling of sexual victimization. *Violence and Victims, 28*, 940–958.

Palmer, R. S., McMahon, T. J., Rounsaville, B. J., & Ball, S. A. (2010). Coercive sexual experiences, protective behavioral strategies, alcohol expectancies and consumption among male and female college students. *Journal of Interpersonal Violence, 25*, 1563–1578.

Payne, D. L., Lonsway, K. A., & Fitzgerald, L. F. (1999). Rape myth acceptance: Exploration of its structure and its measurement using the Illinois Rape Myth Acceptance Scale. *Journal of Research in Personality, 33*(1), 27–68.

Potter, S. J. (2012). Using a multimedia social marketing campaign to increase active bystanders on the college campus. *Journal of American College Health, 60*, 282–295.

Potter, S. J., Moynihan, M. M., Stapleton, J. G., & Banard, V. L. (2009). Empowering bystanders to prevent campus violence against women: A preliminary evaluation of a poster campaign. *Violence Against Women, 15*, 106–121.

Pumphrey-Gordon, J. E., & Gross, A. M. (2007). Alcohol consumption and female's recognition in response to date rape risk: The role of sex-related alcohol expectancies. *Journal of Family Violence, 22*, 475–485.

Rothman, E., & Silverman, J. (2007). The effect of a college sexual assault prevention program on first-year student victimization rates. *Journal of American College Health, 55,* 283–290.

Sabina, C., & Ho, L. Y. (2014). Campus and college victim response to sexual assault and dating violence: Disclosure, service utilization, and service provision. *Trauma, Violence, & Abuse, 15,* 201–226.

Sable, M. R., Danis, F., Mauzy, D. L., & Gallagher, S. K. (2006). Barriers to reporting sexual assault for women and men: Perspectives of college students. *Journal of American College Health, 5,* 157–162.

Silbaugh, K. (2015). Reactive to proactive: Title IX's unrealized capacity to prevent campus sexual assault. *Boston University Law Review, 95,* 1049–1076.

Smith, A. (2005). *Conquest: Sexual violence and American Indian genocide.* Cambridge, MA: South End Press.

Snipes, D. J., Green, B. A., Javier, S. J., Perrin, P. B., & Benotsch, E. G. (2014). The use of alcohol mixed with energy drinks and experiences of sexual victimization among male and female college students. *Addictive Behaviors, 39,* 259–264.

Stappenbeck, C. A., Hassija, C. M., Zimmerman, L., & Kaysen, D. K. (2015). Sexual assault related distress and drinking: The influence of daily reports of social support and coping control. *Addictive Behaviors, 42,* 108–113.

Stein, J. L. (2007). Peer educators and close friends as predictors of male college students' willingness to prevent rape. *Journal of College Student Development, 48,* 75–89.

Sudderth, L. K., Leisring, P. A., & Bronson, E. F. (2010). If they don't tell us, it never happened: Disclosure of experiences of intimate violence on a college campus. *Canadian Women's Studies, 28*(1), 56–64.

Title IX of the Education Amendments, 20 U.S.C. §1681 et seq. (1972).

Truman, D. M., Tokar, D. M., & Fisher A. R. (1996). Dimensions of masculinity: Relations to date rape supportive attitudes and sexual aggression in dating situations. *Journal of Counseling and Development, 74,* 555–562.

Tuliao, A. P., & McChargue, D. (2014). Problematic alcohol use and sexual assault among male college students: The moderating and mediating roles of alcohol outcome expectancies. *American Journal on Addictions, 23,* 321–328.

Turchik, A., Probst, D. R., Irvin, C. R., Chau, M., & Gidycz, C. A. (2009). Prediction of sexual assault experiences in college women based on rape scripts: A prospective analysis. *Journal of Counseling and Clinical Psychology, 77,* 361–366.

Turchik, J. A. (2012). Sexual victimization among male college students: Assault severity, sexual functioning, and health risk behaviors. *Psychology of Men & Masculinity, 13,* 243–255.

Turchik, J. A., Probst, D. R., Chau, M., Nigoff, A., & Gidycz, C. A. (2007). Factors predicting the type of tactics used to resist sexual assault: A prospective study of college women. *Journal of Consulting and Clinical Psychology, 35,* 605–614.

U.S. Department of Education. (2011). *Dear colleague letter: Sexual violence.* Retrieved from https://www2.ed.gov/about/offices/list/ocr/letters/colleague-201104.html

Untied, A. S., Orchowski, L. M., Mastroleo, N., & Gidycz, C. A. (2012). College students' social reactions to the victim in a hypothetical sexual assault scenario: The role of victim and perpetrator alcohol use. *Violence and Victims, 27,* 957–972.

Walsh, K., Blaustein, M., Knight, W. G., Spinazzola, J., & van der Kolk, B. A. (2007). Resiliency factors in the relation between childhood sexual abuse and adulthood sexual assault in college age women. *Journal of Child Sexual Abuse, 16*(1), 1–17.

White, B. H., & Kurpius, S. E. R. (2002). Effects of victim sex and sexual orientation on perceptions of rape. *Sex Roles, 46*, 191–200.

Yeater, E. A., & O'Donohue, W. (1999). Sexual assault prevention programs: Current issues, future directions, and the potential efficacy of interventions with women. *Clinical Psychology Review, 19*, 739–771.

Yung, C. R. (2015). Concealing campus sexual assault: An empirical examination. *Psychology, Public Policy, and Law, 21*(1), 1–9.

Zinzow, H. M., & Thompson, M. P. (2015a). Factors associated with use of verbally coercive, incapacitated, and forcible sexual assault tactics in a longitudinal study of college men. *Aggressive Behavior, 41*, 34–43.

Zinzow, H. M., & Thompson, M. P. (2015b). A longitudinal examination of risk factors for repeated sexual aggression in college men. *Archives of Sexual Behavior, 44*, 213–222.

PART ONE

HISTORICAL CONTEXT

I

DIGGING UP THE ROOTS, RUSTLING THE LEAVES

A Critical Consideration of the Root Causes of Sexual Violence and Why Higher Education Needs More Courage

Luoluo Hong

Washing one's hands of the conflict between the powerful and the powerless means to side with the powerful, not to be neutral. (Freire, 1985, p. 122)

I am a campus rape survivor who has been an activist and protestor on issues of sexual violence. I have subsequently devoted the entirety of my professional life to the intervention and prevention of sexual violence on campuses and in our communities. I have served as a rape crisis counselor and domestic violence advocate, led several committees in drafting and revising sexual assault policies for campuses, adjudicated student conduct cases involving sexual assault, and implemented a wide range of primary prevention programs in an effort to reduce the incidence and prevalence of sexual assault among college students with a particular emphasis on empowering college men to recognize and act on their unique responsibility to end sexual violence.

In 2013, life changed dramatically for many of us working in higher education administration when President Barack Obama signed the Campus SaVE Act into law. This act imposed new obligations on U.S. college and university administrators, including the addition of categories (domestic violence, dating violence, and stalking) and requirements for reporting crime on campus, stipulations regarding notifying victims of their rights as part of student disciplinary procedures, and increasing expectations for having campus policies and providing comprehensive education and training. Many of these new mandates were foreshadowed in the Dear Colleague letter issued by the U.S. Department of Education (2011). This communication unequivocally established that in principle sexual violence at institutions of higher education was inconsistent with equitable access on the basis of gender, linking violence to Title IX of the Education Amendments of 1972. Prior to this, sexual violence was regarded as the purview of the U.S. Department of Health and Human Services or the U.S. Department of Justice and, therefore, on many campuses was seen as an issue of health, student conduct, or campus safety rather than an issue of civil rights.

I have observed this shift in higher education law with great interest and intense hope. I have wondered if the legislative interest that has burgeoned at the federal and state levels might be used for transformational change and generate more genuine attention to this issue among college and university administrators, faculty, and staff. I applaud and appreciate the intention that federal and numerous state entities are demonstrating when it comes to reducing sexual violence on our campuses. Yet I continue to feel a deep sense of dissatisfaction over what I feel is a lack of sufficient courage to tackle the root causes of sexual violence, and I fear that we have not been adequately imaginative or forward thinking in our policy and legislative efforts.

The current research documents how little has changed in regard to ending campus sexual violence. As mentioned in the preface, rates of sexual violence among college students have remained consistently high since the 1960s (Adams-Curtis & Forbes, 2004). That colleges and universities as a collective community have not reduced the incidence and prevalence of sexual misconduct is troubling and raises questions about the effectiveness of current sexual violence prevention.

In this chapter, I review state and federal legislation and federal reports to illustrate four unsupported narratives about sexual violence on campus. Next, I introduce a social justice framework for addressing sexual violence on campus, providing examples of strategies for campus administrators and educators. Finally, I conclude with implications for leadership practice.

Legislative and Policy Narratives About Campus Sexual Violence

Legislative bodies, by virtue of the mandates and regulations they impose, define the agendas and priorities for universities in relation to campus violence in powerful ways. These agendas reflect a story that has permeated much of the national attention on this issue and demonstrated a consistent contradiction: End violence, but focus on victims after the violence has occurred. In this section, I analyze a series of federal reports and state and federal legislation to introduce four unsupported narratives about campus sexual violence.

The report *Not Alone* (White House, 2014b) suggests four areas for campus educators to focus on to end sexual violence. These areas are

1. identifying the problem through the administration of regular campus climate surveys;
2. preventing sexual assault, in particular through engaging boys and men;
3. effectively responding when a student reports an incident of sexual assault, including the provision of confidential advocates, a comprehensive sexual misconduct policy, trauma-informed practices, more responsive disciplinary processes, and partnerships with community-based organizations; and
4. increasing transparency by more readily sharing data and improving enforcement by strengthening the Office of Civil Rights' oversight of Title IX implementation on campuses.

Although all are important to achieve, only the second recommendation addresses the need to provide prevention programming and does so rather broadly and vaguely. For example, how exactly should boys and men be engaged, and what should the goal or focus of these engagements be? Will the focus be on negotiating consent and understanding the law, or will the educational efforts also help boys and men understand gender role socialization and gender stereotyping, deconstruct male privilege and patriarchy, debunk rape myths, and critically analyze aspects of rape culture and violence culture, all of which are root causes of sexual violence?

Similarly, a report commissioned by Senator Claire McCaskill, *Sexual Violence on Campus: How Too Many Institutions of Higher Education Are Failing to Protect Students* (U.S. Senate Subcommittee on Financial & Contracting Oversight, 2014), contained the word *protect* in the title, implying some notion of prevention; that is, that we keep students from being harmed in the first place by violence. Yet, the eight key findings cited in the report focused on intervention (response)-focused programs and services, including a lack of coordination and oversight, with 10% of higher education institutions failing to designate a Title IX coordinator. Not one of the findings had a demonstrable connection to reducing the occurrence of sexual violence. Yet on her Web page, McCaskill indicates that she believes addressing these shortfalls will "ultimately lead to increased confidence by victims in judicial systems, and therefore to a higher rate of reporting of sexual crimes" (U.S. Senator Claire McCaskill, 2015, para. 3).

The overwhelming majority of federal legislation and guidance that has been passed, issued, or is under consideration (e.g., Campus Accountability and Safety Act, 2015; Safe Campus Act, 2015) falls under the following four functional areas:

1. improving the quality and accessibility of services for victims/survivors of campus sexual violence;
2. enhancing due process protections for both complainants and respondents in the campus administrative and/or disciplinary proceedings;
3. strengthening collaborations and partnerships between community-based organizations, including law enforcement agencies, and campuses; and
4. expanding reporting and data collection requirements as they relate to campus sexual violence.

Although it is laudable to focus on services for survivors and accountability for perpetrators, there is insufficient evidence to demonstrate that these efforts lead to declines in sexual violence perpetration (World Health Organization, 2009). Further, none of these services address the root causes of sexual violence, which include a wide range of individual, interpersonal, community, and societal contributing and sustaining factors (Berkowitz, 1994; Centers for Disease Control and Prevention [CDC], 2015; Krug, Dahlberg, Mercy, Zwi, & Lozano, 2002).

Finally, a review of state-based legislation under consideration as of December 2015 reveals the most common policies being proposed included establishing affirmative consent standards, requiring transcript notations or transcript withholding for those found responsible for campus sexual violence, ensuring access to medical attention for sexual assault victims, developing memorandums of understanding with local rape crisis centers and other community-based agencies, providing confidential victim advocates, and instituting Good Samaritan provisions for those who report sexual assault (American Association of State Colleges and Universities, 2015). Except for proposals addressing affirmative consent, virtually all the state legislation reviewed addresses sexual violence after it has occurred and focuses minimally on prevention. These after-the-violence efforts fail to stop or interrupt incidents of sexual violence before they occur.

Although these are all critically important efforts in which campus officials and staff must participate, college educators know that these kinds of initiatives do not lead to the prevention and reduction of sexual violence on campus. In a content analysis of these initiatives, I observed the following four problematic and concerning narratives in the legislative landscape, explicitly and implicitly, that warrant examination and disruption:

1. Improving victim services will encourage reporting.
2. Increased reporting leads to reduced perpetration.
3. Bystander intervention is a form of primary prevention.
4. Everyone in society shares equal responsibility to end sexual violence.

Next, I examine each of these dominant beliefs individually. This analysis is intended to help higher education institutions and professionals who are responsible for compliance to be critically reflective about what these efforts do and do not accomplish for their students in terms of prevention.

Unsupported narrative 1: Improving victim services will encourage reporting. The efforts to ensure that victims have access to confidential reporting resources, trauma-informed advocacy services, and timely disciplinary proceedings that acknowledge their rights are definitely essential to creating a campus climate that facilitates victims coming forward. For some campuses, these changes are much needed and long overdue. However, what has not been as clearly and carefully considered is that victims come from a diverse range of backgrounds and identities. Yet from my own observation, much of the dialogue on improving the conditions for reporting address the needs and realities of white heterosexual middle-class victims who identify as women. Policies that are being mandated as a result may not reflect the needs and realities of women of color and their intersecting identities. Wagatwe Wanjuki (2013) raises similar concerns about the notable absence of the voices and realities of Black women in sexual violence prevention.

Students who experience any sort of additional oppression or marginalization as a result of their intersecting identities, such as victims who are racialized and ethnic minorities; trans* students; students who identify as lesbian, gay, bisexual, and queer; or students from the lowest socioeconomic backgrounds, often perceive and experience available resources and campus processes as risk laden and unsafe. Their marginalized identity status often makes them more vulnerable to sexual violence. Sexual violence victims and survivors from these historically marginalized communities are far less likely to come forward for a variety of reasons (Olive, 2012; Walters, Chen & Breiding, 2013; Women of Color Network, 2006).

Yet the formulation of campus policies and procedures, as well as state and federal legislation, is informed by the testimony of those who feel safe enough or comfortable enough to come forward and share their perspectives because they are more likely to be believed or supported with care and empathy. Unless our efforts to expand facilitating conditions for reporting also take into account the varying identities and realities of our students, we will not equitably support all victims.

Unsupported narrative 2: Increased reporting leads to reduced perpetration. Policy and legislative requirements have generated what appears to be an almost singular focus on identifying those who are perpetrators of sexual violence on our campuses. The emphasis on mandated reporting means that we are asking victims to come forward about their experiences so we can remove the offending individuals from our institutions of higher education, assuming removal or some other sanction is in fact levied. Forensic consultant David Lisak has spearheaded the growing notion that campus rapists represent a select number of repeat offenders who possess a distinctly predatory nature (Lisak & Miller, 2002). Consequently, many administrators and policymakers are under the false belief that rooting out these perpetrators and removing them from campus will end sexual violence on campus. Yet, this contradicts a sustained body of research that indicates that sexual violence perpetration is more broadly engrained in a U.S. "rape culture" (Buchwald, Fletcher, & Roth, 2005, p. 8), gender-role socialization, and stereotypical expectations of boys and men starting from an early age (Berkowitz, 2002; Katz, 2006; Kimmel, 2008).

Ultimately, encouraging reporting is likely to lead to increased reporting. At my institution, our reporting rates escalated significantly from academic years 2013–2014 to 2014–2015 following an aggressive outreach and education campaign with students, faculty, and staff in the second year. However, I know of no data or evidence that demonstrates that increased reporting leads to decreased rates of perpetration. Prevention programs have the potential to reduce violence, but despite the call for more prevention efforts, the overwhelming focus has still largely remained on intervention and investigative efforts. Legislation maintains broad expectations that campuses should provide education and training to their students but has not provided the level of specific guidance present in other recommendations associated with intervention and response. Further, virtually no legislation allocates funding to campuses to meet what is becoming an increasingly burdensome administrative and operational responsibility associated with complying with all the guidance and mandates. On many campuses, in the face of limited or shrinking fiscal resources, external mandates require dollars to be invested first in compliance efforts, and understandably so. But this means that prevention efforts remain second in the allocation of human and fiscal resources for many campuses.

Unsupported narrative 3: Bystander intervention is a form of primary prevention. According to the CDC (2004), the following are three levels of sexual violence prevention:

1. *Primary Prevention:* Approaches that take place before sexual violence has occurred to prevent initial perpetration or victimization;
2. *Secondary Prevention:* Immediate responses after sexual violence has occurred to deal with the short-term consequences of violence; and
3. *Tertiary Prevention:* Long-term responses after sexual violence has occurred to address the lasting consequences of violence and sex offender treatment interventions. (p. 3)

Despite the proliferation of a wide range of programs implemented to reduce or prevent sexual violence, the CDC has identified only a handful of programs that have demonstrated efficacy or potential to affect behaviors, most notably Safe Dates (aims to prevent abuse in adolescent dating relationships), Shifting Boundaries (aims to reduce the likelihood of sexual harassment and dating violence among teens), and RealConsent (aims to reduce sexual violence perpetration by college men through the application of social cognitive and social norms theories; DeGue et al., 2014).

Even with the CDC's lackluster body of evidence to support their efficacy, bystander intervention strategies have emerged as a popular new way to address prevention programming needs on campus, such as Green Dot (www .livethegreendot.com), White Ribbon (www.whiteribbon.ca), and Mentors in Violence Prevention (www.mvpnational.org). Bystander approaches attempt to develop communal responsibility for preventing sexual violence by encouraging those who are potential witnesses to take action or intervene so they can potentially challenge cultures of violence and gender inequality (Powell, 2014).

It is important to keep in mind that based on the CDC's definition of *primary prevention*, bystander interventions are far more likely to serve as a form of secondary prevention in incidents of sexual violence. As a university administrator who has long been involved with student conduct, I and my colleagues recognize that many incidents of sexual violence happen away from the observation of others, that is, away from bystanders. This is one reason why investigations into campus sexual violence allegations often require an analysis of word-against-word evidence. However, I do believe that bystander intervention does have the potential to interrupt and counter actions and communication that contribute to a rape-supportive culture. But in adopting bystander education programs as a primary or predominant initiative in the effort to stop violence, universities and practitioners shift the accountability away from the actual perpetrator(s).

In the end, the only individual or groups capable of the primary prevention of sexual violence are potential offenders. Although bystander interventions are important to a comprehensive, ongoing campaign to end sexual violence, they are insufficient and do not adequately address the root causes of sexual violence. Further, the norms, values, and beliefs that foster campus violence are seeded in childhood and adolescence as well as in the history of the United States and in the foundations of higher education, dating from colonial colleges. College students arrive already predisposed to certain attitudes, ideologies, and behaviors. The singular legislative focus on institutions of higher education is shortsighted and inadequate.

Unsupported narrative 4: Everyone in society shares equal responsibility to end sexual violence. This simple message is understandably appealing. It does not require students, faculty, staff, and administrators in higher education to have the difficult conversations to delve into who actually perpetrates the majority of sexual violence on our campuses and in our communities, and in many ways helps immunize us against examining the foundational context of sexual violence. Addressing root causes is challenging and overwhelming work, and the process of leading this kind of transformative, deep-level change often comes at the expense of political resistance and personal attacks. Yet if everyone is responsible, then one could conclude that victims share equal responsibility with their assailants, which is especially troubling when we consider acts of child sexual assault or incest. If everyone is responsible, then witnesses bear as great a burden as perpetrators, yet research shows that sexual violence by its nature is often committed in environments where there are no witnesses. The problem with a message that makes everyone responsible is that ultimately nobody feels accountable; this mind-set presumes everyone is equitably situated in regard to power and privilege in our society and therefore equally able to act or speak up, which they are not. Further, bystander interventions, which claim that everyone has the same degree of responsibility to end sexual violence, ignores a data-supported reality about sexual violence: Boys and men are the predominant perpetrators.

The popularity of the everyone-as-bystander intervention approach has been catalyzed in many ways by the White House's own version of this campaign. The release of the *Not Alone* report (White House, 2014b) was followed by the launch of the It's On Us campaign (White House, 2014a). Ironically, the campaign in its earlier iterations appeared to more affirmatively emphasize the role of men in helping end sexual violence, recognizing that men constitute the overwhelming proportion of perpetrators of sexual violence regardless of the gender of the victims. Yet as the campaign progressed, the approach softened and focused more on the responsibility all of us have to end sexual violence. I surmise this was adjusted to respond to criticism and public discomfort about the original message and make the revised message more palatable for those who benefit from patriarchy, whiteness, and other systems of oppression upheld by sexual violence.

It is vital in our educational efforts to build the leadership and citizenship capacity of all individuals to contribute toward deconstructing societal norms that support sexual violence directly and indirectly. As university educators and administrators, we cannot and should not blur or make invisible the unique ways that those with much power at individual and institutional levels bear great responsibility to interrupt the status quo and promote change. These unsupported narratives require educators and policymakers to shift away from a traditional paradigm for prevention, education, and outreach and recognize that sexual violence is ultimately rooted in power, privilege, and socially determined injustices that should be grounded in a social justice framework.

Embracing a Social Justice Paradigm for Sexual Violence Prevention

I recommend a social justice paradigm to inform college and university educators' approaches in leading and guiding the work of campus sexual violence intervention and prevention on their campuses, It challenges educators to move beyond the rhetoric of prevention conflated with efforts to improve the institutional response to a comprehensive approach that engenders transformational change that fully implements all that higher education administrators and student development professionals know about the root causes of sexual violence. The paradigm incorporates a systemic set of sustained initiatives to address sexual violence on multiple levels, moving beyond traditional notions of how to do sexual violence work.

This proposed model, summarized in Table 1.1, is the culmination of a program delivery model I developed and refined over more than two decades of observation, reflection, and application while working in the field of sexual violence intervention and prevention at six different campuses in various roles and responsibilities, for example, as prevention educator, crisis responder and victim advocate, dean of students conduct officer, senior student affairs officer policy developer, and now Title IX coordinator.

Traditional Prevention Paradigm

Historically, the paradigm for sexual violence prevention on most campuses has focused primarily and nearly exclusively on individual responsibility, usually that of the victim and now increasingly that of the bystander. A handful

TABLE 1.1
Social Justice Paradigm for Violence Prevention

Traditional Paradigm	*Social Justice Paradigm*
Focuses primarily on individual responsibility (usually that of the victim, as well as that of the bystander)	Focuses on individual actions plus systemic/cultural factors, institutional policies, political context, and their interrelationship
Agency of the perpetrator is largely invisible or unacknowledged	Agency of the perpetrator and the system that supports the perpetrator's actions are named and made transparent
Does not acknowledge the salience of identity, power, and privilege in human interactions	Intersections of identity, power, and privilege are essential to understanding and deconstructing interpersonal dynamics
Violence and its prevention are defined from the perspective of and controlled by the dominant group	The single story is challenged, and understandings of violence are complex and informed by many counternarratives
Peer health educators implement programming	Peer health leaders are embedded in existing social groups
Prevention work tends to occur in isolation; efforts are fragmented and inconsistent	Prevention work is infused across multiple entities working collaboratively to build and sustain community capacity
Focuses almost exclusively on transactional effectiveness	Focuses on transformational and transactional impact
Is an overlay on the institution's existing practices, programs, policies, and procedures	Infiltrates and disrupts the systems, structures, culture, and core values of the institution
Sustained as long as the champion is present	Sustainable over time, with many champions
Requires care and competence	Requires care, competence, and courage

of campuses have focused on the unique responsibility of men, such as those affiliated with the Men Can Stop Rape's Men of Strength Clubs (www .mencanstoprape.org). In the traditional approach, the agency of the perpetrator is largely invisible or unacknowleged; for example, statistics and data are reported from the perspective of who has been victimized, whereas sexual assault and sexual misconduct are described as experiences that happen *to* the victim or survivor as opposed to actions or choices made by a perpetrator. This also means that the conceptualization of, and therefore education about, sexual violence does not acknowledge the salience of identity, power, and privilege in shaping and defining human interactions as well as how we perceive or interpret them.

In fact, in a traditional paradigm, violence and its prevention are defined from the perspective of and controlled by the dominant group or group in authority, which in many cases is men. For instance, law enforcement gets to decide whether a case is unfounded, and legislators and courts decide what constitutes sexual violence, usually from a heterosexist normative model (overemphasizing penetration as harmful over other forms of violation). Children, girls, and women are told how they should or should not act, behave, dress, and drink, and people of all genders are taught how they should conform to traditional concepts of gender identity.

In this traditional approach, more often than not, perpetrators are regarded as unusual others who have deficits in moral judgment, character, or family upbringing. The gendered nature of sexual violence is not named or acknowledged; it is almost incidental. This is the story those who are committed to the status quo need to believe, as it would be unfathomable to think that entire cohorts of boys and men are socialized since childhood to regard violence as a viable pathway to negotiate relationships. Further, the route to prevention assumes an equity in the ability to act and communicate among all parties involved in the sexual encounter; it does not account for how positional authority, age, physical size and strength, or induced incapacitation can be coercive implicitly if not explicitly in negotiating consent, and that teaching college students about consent is insufficient as a risk-reduction tool.

Many campuses also use a cadre of concerned, committed, and caring peer educators to spearhead their educational efforts, training them through a weekend retreat, weekly meetings, or even a course for credit, following the false illusion that arming their undergraduate peers with more information or statistics will help shield them from perpetration or victimization. These peers may facilitate discussions about recognizing the signs of an abusive relationship, knowing how to have a healthy one, or negotiating affirmative consent. These skill sets are important but do not take into account the difficulties of applying them in real-world and real-time situations where the weight of 18-plus years of socialization and messaging overcomes the vaguely recalled bullet points of a 50-minute workshop. Such educational approaches neglect that salience of culture, gender role socialization, peer group norms, and prevailing social mores in influencing behaviors and other factors cannot be easily diminished by the provision of facts or recitation of laws and policies. In other words, this approach implicitly accepts the world as it is and attempts to teach students how to cope, survive, and thrive despite the realities; it does not empower or encourage students to challenge and use their agency to promote change.

Prevention work in the traditional model is often conducted in silos and in isolation, with a cadre of the usual suspects: student health services, counseling centers, health education/health promotion programs, university police or campus security departments, and perhaps the dean of students office and now by Title IX coordinators. Even with multiple prevention partners, efforts are often fragmented and uncoordinated, with the messages from the police officers contradicting those provided by health promotion professionals. And nearly all the efforts are marginalized in some way, predictably touted and praised by university executives when an incident of sexual assault occurs and the media catches wind but largely unfunded and unnoticed at other times as long as the compliance checklists are completed.

Traditional prevention efforts focus almost exclusively on transactional effectiveness, often because these are the easiest to measure and cause the least disuption to the institution. Such efforts include determining the number of workshops conducted, the number of people who attended, how many incidents were reported and how many were investigated, and if the policy was posted online. Of course, it would be difficult to measure outcomes associated with transformational change, because prevention efforts are usually just an overlay on the institution's existing practices, programs, policies, and procedures. For example, a provision or statement prohibiting sexual misconduct may be added to the student conduct code or an entirely new policy may be developed, but there is no preparatory content analysis of the body of existing student life policies to find out how they may or may not contribute to an institutional climate that supports, encourages at worst, or ignores at best incidents of sexual violence.

Campus officials may provide confidential victims' advocates yet not consider that many faculty and staff who are often the first responders for students and the likely recipients of a student's report of sexual assault (especially on commuter campuses) lack the comfort level or capacities to respond empathetically or appropriately when a student discloses an incident of sexual violence. Administrators may find the will and the funds to hire a Title IX coordinator, who arrives on campus to find lots of goodwill and psychological support but no staffing, no funding, and barely an office. The changes are incremental and somewhat cosmetic, and do not require campus officials to become uncomfortable to have to ask difficult questions or have challenging conversations.

Finally, in the traditional approach to violence prevention, campus officials will find they have many colleagues and student leaders who are caring and competent and contribute in meaningful ways to intervention services in the aftermath of sexual violence and to prevention programs. There may be a well-respected or well-regarded champion on campus who is leading the charge and holding efforts together, finding ways to scrape together funding. Yet, the institutional support is fragile because ownership is not embedded at the top and throughout the institution; students graduate, staff may take on new responsibilities or get promoted, and faculty may have to (re)focus on teaching or research responsibilities, all while administrators come and go.

This structure supporting sexual violence prevention efforts is inherently not sustainable; in addition, it redirects energy that could be invested in primary prevention efforts on mandated programs and services that ultimately do not change cultural norms. As a result, sufficient change momentum cannot be generated, and the status quo is maintained. To use Jim Collins's (2001) metaphor for how organizations achieve excellence, the proverbial "flywheel" (p. 164) cannot be rotated enough to reach breakthrough. Even the most caring and competent group of individuals working hard and with the best intentions will not be able to move it on reducing the incidence and prevalence of sexual violence, not without something more.

The Social Justice Paradigm

The social justice paradigm for sexual violence prevention begins with a close examination of the existing body of scholarship about prevention strategies with demonstrated efficacy and relies on a culture of evidence; a recommended place to begin is with the CDC's (2014) own summary paper as well as its website summarizing research on sexual violence prevention. The CDC focuses on individual actions as well as those systemic and cultural factors that shape individual and group behaviors, including but not limited to institutional policies, political contexts, and their interrelationship.

I have observed how communications and educational messages about sexual violence frequently present the issue in terms of statistics and numbers, dehumanizing the aspects and causes of sexual violence. In these practices, it is almost as if the perpetrators were unknown or invisible. By contrast, in a social justice approach, the perpetrators' agencies are specifically named, examined, and made transparent, along with the structures, beliefs, values, and attitudes that encourage, endorse, or otherwise support their behaviors. A social justice paradigm focuses on the frequency of perpetration and the risk factors associated with the commission of acts of sexual violence.

The consideration of identity is not linear or simple in the social justice paradigm. The intersections of identity are fully considered, and the complexities of our realities are acknowledged. For example, social justice–minded prevention educators grapple with what Angela Davis (2000) refers to as the "race of gender" and the "gender of race."

> We must also learn how to oppose the racist fixation on people of color as the primary perpetrators of violence, including domestic and sexual violence, and at the same time to fiercely challenge the real violence that men of color inflict on women. (para. 10)

As a woman of color, I find this observation particularly significant. First, as noted earlier in this chapter and in this book, women of color are at an increased risk for sexual violence. Second, women in communities of color are often implicitly and explicitly asked to demonstrate racial or ethnic solidarity against racism, which often means remaining silent about sexual violence experienced at the hands of men from our communities of color (Olive, 2012).

Davis (2000) appeals to us to address both forms of social injustice, accounting for gender-based and race-based oppression.[1] Sexual violence prevention through a social justice framework works to deconstruct interpersonal dynamics as a way to understand and end violence. This paradigm also takes into account that although all sexual violence perpetration and victimization may share common roots, each incident has differential impacts on individuals and communities because of the realities of how intersecting identities shape lives.

In a social justice approach to sexual violence prevention work, educators and practitioners understand that violence is the outcome of a complex interplay of many factors, visible and unknown, and as such, they resist adhering to one narrative. The single story or master narrative is challenged, and a purposeful effort is made to understand violence through a diverse array of counternarratives, or narratives that counter dominant ways of knowing. Root causes, including but not limited to gender role socialization, acculturation into rape-supportive myths and misconceptions, and implicit and unconscious acceptance of male privilege and patriarchy, require multiple conversations and several years to examine, understand, and deconstruct.

Prevention education that intends to have an impact must be sustained over time and be multifaceted, leaning into the complexity of how and why sexual violence occurs. Simple or single-message, onetime, narrowly focused programs will not generate behavior change. Online education modules for sexual violence prevention are efficient at reaching large numbers of students in one implementation and are therefore understandably popular among institutions of higher learning. Yet, their proliferation raises concerns about their efficacy in bringing about actual behavior change.

In a social justice approach, college students are used as peer health leaders rather than peer health educators because of their potential power to influence norms, attitudes, beliefs, and ideas in real time while interacting with their peers through everyday academic, social, experiential learning, and employment-related activities. Peer health leaders are often selected so that they can be inserted into existing student affinity groups or living-learning communities; their potential to affect others is predicated less on knowledge and more on capacities such as courage, tenacity, vulnerability, and critical thinking that allow them to meaningfully and strategically interrupt the status quo of students' everyday lives and catalyze fearless dialogue and self-reflection in search of a new vision for how the world might and ought to be if it were free of sexual violence.

When a campus adopts a social justice framework, prevention work is embedded across multiple entities working collaboratively and simultaneously to build and sustain community capacity. Senior leadership must take responsibility to ensure that these efforts are coordinated and that resources are appropriately allocated and effectively institutionalized. Actors in these efforts can produce transformational change as well as transactional impacts because the campus is open to being infiltrated and having its systems, structures, culture, and core values disrupted. Efforts are not just an overlay—they are embedded, and the foundations of the institution are fundamentally uprooted and replanted; new trees are not simply planted on top of what is there and expected to grow. Because of this institutional ownership, there are many champions across the institution, so efforts are sustained over time and forward progress is maintained; the departure of one champion does not signal the end of initiatives, programs, services, or other efforts that make a notable difference in moving the needle. Individuals contributing to the effort not only remain caring and competent but also possess one additional essential characteristic: courage.

Conclusion: From Conviction to Courage

I remember distinctly many of the conversations I had when I first began working in 1995 with the student organization Men Against Violence at Louisiana State University, which, as I knew, was the first organization of its kind. The program was distinguished by its adoption of a social justice approach to violence prevention. The group's emergence generated several interesting conversations, reflective of my colleagues' significant concerns about what creating such a group meant. Two conversations stood out for me. The first was in the form of a frantic phone call from a colleague at the local domestic violence shelter who was skeptical about what a "group of college men" were going to be doing when they got together and how they could possibly contribute in any way to ending violence. She was reassured when I told her that I had been asked to be their adviser and that resources would not be drawn from victims' services. Her concerns were understandable, yet our exchange caused much reflection.

The second conversation occurred when we asked the campus committee that recognizes student organizations for their endorsement of this new club. One faculty member was disturbed by the proposed name and wondered why we did not use Students Against Violence. The inaugural officers of the club quickly responded that it was because men are responsible for perpetrating most of the interpersonal violence on campus. The faculty member remained skeptical and asked that we not tarnish the good reputation of the university, specifically the male students enrolled at the institution. Those conversations taught me that using a social justice approach to violence prevention requires moral courage, and now in 2016, as I continue to do the work of sexual violence prevention from a social justice perspective, I find myself having many of the same challenging conversations.

The Institute for Global Ethics defines *moral courage* as "the quality of mind and spirit that enables one to face up to ethical dilemmas and moral wrongdoings firmly and confidently, without flinching or retreating" (Kidder & Bracy, 2001). Moral courage differs from physical courage in that it addresses intangible versus tangible matters; the risk is inherent in success rather than failure; and it can be practiced by anyone regardless of age, gender, physical ability, or surroundings. Further, moral courage exists at the intersection of three things. First, we as individuals and institutions must have a clear core or guiding principle to aspire to; second, some element of danger, threat, or risk to ourselves or those we care about is either implicitly or explicitly associated with implementing this principle. These two elements combined with the third—endurance, resilience, and tenacity to sustain our principled action through the risk—constitute moral courage (Kidder, 2005).

Much of the discourse about sexual violence focuses on college, giving only cursory attention and acknowledgment to the 18 or so years of gender-role socialization and cultural training that precede an individual's entry into college. Yet the story does not begin in college, nor does it begin when we are born. The society that socializes us has deep roots in institutions, systems, and structures. Our strategies for responding to campus sexual violence are still focused predominantly on what happens after sexual violence has taken place, which we must do until sexual violence ends. Yet, we must do more and in new ways.

I suspect we feel a collective sense of helplessness and powerlessness in the face of what to do to end sexual violence. As with all social change efforts, simplifying the solution will not achieve the desired results, nor will taking shortcuts. The prevailing national dialogue about sexual violence on campuses carries elements of truth; however, these stories are incomplete in terms of why and how sexual violence proliferates and persists. Let us begin by broadening the narratives and learning from all of them to bring our best intentions for campuses free of sexual violence to full fruition.

Note

1. For more on this topic, sec the National Alliance to End Sexual Violence (http://endsexualviolencc.org/where-we-stand/racism-and-rape), Women of Color Network (www.wocninc.org/about-wocn/working-asstimprions), and INCITE! (www .incite-national.org/page/dangerous-intersections).

References

Adams-Curtis, L. E., & Forbes, G. B. (2004). College women's experiences of sexual coercion: A review of cultural, perpetrator, victim, and situational violence. *Trauma, Violence, & Abuse, 5*(9), 91–22.

American Association of State Colleges and Universities. (2015). *Policy matters: A higher education policy brief: State policy proposals to combat campus sexual assault.* Washington, DC: Author.

Berkowitz, A. D. (1994). A model acquaintance rape prevention program for men. In A. D. Berkowitz, *Men and rape: Theory, research, and prevention programs in higher education* (pp. 35–42). San Francisco, CA: Jossey-Bass.

Berkowitz, A. D. (2002). Fostering mens' responsibility for preventing sexual assault. In P. A. Schewe, *Preventing violence in relationships: Interventions across the life span* (pp. 163–196). Washington, DC: American Psychological Association.

Buchwald, E., Fletcher, P., & Roth, M. (2005). *Transforming a rape culture* (Rev. ed.). Minneapolis, MN: Milkweed Editions.

Campus Accountability and Safety Act, S.590, 114th Congress of the United States of America. (2015). Retrieved from www.congress.gov/bill/114th-congress/ senate-bill/590/text-

Centers for Disease Control and Prevention. (2004). *Sexual violence prevention: Beginning the dialogue.* Atlanta, GA: Author.

Centers for Disease Control and Prevention. (2014). *Preventing sexual violence on college campuses: Lessons from research and practice.* Retrieved from www.cdc.gov/ violenceprevention/sexualviolence/prevention.html

Centers for Disease Control and Prevention. (2015). *The social-ecological model: A framework for prevention.* Retrieved from www.cdc.gov/violenceprevention/overview/social-ecologicalmodel.html

Collins, J. (2001). *Good to great: Why some companies make the leap . . . and others don't.* New York, NY: HarperCollins.

Davis, A. (2000). *The color of violence against women.* Retrieved from www.colorlines.com/articles/color-violence-against-women

DeGue, S., Valle, L. A., Holt, M. K., Massetti, G. M., Matjasko, J. L., & Tharp, A. T. (2014). A systematic review of primary prevention strategies for sexual violence perpetration. *Aggression and Violent Behavior, 19,* 346–362.

Freire, P. (1985). *The politics of education: Culture, power, and liberation.* Westport, CT: Bergin & Garvey.

Katz, J. (2006). *The macho paradox: Why some men hurt women and how all men can help.* Naperville, IL: Sourcebooks.

Kidder, R. M. (2005). *Moral courage.* New York, NY: William Morrow.

Kidder, R. M., & Bracy, M. (2001). *Moral courage: A white paper.* Retrieved from ww2.faulkner.edu/admin/websites/jfarrell/moral_courage_11-03-2001.pdf

Kimmel, M. (2008). *Guyland: The perilous world where boys become men.* New York, NY: HarperCollins.

Krug, E. G., Dahlberg, L. L., Mercy, J. A., Zwi, A. B., & Lozano, R. (2002). *World report on violence and health.* Geneva, Switzerland: World Health Organization.

Lisak, D., & Miller, P. M. (2002). Repeat rape and multiple offending among undetected rapists. *Violence and Victims, 17*(1), 73–84.

McCaskill, C. (2015). *Combating sexual violence.* Retrieved from https://www.mccaskill.senate.gov/violence

Olive, V. C. (2012). Sexual assault against women of color. *Journal of Student Research, 1,* 1–9.

Powell, A. (2014). Bystander approaches: Responding to and preventing men's sexual violence against women. *Australian Centre for the Study of Sexual Assault Issues, 17,* 1–20.

Safe Campus Act of 2015, H.R.3403, 114th Congress of the United States of America. (2015). Retrieved from www.congress.gov/bill/114th-congress/house-bill/3403/text

Title IX of the Education Amendments, 20 U.S.C. §1681 et seq. (1972).

U.S. Department of Education. (2011). *Dear colleague letter.* Retrieved from http://www2.ed.gov/about/offices/list/ocr/letters/colleague-201104.html

U.S. Senate Subcommittee on Financial & Contracting Oversight—Majority Staff. (2014). *Sexual violence on campus: How too many institutions of higher education are failing to protect students.* Retrieved from www.mccaskill.senate.gov/Survey ReportwithAppendix.pdf

U.S. Senator Claire McCaskill. (2015). *Combatting sexual violence.* Retrieved from www.mccaskill.senate.gov/violence

Violence Against Women Reauthorization Act of 2013, 113th Congress of the United States of America. (2013, March 7). S. 47. Retrieved from www.govtrack.us/congress/bills/113/s47

Walters, M., Chen, J., & Breiding, M. (2013). *The National Intimate Partner and Sexual Violence Survey (NISVS): 2010 findings on victimization by sexual orientation.* Atlanta, GA: National Center for Injury Prevention and Control, Centers for Disease Control and Prevention.

Wanjuki, W. (2013, November 25). *Is there no room for Black women in the rape and alcohol debate?* Retrieved from https://rewire.news/article/2013/11/25/is-there-no-room-for-black-women-in-the-rape-and-alcohol-debate

White House. (2014a, Sebtember 19). *Fact sheet: Launch of the "It's On Us" public awareness campaign to help prevent campus sexual assault.* Retrieved from https://www.whitehouse.gov/the-press-office/2014/09/19/fact-sheet-launch-it-s-us-public-awareness-campaign-help-prevent-campus-

White House. (2014b, April). *Not alone: The first report of the White House Task Force to Protect Students From Sexual Assault.* Retrieved from https://www.notalone.gov/assets/report.pdf

Women of Color Network. (2006). *Women of Color Network: Facts & stats collection.* Retrieved from www.doj.state.or.us/victims/pdf/women_of_color_network_facts_sexual_violence_2006.pdf

World Health Organization. (2009). *Reducing violence through victim identification, care and support programmes.* Retrieved from www.who.int/violence_injury_prevention/violence/programmes.pdf

2

CENTERING WOMEN OF COLOR IN THE DISCOURSE ON SEXUAL VIOLENCE ON COLLEGE CAMPUSES

Jessica C. Harris

White women students are foregrounded in the majority of college sexual violence prevention and response efforts and in media stories concerning sexual violence on campus (Barrick, Krebs, & Lindquist, 2013; Wanjuki, 2013). Focusing on sexual violence on college campuses is necessary, yet the unilateral focus on white women obscures other student populations' experiences with sexual violence. This chapter concentrates on one such population: women students of color and their experiences with sexual violence. The term *women of color* refers to all women who do not have white privilege and are discriminated against based on their race or gender. The term *experiences with sexual violence* includes any unwanted sexual experience.

Knowledge and recognition of the experiences of women of color and sexual violence on college campuses is in desperate need of increased attention. College women of color experience higher rates of sexual violence than white women (Gross, Winslett, Roberts, & Gohm, 2006; Testa & Dermen, 1999), and the effects of this violence are nuanced for women of color because they "do not just face quantitatively more issues when they suffer violence, . . . but their experience is qualitatively different from that of white women" (Smith, 2005, p. 8). Yet, minimal scholarship is dedicated to women of color and sexual violence in college.

Using critical race theory (CRT) and critical race feminism (CRF), this chapter builds a foundation to examine women students of color's experiences with sexual violence. The chapter elucidates how college educators can address and deconstruct oppressive systems that maintain sexual violence on college campuses for women students of color. To do this, I first provide an overview of how CRT and CRF have been used in higher education and how they frame sexual violence for women of color. Second, I explore how several tenets of CRT and CRF, such as challenging ahistoricism, intersectionality, and the endemic nature of racism, can be used to deconstruct interlocking systems of domination that influence women of color's experiences with sexual violence in society and how this translates to college campuses. Third, I offer implications informed by CRT and CRF that aim to prevent and address sexual violence for women students of color in higher education.

Critical Race Theory and Critical Race Feminism

CRT is a movement and a framework that aims to destabilize white supremacy and address racial inequity (Delgado & Stefancic, 2012). CRT provides an exploration of "how a regime of white supremacy and its subordination of people of color have been created and maintained in America . . . not merely to understand the vexed bond between law and racial power but to change it" (Crenshaw, Gotanda, Peller, & Thomas, 1995, p. xiii). Although CRT was originally conceptualized to critique the American legal system's role in upholding white supremacy (Delgado, 1989), the theory has more recently been applied to education to interrupt racist structures that are deeply ingrained in the U.S. educational pipeline (Ladson-Billings, 1998; Ladson-Billings & Tate, 1995).

As educational scholars have begun to use CRT as a framework to critique institutionalized racism in higher education, core tenets of the theory have emerged (Lynn & Adams, 2002). However, CRT scholars do not subscribe to one set of tenets. Instead, they use several different tenets including whiteness as property, interest convergence, intersectionality, and several others that allow for a critique of oppressive systems embedded in the U.S. educational pipeline. As the tenets of CRT expanded, so too did the application of the theory. CRF, an offshoot of CRT, calls attention to the intersections of race and gender in the lived experiences of women of color (Wing, 1997). Drawing from CRT, CRF calls for a targeted focus on the intersections of race, gender, and other social identities in the lives of women of color (Wing, 2003). Although "CRF has much in common with CRT" (Wing, 1997, p. 948), CRF explicitly critiques and deconstructs interlocking systems of domination, specifically white supremacy and patriarchy, that affect the daily experiences of women of color. CRF draws from the tenets of CRT and builds a foundation on the concepts of intersectionality and antiessentialism, both of which are explored in detail later in this chapter.

Educational scholars have used CRT to better understand students' racialized experiences (Ladson-Billings, 1998; Ladson-Billings & Tate, 1995), but the use of CRF within higher education is harder to locate. A growing body of scholarship outside education uses CRF to analyze sexual violence and other forms of violence against women of color in U.S. society (Crenshaw, 1991; Ghavami & Peplau, 2012; Olive, 2012; Wing, 1997). Furthermore, Kimberlé Crenshaw (1989) grounded the concept of intersectionality in research concerning violence against women of color. CRF, therefore, is well positioned to center women students of color's experiences, affording a more nuanced and complete understanding of sexual violence on college campuses. In sum, CRF places "women of color at the center rather than the margins or footnotes of the analysis. . . . CRF attacks the notion of the essential woman (i.e., the white middle class woman) and explores the lives of those facing multiple discrimination" (Wing, 1997, p. 948). In the next section, I use CRF and CRT as frameworks to focus on women of color's experiences with sexual violence in U.S. society. This approach explores intersecting systems of domination that contribute to women of color's everyday experiences with sexual violence and maintain women's invisibility in the discourse of campus sexual violence.

Intersectionality and Antiessentialism

Intersectionality and antiessentialism "embody what is essentially the same critique, but made from two different starting points" (Grillo, 1995, p. 16). The theory of intersectionality originated in the works of Kimberlé Crenshaw (1989, 1991), who focused on the intersections of race and gender in shaping women of color's experiences with domestic and sexual violence. Crenshaw (1989) emphasized how women of color are rendered invisible because antiracist discourse focuses on men of color and fails to address patriarchy. Additionally, feminist discourse, which centers on white women, fails to critique structures of racism. Because women of color do not experience racism in the same manner as men of color, nor do they experience sexism in the same manner as white women, they fall into a chasm created by these competing discourses (Crenshaw, 1989, 1991). Intersectionality theory also recognizes that women of color's experiences do not equate to the addition of these two separate experiences, that is, men of color plus white women. Instead, these experiences are understood when the intersections of multiple identities are accounted for. Although intersectionality theory focuses on how individual identities intersect to inform experiences, the theory also explores how these microlevel experiences connect to macrolevel systems of domination. For instance, Crenshaw described how institutions, such as the law, reproduced power structures and "how discourses of resistance (e.g., feminism and antiracism) could themselves function as sites that produced and legitimized marginalization" (Carbado, Crenshaw, Mays, & Tomlinson 2013, p. 304). In short, an intersectional approach accounts for women of color's identity-specific experiences and the social process that shape these experiences (Crenshaw, 1989, 1991; Thornton-Dill & Zambrana, 2009).

Intersectionality is a useful tool in framing women of color's experiences with sexual violence on college campuses. First, it allows a closer critique of how and why women of color are left out of the discourses, including policies, practices, and programming, surrounding sexual violence. Research, media, and policies and procedures, which are informed by and uphold intersecting systems of domination, unilaterally focus on white women survivors of sexual violence (Crenshaw, 1991). This unilateral focus frames sexual violence as a white-women-only issue, pushing women of color to the margins of the discourse on sexual violence on a systemic and an individual level. For example, women of color's experiences with sexual violence are not often accounted for in governmental and campus policies whether through negation or color-blind rhetoric. This macro level invisibility and exclusion informs women of color's everyday experiences of invisibility and exclusion on campus.

Second, the theory of intersectionality expands educators' understandings of sexual violence on college campuses to account for women of color's unique experiences with sexual violence, influenced by patriarchy, white supremacy, and other interlocking systems of domination. For instance, an intersectional lens exposes how women of color's bodies have been constructed throughout time, via patriarchal and white supremacist structures, to serve the needs of dominant society. Viewing this construction through an intersectional lens allows college educators to address the multiple systems that influence women of color's individual experiences with sexual violence.

Antiessentialism furthers the intersectionality critique by refuting the ideology that there is one group experience in which all women can be categorized (Grillo, 1995). Essentialism states that all women, regardless of race, class, ability status, and other intersecting identities, have the same experiences. Essentialism is damaging because "the perceived need to define what 'women's' experience is and what oppression 'as women' means has prompted some feminists to analyze the situation of woman by stripping away race and class" (Grillo, 1995, p. 19). When race, class, and other minoritized identities are stripped away from the identity of woman, the identity that remains is white woman. Essentialism equates all women's experiences with white women's experience.

Antiessentialism is a useful tool to deconstruct the disproportionate representations of white women in the discourses on sexual violence. Essentialism is widespread in college educators' understandings of and approaches to sexual violence on college campuses. For instance, several programs and policies are geared toward an essentialized notion of survivors of sexual violence: white cisgender heterosexual women (see Chapter 12). When white women are essentialized as the sole survivors of sexual violence, the experiences of women of color become unnecessary to telling the story of sexual violence on campus. This is because a unilateral focus on white women creates a paradigm that "theoretically erases" (Crenshaw, 1989, p. 57) women of color from the conversation of sexual violence in higher education. Essentialist notions guide the policies, practices, procedures, and campaigns that aim to prevent, address, and redress sexual violence on campus. In other words, if college educators' approaches to sexual violence are filtered through an (un)conscious essentialist lens that frames white women as the only survivors of sexual violence, then support will be exclusively targeted toward white women, further marginalizing women students of color who experience sexual violence.

Although it is paramount to focus on the essentialism of white women as "all women," it would be hypocritical not to acknowledge that the term *women of color* may also essentialize women with multiple intersecting identities. The term *women of color* grew out of a movement of resistance and a need for solidarity among a group of racially minoritized women in the United States (Roshanravan, 2010). Recently, this term has come to reference a biological group rather than a political group, which risks placing women of color into a monolithic community of people who share the same experiences because of their race *and* gender. Although I continue to refer to women who must navigate racism and sexism as women of color, I offer this caveat in an attempt at transparency and awareness. We as college educators must acknowledge that Latina, Black, Native, Asian, Multiracial, and all other racially minoritized women's experiences of sexual violence are different from one another (and further nuanced within these groups). However, the term *women of color* remains powerful in building a foundation to support larger, more intricate discussions on sexual violence at the intersections of other identities, such as ability, age, and class. In the end, college educators must use antiessentialism and intersectionality to "define complex experiences as closely to their full complexity as possible and . . . not ignore voices at the margin" (Grillo, 1995, p. 22).

Ahistoricism

In this section, I shed light on more accurate and less comforting histories of sexual violence for women of color in a U.S. context (Delgado & Stefancic, 2012). Often, sexual violence is interpreted through an ahistoric framework, which disregards the history of sexual terrorization for women of color in the United States (Crenshaw, 1988). Ahistoric approaches ignore inequities of the past and separate women of color's current realities of sexual violence from the influence of a larger sociohistorical and institutionalized system (Crenshaw, 1988). Approaching women of color students' experiences with sexual violence from an ahistoric framework makes it impossible for college educators to understand, let alone address and deconstruct, historical influences of sexual violence on college campuses. Moreover, ahistoricism contributes to a restrictive view of equality (Crenshaw, 1988), which focuses on equality as a process and not as an outcome. A restrictive view of equality "applauds affording everyone equality of opportunity but resists programs that assure equality of results" (Crenshaw, 1988, p. 28). For instance, although campus sexual violence policies may provide all students, including women of color, with the opportunity to report and seek redress, these policies rarely account for women of color's unique histories and identities, which fail to "assure equality of results" throughout the reporting process. Moreover, these restrictive policies allow colleges to blame women of color for their failure or unwillingness to report sexual violence, rather than critique the historically constructed oppressive structures that deter these women from reporting sexual violence.

To address ahistoricism and the restrictive view it constructs, CRT scholars (Delgado & Stefancic, 2012; Solórzano & Yosso, 2002) encourage the positioning of current-day racial inequities within a historical and contextual framework. This repositioning "reexamines America's historical record, replacing comforting majoritarian interpretations of events with ones that square more accurately with minorities' experiences" (Delgado & Stefancic, 2012, p. 24). An exhaustive revisionist history is not possible here because of space limitations, but I attempt to briefly shed light on less comforting interpretations of the rape of women of color throughout U.S. history. In short, this section exposes how the rape of women of color centers on terrorization, white supremacy, male supremacy, and power, and less (if at all) on alcohol, athletes, and campus parties.

The history of sexual violence against women of color, specifically rape, is about economic, political, and cultural colonization and power. Put simply, the rape of women of color by white men was and is used as a way to control women's bodies and gain power and secure the status quo (Freedman, 2013; Smith, 2005). Prior to the colonization of the United States by white male Europeans, gendered and raced hierarchies were foreign to Native cultures, but this egalitarian society threatened the European belief of a patriarchal, white-male-dominated society (Smith, 2005). Therefore, "in order to colonize a people whose society was not hierarchal, colonizers must first naturalize hierarchy through instituting patriarchy" (Smith, 2005, p. 23). White men introduced the naturalization of patriarchy through the rape of Native women's bodies. This terrorization emphasized control and domination over Native women's bodies as well as over Native culture.

While the rape of Native women was used as a tool for cultural genocide, the rape of Black slave women was often used as a way to gain economic capital. To gain economic power, white slave masters raped Black slave women to produce children who were born into slavery and added to the slave owner's labor force (Freedman, 2013; Hunter, 2005; Smith, 2005). The rape of Black women's bodies was seen as permissible because they were the property of white slave masters (Freedman, 2013). Asian women have also been, and continue to be, economic pawns in the game of patriarchy and white supremacy (Lloyd, 2000). Some Asian immigrant women entered the United States as mail-order brides, advertised "as exotic sexual toys for white-male consumption" (Lloyd, 2000, p. 341). Still other Asian women faced poverty because of restrictive U.S. employment laws and were forced or sold into prostitution in order to survive (Smith, 2005). Men bought, sold, and treated Asian women's bodies as if they were commodities, conferring white men with even more power while robbing power from Asian women and Asian communities.

Placing the experiences of women of color with sexual violence in a historical context exposes how this violence has little to do with sex and everything to do with power, control, and colonization. As Smith (2005) stated, "The history of sexual violence and genocide . . . illustrates how gender violence functions as a tool for racism and colonialism for women of color in general" (p. 15). College educators must understand how the history of racism, sexism, and colonialism in the United States continues to influence sexual violence on campus. Understanding how the rape of women students of color reinforces patriarchal and white supremacist structures on campus allows for more expansive, rather than restrictive, approaches to addressing and redressing sexual violence for women students of color. College educators must design policies and programs that allow women of color to feel empowered and vocal on campus. Educators must also improve prevention strategies with the knowledge that sexual violence is about domination, colonization, and power, and not solely, if ever, about sex. A focus on deconstructing a hierarchal and colonized campus culture is critical in these prevention strategies. Educators must decolonize our campuses to effectively address and root out sexual violence for all peoples. One way we can begin this decolonization is through the deconstruction of racialized and gendered stereotypes that continue to control women of color's bodies.

Constructing Women of Color via Stereotypes

Race is a socially constructed concept that has been invented and reinvented by white people in positions of power to maintain a social order that preserves white privilege (Delgado & Stefancic, 2012). Delgado and Stefancic (2012) wrote, "Races are categories that society invents, manipulates, or retires when convenient" (p. 8). Over time, as racial categories have been socially constructed, stereotypes have become attached to these categories, leading people to rely on a "series of unsubstantiated beliefs" (Omi & Winant, 1986, p. 62) about how certain racial groups and individuals should behave, operate, and exist in U.S. society. These racial myths also dictate how to treat individuals and groups on the basis of skin color and other physical features. Further, white society uses these myths to explain away the ill treatment of racialized groups associated with each racial category (Omi & Winant, 1986).

Stereotypes concerning women of color are often raced and gendered. Throughout history, unsubstantiated beliefs have been assigned to women of color as a monolithic group as well as to each individual racial group under the umbrella term of *women of color*. Since the founding, or rather, the *finding and taking*, of the United States, Native women's bodies have been constructed as "dirty," which communicated to white colonizers that they were "sexually violable and 'rapeable,' and the rape of bodies that are considered inherently impure or dirty simply does not count" (Smith, 2005, p. 10). Black women are portrayed as Jezebels, or sexually promiscuous, oversexed, and corrupt women (West, 1995, 2008). As with Native women, the stereotype of the Jezebel "gave the impression that Black women could not be rape victims because they always desired sex" (West, 2008, p. 294). Throughout time, Asian women have been constructed as "exotic, inferior . . . passive, in need of domination, and eager to please" (Park, 2012, p. 495). Latina women have been portrayed as harlots and spitfires who lust after white men and have uncontrollable sexualities (Vargas, 2010). Multiracial women are stereotyped as tragic and "vulnerable in the sense that they are mentally, emotionally, and socially weak, powerless, and tormented, and very often the product of sexual and racial domination" (Nakashima, 1992, p. 169). Together, women of color have often been stereotyped as a population that is hypersexual, sexually permissive and passive, and, therefore, unrapeable. In other words, because women of color are constructed as always looking for sex, the rape of their bodes is not seen as a violation and, therefore, does not "count" (Smith, 2005, p. 10).

White women, however, are constructed as pure and virginal, not sexual beings (Hale, 1998). Therefore, the rape of their bodies does count and is seen as an extreme violation. This violation is as much a threat to white women as it is a threat to white men and the overall supremacy of whiteness and patriarchy. Hale (1998) explained, "Rape of white women signaled metaphorically white men's fear of the loss of ability to provide for white women and . . . the loss of white racial purity" (p. 253). When white women are raped, regardless of the perpetrator's race, the white patriarchal structure the nation was founded on, the same structure that continually confers supremacy to white men, is threatened. The rape of white women makes whiteness impure. It also challenges white men's ownership over white women's bodies and their ability to exert sole control over this property. The rape of white women as a threat to whiteness and patriarchy is one of many reasons that this rape is framed as a greater offense than the rape of women of color (Burrell, 1993). This correlates directly to the disproportional coverage of white women as the sole victims of sexual violence on college campuses. Acts of sexual violence against white women are more believable but also more tragic and compelling because they, unlike the stereotypes of women of color, have never asked for sex.

Although stereotypes are unsubstantiated beliefs, they are embedded in and significant to the operation of U.S. society (Omi & Winant, 1986). The racially charged stereotypical understandings of sexual violence for women on college campuses have seeped into the very fabric of education, affecting the ways that all individuals involved in higher education perceive, address, prevent, and respond to sexual violence for women of color. With this understanding, the next section explores how racism and sexism, which manifest in stereotypes concerning women of color and white women, are endemic, ingrained, and permanent to U.S. society and institutions of higher education.

The Endemic Nature of Racism and Sexism

Although race and gender are social constructs, these constructed identities have become real and normalized systems that shape everyday experiences for women living in a U.S. context (Delgado & Stefancic, 2012). Put simply, racism and sexism are endemic, embedded in, and permanent to U.S. society (Bell, 1992) and, more specifically higher education (Harper & Patton, 2007). The endemic nature of racism and sexism shapes individuals' experience with, perceptions of, and responses to sexual violence for women of color on college campuses. Olive (2012) explained:

> Our culture's views affect how women of color are evaluated and how they respond to their trauma. These images serve to reinforce rape myths and mark victims of color as responsible for their assaults. Particular stereotypes develop a culture of silence around assault. (p. 3)

Starting from a young age, these cultural views are tacitly communicated so that understandings and values concerning race, gender, and women of color are ingrained in societies' developing minds (see Lawrence, 1987). Cultural stereotypes, such as the passive Asian and the Latina spitfire, are images that aid in the construction of our inherently racist and sexist cultural views as a collective nation and as individual people. These stereotypes are "tacitly transmitted" (Lawrence, 1987, p. 343) via television, movies, print media, news broadcasts, books, and music. With each passing second, stereotypes about women of color become more ingrained in the fabric of the United States.

The manifestations of these stereotypes are apparent in the perceptions others hold of women's sexuality. For instance, college students perceive white women as "sexually liberal" whereas Black women are described as promiscuous; Latinas are seen as sexy and feisty, and Asian women are viewed as submissive (Ghavami & Peplau, 2012, p. 120). Racist and sexist tacit understandings support the belief that white women when raped by a Black perpetrator are less responsible than Black women for their rape (Varelas & Foley, 1998). These perceptions stem from the deleterious stereotype of "Black women as promiscuous, thereby leading participants to judge the interracial Black victim as more blameworthy" (George & Martinez, 2002, p. 115) and less deserving of reporting their victimization.

Although college students' perceptions and understandings of sexual violence for women of color and white women are alarming, what may be even more troubling is the internalization of these endemic racist and sexist stereotypes by women of color. For instance, Latinas may blame other Latinas for rape "because of the way they dress, lead men on, or take risks by going out alone or to dangerous places" (Lira, Koss, & Russo, 1999, p. 253). Additionally, Hispanic American women (Jimenez & Abreu, 2003) and first-generation Asian American women (Devdas & Rubin, 2007) display a higher acceptance for rape myths. Hispanic American women also hold less positive attitudes toward rape victims than white women (Jimenez & Abreu, 2003). Finally, Black women may be hesitant to report sexual violence because they place blame on themselves or are aware of the hypersexualization of Black women and are afraid that others will blame them for being sexually violated (McGuffey, 2013; Tillman, Bryant-Davis, Smith, & Marks, 2010). The endemic nature of stereotypes concerning women of color, which are produced at the intersections of race and gender, are so normalized that women of color internalize them, resulting in their own victim blaming and hesitancy to report assault. College educators must explore the endemic nature of racism and sexism that is undoubtedly prevalent on campus but also in their own minds, informing their approaches to sexual violence.

Implications and Conclusions

The preceding sections explored CRT and CRF as useful frameworks that help to expose and deconstruct oppressive, interlocking systems influencing women of color's experiences with sexual violence. CRT and CRF are also useful in guiding action steps college educators may take to actively dismantle systems of oppression and effectively address the experiences of women students of color and sexual violence. Next, I offer recommendations, informed by CRT and CRF, that aim to prevent and address sexual violence for women students of color on college campuses.

Education and Visibility

People living, working, and learning on college campuses are not immune to the endemic nature of racism and sexism that plagues U.S. society. Lawrence (1987) may have put it best: "To the extent that this cultural belief system has impacted all of us, we are all racist. At the same time, most of us are unaware of our racism" (p. 322). It is imperative for college educators to explore avenues to offer education to all campus constituents that expose and deconstruct dominant ideologies that have an impact on women of color and other communities historically constructed as subordinate by dominant groups.

The education offered by colleges can be achieved through various avenues. For instance, curricula must reflect the voices of women of color, past and present. Faculty must explore race, gender, and the intersections of identity in their courses so all students may gain a diverse understanding of experiences and histories. Moreover, courses that address race, gender, and intersectionality will challenge dominant ideologies by focusing on topics such as the social construction of stereotypes to maintain the status quo, violence as a tool used by colonizers to terrorize communities of difference, and the revisionist history of women of color in a U.S. educational context. Educators should supplement academic curricula with campus events that allow campus constituents to explore a diversity of identities and experiences. Lecturers, poets, and theater productions that focus on women of color's experiences must be invited to campus. Finally, visual education of sexual violence, including posters, videos, and newspaper articles, must highlight populations beyond white women. Visual representations nonverbally convey who matters in campus conversations about sexual violence, making it imperative that women of color are represented in these visual messages.

It may be even more important for campus educators to remain cognizant of and educated on the endemic and internalized sexism and racism that affects their own work. Self-reflection and education is achieved on individual, institutional, and organizational levels. Individually, educators must read current issues, events, and research surrounding sexual violence on college campuses. Educators can find this information in realms specific to higher education, such as *The Chronicle of Higher Education* and the *Journal for College Student Development*. However, I also urge educators to look to other disciplines, such as women's studies and ethnic studies, and organizations such as INCITE! and the National Organization of Sisters of Color Ending Sexual Assault, and follow blogs and news outlets, such as *Colorlines*, that center women of color.

At the institutional level, administrators must also provide resources that allow college educators to remain knowledgeable about sexual violence for differing populations. For instance, institutional leaders should offer annual retreats for faculty, staff, and administrators who aim to be advocates for all students who are sexually assaulted. Higher education and student affairs organizations, such as the Association for the Study of Higher Education and the National Association of Student Personnel Administrators, also have a responsibility to address the endemic nature of racism and sexism in higher education as well as focus on women of color and sexual violence on college campuses. Conference sessions, task forces, and podcasts must be dedicated to educating researchers and practitioners on the root causes of sexual violence for multiple student populations and explore how practice and research can be tailored to focus on students with multiple minoritized identities.

Empowerment Through Narrative Voice

Although focusing on the lived experiences of women of color is integral for the entire campus community to recognize and root out dominant ideologies, educators must do more to support women of color as a community. Women of color internalize racism, sexism, and rape myth ideologies. It is necessary for college educators to work with this population to empower its members to have a voice and visibility on campus but also work to root out their own embedded understandings of sexism and racism. By focusing on the experiential knowledge of women students of color on campus, educators may support these women in addressing internalized racism and sexism. Critical race theorists and critical race feminists agree that sharing the narratives of marginalized populations brings power to these communities and "are essential to the task of exposing the impact of systemic racism" (Arriola, 2003, p. 408). Experiential knowledge and narrative voice are beneficial in building stronger communities from within and relationships between women of color. Delgado and Stefancic (2012) agreed: "Stories also serve a powerful additional function for minority communities. Many victims of racial discrimination suffer in silence or blame themselves for their predicament. Stories can give them a voice and reveal that others have similar experiences" (p. 49). By sharing stories with one another, women of color may combat the internalized racism and sexism that is endemic in communities of color. College educators must ensure women of color have the resources and support to build organizations, groups, and events specific to this community.

For instance, Barnard College sponsors a women of color support group that aims to "provide a supportive atmosphere where women of diverse cultural backgrounds can engage in discussion and self-expression related to the challenges, celebrations, and complexities related to their life at Barnard" (Barnard College, 2015). Other campuses may find alternate initiatives more influential, such as dedicating a residence hall floor for women of color, developing a campus organization that creates programs about and for women of color, and holding an annual retreat for women of color students, faculty, and staff. Educators must build a space where women of color may come together in an environment that feels supportive enough to talk openly about sexism, racism, sexual violence, and other issues facing this population on college campuses. It should be noted that these spaces and programs might require time and energy from faculty and staff of color on campus. The dedication of these campus employees to women of color students must be recognized with possible monetary compensation, a course release, or approved time away from the office.

Policies, Procedures, and Programs

Women of color students are often further silenced by campus sexual violence policies, procedures, and programs, which lack an intersectional analysis and are generated from the understanding that the essential woman is white. Essentialist discourses concerning sexual violence on college campuses must be critiqued and deconstructed so women of color feel visible and supported on campus. To begin this deconstruction and reconstruction of approaches to sexual violence on campus, it is particularly important that every college educator "looks to the needs of the bottom" (Matsuda, 1987, p. 397) to develop policies, procedures, and programs. Looking to the bottom requires educators to create policies, procedures, and programs that address the needs of "the poorest group" (Delgado & Stefancic, 2012, p. 27). If policies, procedures, and programs do not address the needs of minoritized students, then the policies, procedures, and programs are ineffective.

Understanding the needs of women of color on campus is critical in forming policies that look to the bottom, address all campus communities, and critique interlocking systems of oppression. Listening to women of color's experiences and asking them directly about their needs regarding approaches to sexual violence on campus is one way college educators can begin to build this understanding. Once again, the narratives of women of color are central to identifying and exposing oppressive structures that affect their experiences (Solórzano & Yosso, 2002; Yosso, 2006), specifically with sexual violence. Understanding also stems from reading the narratives of women of color who are sexually assaulted. For instance, research (see Amar, 2009) suggests that Black women students are more willing to report forced sexual violence when they perceive they have more control and support in the reporting process. Research findings such as this guide educators' tailored approaches to sexual violence for different populations on campus. Moreover, CRT encourages an interdisciplinary approach to understanding racism and sexism on campus. College educators must look to other disciplines, organizations, and institutional types for information on sexual violence for women of color. Sexual violence on college campuses does not exist in a silo. Therefore, it will take alternate tools from outside higher education to more fully understand and address this issue.

Look Beyond the "Master's Tools"

College educators must use tools that center on sexism, racism, and the intersections of identity if they truly aim to address and eradicate sexual violence on the college campus. CRT and CRF are two such tools that allow us to "rethink and recast" (Crenshaw, 1989, p. 58) sexual violence in higher education and center on women of color in this discourse. For instance, the theory of intersectionality "provides an important lens for reframing and creating new knowledge because it asserts new ways of studying power and inequality and challenges conventional understandings of oppressed and excluded groups and individuals" (Thornton-Dill & Zambrana, 2009, p. 5). College educators must continue to learn about and apply nondominant tools, such as CRT and CRF, that allow for the critique and deconstruction of dominant structures. If educators continue business as usual, approaching sexual violence from a white patriarchal paradigm, women students of color will remain invisible and unheard in the discourses on sexual violence. Audre Lorde (2007) may have said it best: "The master's tools will never dismantle the master's house." We must push ourselves and one another to look beyond the master's tools to root out the systems of oppression that are deeply embedded on our college campuses and have an impact on women of color students' experiences with sexual violence.

References

Amar, A. F. (2009). Applying the theory of planned behavior to reporting of forced sex by African-American college women. *Journal of the National Black Nurses Association, 20*(2), 13–19.

Arriola, E. R. (2003). Voices from the barbed wires of despair: Women in the maquiladoras, Latina critical legal theory, and gender at the U.S.-Mexico border. In A. K. Wing (Ed.), *Critical race feminism: A reader* (pp. 406–426). New York: New York University Press.

Barnard College. (2015). *Barnard college student life: Women of color support group.* Retrieved from barnard.edu/studentlife/diversity/programs/women-of-color-support-group

Barrick, K., Krebs, C. P., & Lindquist, C. H. (2013). Intimate partner violence victimization among undergraduate women at historically Black colleges and universities (HBCUs). *Violence Against Women, 19*, 1014–1033.

Bell, D. A. (1992). *Faces at the bottom of the well: The permanence of racism.* New York, NY: Basic Books.

Burrell, D. E. (1993). Myth, stereotypes, and the rape of Black women. *UCLA Women's Law Journal,* 87–99.

Carbado, D. W., Crenshaw, K. W., Mays, V. M., & Tomlinson, B. (2013). Intersectionality: Mapping the movements of a theory. *Du Bois Review, 10*(2), 303–312.

Crenshaw, K. (1988). Race, reform, and retrenchment: Transformation and legitimation in antidiscrimination law. *Harvard Law Review, 101*, 1331–1387.

Crenshaw, K. (1989). Demarginalizing the intersection of race and sex: A Black feminist critique of antidiscrimination doctrine, feminist theory, and antiracist politics. *University of Chicago Legal Forum,* 139–167.

Crenshaw, K. (1991). Mapping the margins: Intersectionality, identity politics and violence against women of color. *Stanford Law Review, 43*, 1241–1299.

Crenshaw, K., Gotanda, N., Peller, G., & Thomas, K. (Eds.). (1995). *Critical race theory: The key writings that formed the movement.* New York, NY: New Press.

Delgado, R. (1989). Storytelling for oppositionists and others: A plea for narrative. *Michigan Law Review, 87*, 2411–2441.

Delgado, R., & Stefancic, J. (2012). *Critical race theory: An introduction* (2nd ed.). New York: New York University Press.

Devdas, N. R., & Rubin, L. J. (2007). Rape myth acceptance among first-generation and second-generation South Asian American women. *Sex Roles, 56*, 701–705.

Freedman, E. B. (2013). *Redefining rape: Sexual violence in the era of suffrage and segregation.* Cambridge, MA: Harvard University Press.

George, W. H., & Martinez, L. J. (2002). Victim blaming in rape: Effects of victim and perpetrator race, type of rape, and participant racism. *Psychology of Women Quarterly, 26*, 110–119.

Ghavami, N., & Peplau, L. A. (2012). An intersectional analysis of gender and ethnic stereotypes: Testing three hypotheses. *Psychology of Women Quarterly, 37*, 113–127.

Grillo, T. (1995). Anti-essentialism and intersectionality: Tools to dismantle the master's house. *Berkeley Journal of Gender, Law, and Justice, 10*, 16–30.

Gross, A. M., Winslett, A., Roberts, M., & Gohm, C. L. (2006). An examination of sexual violence against college women. *Violence Against Women, 12*, 288–300.

Hale, G. E. (1998). *Making whiteness: The culture of segregation in the South, 1890–1940.* New York, NY: Random House.

Harper, S. R., & Patton, L. D. (2007). Editors' notes. *New Directions for Student Services, 120*, 1–5.

Hunter, M. L. (2005). *Race, gender, and the politics of skin tone.* New York, NY: Routledge.

Jimenez, J. A., & Abreu, J. M. (2003). Race and sex on attitudinal perceptions of acquaintance rape. *Journal of Counseling Psychology, 50*, 252–256.

Ladson-Billings, G. (1998). Just what is critical race theory and what's it doing in a nice field like education? *International Journal of Qualitative Studies in Education, 11*(1), 7–24.

Ladson-Billings, G., & Tate, W. G. (1995). Toward a critical race theory of education. *Teachers College Record, 97*(1), 47–68.

Lawrence, C. R. (1987). The id, the ego, and the equal protection: Reckoning with unconscious racism. *Stanford Law Review, 39*, 317–388.

Lira, L. R., Koss, M. P., & Russo, N. F. (1999). Mexican American women's definitions of rape and sexual abuse. *Hispanic Journal of Behavioral Sciences, 21*, 236–263.

Lloyd, K. A. (2000). Wives for sale: The modern international mail-order bride industry. *Northwestern Journal of International Law & Business, 20*, 341–368.

Lorde, A. (2007). *Sister outsider: Essays and speeches by Audre Lorde.* Berkeley, CA: Crossing Press.

Lynn, M., & Adams, M. (2002). Critical race theory and education: Recent developments in the field. *Equity and Excellence in Education, 35,* 119–130.

Matsuda, M. J. (1987). Looking to the bottom: Critical legal studies and reparations. *Harvard Civil Rights-Civil Liberties Law Review, 22,* 323–399.

McGuffey, C. S. (2013). Rape and racial appraisals: Culture, intersectionality, and Black women's accounts of sexual assault. *Du Bois Review, 10*(1), 109–130.

Nakashima, C. L. (1992). An invisible monster: The creation and denial of mixed-race people in America. In M. P. P. Root (Ed.), *Racially mixed people in America* (pp. 162–179). Newbury Park, CA: Sage.

Olive, V. C. (2012). Sexual assault against women of color. *Journal of Student Research, 1,* 1–9.

Omi, M., & Winant, H. (1986). *Racial formation in the United States: From the 1960s to the 1980s.* New York, NY: Routledge.

Park, H. (2012). Interracial violence, western racialized masculinities, and the geopolitics of violence against women. *Social & Legal Studies, 21,* 491–509.

Roshanravan, S. M. (2010). Passing-as-if: Model-minority subjectivity and women of color identification. *Meridians, 10,* 1–31.

Smith, A. (2005). *Conquest: Sexual violence and American Indian genocide.* Cambridge, MA: South End Press.

Solórzano, D., & Yosso, T. (2002). Critical race methodology: Counter-storytelling as an analytical framework for educational research. *Qualitative Inquiry, 8*(22), 22–44.

Testa, M., & Dermen, K. H. (1999). The differential correlates of sexual coercion and rape. *Journal of Interpersonal Violence, 14,* 548–561.

Thornton-Dill, B., & Zambrana, R. E. (2009). Critical thinking about inequality: An emerging lens. In B. Thornton-Dill & R. E. Zambrana (Eds.), *Emerging intersections: Race, class, and gender in theory, policy, and practice* (pp. 1–21). New Brunswick, NJ: Rutgers University Press.

Tillman, S., Bryant-Davis, T., Smith, K., & Marks, A. (2010). Shattering silence: Exploring barriers to disclosure for African American sexual assault survivors. *Trauma Violence Abuse, 11*(2), 59–70.

Varelas, N., & Foley, L. (1998). Blacks' and Whites' perceptions of interracial and intraracial date rape. *Journal of Social Psychology, 138,* 392–400.

Vargas, D. R. (2010). Representations of Latina/o sexuality in popular culture. In M. Ascencio (Ed.), *Latina/o sexualities: Probing powers, passion, practices, and policies* (pp. 117–136). New Brunswick, NJ: Rutgers University Press.

Wanjuki, W. (2013). *College rape: Does the media focus only on White survivors?* Retrieved from mic.com/articles/38363/college-rape-does-the-media-focus-only-on-White-survivors

West, C. M. (1995). Mammy, Sapphire, and Jezebel: Historical images of Black women and their implications for psychotherapy. *Psychotherapy, 32,* 458–466.

West, C. M. (2008). Mammy, Jezebel, Sapphire, and their homegirls: Developing an "oppositional gaze" toward developing the images of Black women. In J. Chrisler, C. Golden, & P. Rozee (Eds.), *Lectures on the psychology of women* (4th ed., pp. 286–299). New York, NY: McGraw-Hill.

Wing, A. K. (1997). A critical race feminist conceptualization of violence: South African and Palestinian women. *Albany Law Review, 60,* 943–976.

Wing, A. K. (2003). Introduction. In A. K. Wing (Ed.), *Critical race feminism: A reader* (pp. 1–19). New York: New York University Press.

Yosso, T. J. (2006). *Critical race counterstories across the Chicana/Chicano educational pipeline.* New York, NY: Routledge.

3

REEXAMINING OUR ROOTS

A History of Racism and Antirape Activism

Chris Linder

Sexual violence activism in the United States has largely been credited to feminist consciousness-raising groups of the 1960s (Bevacqua, 2000; Bohmer & Parrot, 1993; Corrigan, 2013); however, the sexual violence movement of the 1960s is a continuation of a long history of organizing on sexual violence. Consciousness-raising groups of the 1960s largely emerged from college campuses and centered on white women's issues and experiences with sexual violence (Bevacqua, 2000); yet Black women have organized on issues of sexual violence since the late 1800s (Davis, 1971; Freedman, 2013; Giddings, 1984; McGuire, 2010). Failing to acknowledge or recognize Black women's contributions to sexual violence activism contributes to a narrow understanding of sexual violence and minimizes the significance of the intersections of racism and sexism in addressing sexual violence. The implications of this ahistoricism (not understanding or accounting for history) are significant: Namely, failing to understand the relationship between sexual and racial violence leads to incomplete and ineffective strategies for eradicating sexual violence.

Black feminist women's organizing in the late 1800s and early 1900s provided a strong foundation for addressing sexual violence through an intersectional lens (Giddings, 1984; McGuire, 2010). Yet, white feminists ignored this history, creating power-neutral, racist organizing strategies resulting in laws and practices that centered on white women's experiences. Examining a more nuanced history may assist current sexual violence activists and educators to better understand the intersections of racism and sexism related to sexual violence and to consider strategies for addressing sexual violence from a more power-conscious lens on college campuses.

Although much of the history covered in this chapter centers on sexual violence organizing beyond college campuses, this history has implications for campus-based movements as well. In the following sections, I examine the intersections of anti-Black racism and sexual violence in U.S. history by examining four eras: colonization, slavery, and the Victorian era; the Civil War and reconstruction; the civil rights movement of the 1960s; and the tough-on-crime period of the 1970s through the 1990s.

In reviewing literature for this chapter, I struggled to find documentation of histories of groups other than white women and Black women. Additionally, despite numerous attempts, I located only a few historical analyses about sexual violence written by women of color. Both these challenges have additional implications for today's organizing related to sexual violence. For instance, more than just Black women and white women are affected by sexual violence in the United States, yet many of these realities have been silenced or ignored. Additionally, white women historians (and I as the author of this chapter) may have overlooked or misinterpreted some historical events based on our positionalities as white women. Further, the lack of documented history about sexual violence among women of color further illustrates the ways sexual violence has been constructed as an issue primarily affecting white women throughout history.

Colonization, Slavery, and the Victorian Era

Sexual violence in the United States dates from at least colonial times and has been used systemically as a tool of terrorization and economic control (Donat & D'Emilio, 1992; Freedman, 2013; Giddings, 1984; A. Smith, 2005). European colonizers used rape as a tool of colonization directed toward indigenous women and communities (Freedman, 2013; A. Smith, 2005). European colonizers raped indigenous women as a way to exert power over entire Native communities. By demonstrating their power to take or have whatever they wanted, white European men attempted to control and terrorize indigenous communities, using rape as one tool for colonizing what is now known as the United States (A. Smith, 2005; Trask, 2006).

Colonizers also used rape as a tool of terrorization and economic control in relationship to slavery. Slave owners regularly raped women slaves as a way to increase their property ownership (Davis, 1981; Freedman, 2013; Giddings, 1984). Because children of slaves became the property of the slave owner, not the parents, slave owners could increase their labor supply by impregnating women slaves. Slave owners not only increased their labor supply but also used rape as a tool of terrorization, attempting to keep slaves in a constant state of fear (Davis, 1981; Giddings, 1984). Black women slaves engaged in resistance to white patriarchal control of their bodies. For example, slave women took camphor (derived from camphor tree bark) as a contraceptive and aborted their own pregnancies, striving to avoid contributing to the slave owner's desire to increase his labor supply (Giddings, 1984).

British rape laws defining *rape* as "unlawful and carnal knowledge of a woman, by force and against her will" were instituted in the U.S. colonies in the late 1600s (Freedman, 2013, p. 12). These laws required evidence of force and lack of consent but were rarely enforced even in colonial times because of "suspicion about female complicity" (Freedman, 2013, p. 12; Lindemann, 1984). Rape laws were enforced most frequently when the alleged perpetrator was a Black or indigenous man or a man from a lower-class background whose victim was a white woman from an upper-class family (Lindemann, 1984). Further, given that Black women were primarily considered property as in the case of slaves, and indigenous women were considered savages by white colonizers, these laws primarily applied to white women (Donat & D'Emilio, 1992; Giddings, 1984).

During the Victorian era of the early 1800s, politicians developed additional laws related to morality, purity, and sexual behavior. Rooted in Victorian notions of womanhood and closely tied to teachings of the church, laws protecting white women's purity and chastity emerged (Donat & D'Emilio, 1992; Giddings, 1984). These laws were intended for "better classes" (e.g., white middle- and upper-class women and their families; Giddings, 1984, p. 49), resulting in women of color's and poor white women's experiences with sexual violence continuing to be ignored in the legal realm. Examining the ways rape laws were designed to protect white women and their families further illustrates the role of racism in the history of sexual violence organizing, specifically as related to legal issues, as described next.

Seduction laws, centered on white women's chastity and virtue, were "applied in cases when a woman had not consented but had not experienced the level of physical violence required to prove rape" (Freedman, 2013, p. 43). Seduction laws emerged from concerns about white women's chastity and virtue and centered on white fathers' economic stability. Patriarchal values insisted that white women were fragile and needed men (their fathers or husbands) to protect them and required that women remain pure to allow their fathers to find a suitable husband for their daughters (Donat & D'Emilio, 1992). If a woman's sexual reputation was "sullied" prior to marriage, her prospects for marriage plummeted, making her an economic burden to her father because he would have to continue to financially support her (Freedman, 2013, p. 35). Fathers could sue men who seduced their daughters into premarital sex because the reputation she gained "seriously reduced" her "marital prospects by undermining her qualifications to become a virtuous wife and mother" (Freedman, 2013, p. 39).

Laws related to rape and seduction ignored the experiences of women of color in the late 1700s and early 1800s. However, by the late 1800s Black women and some white women worked to raise awareness about the rape of Black women by white men and the violence directed toward Black men falsely accused of raping white women (Davis, 1981; McGuire, 2010).

Civil War and Reconstruction Era

Prior to emancipation, white men used rape as a tool of terrorization and colonization to keep slaves under control (Giddings, 1984). After emancipation, white men continued to use rape as a tool of terrorization to remind former slaves of their place in society (Davis, 1971; Donat & D'Emilio, 1992). Evidence of Black communities gaining increased power, whether through legislation, court proceedings, or economic growth, resulted in white men engaging in violence to maintain their power. Riots, including looting Black-owned businesses, burning Black homes, and raping Black women, were common post-emancipation (Alexander, 2010; Davis, 1971; Giddings, 1984). When Black women attempted to resist sexual violence, or when Black men responded to rape directed toward Black women, they were threatened with death and sometimes killed (Davis, 1971; Freedman, 2013; McGuire, 2010). Although police and legal systems were supposed to protect all citizens, including Black "citizens," they failed to do so. White police officers frequently engaged in, and sometimes led, riots, looting, and rape of Black women (McGuire, 2010). When Black citizens did report crimes they experienced to the police or criminal justice system, they were rarely taken seriously, and when they did go to trial, juries consisted solely of white men (McGuire, 2010).

Black activists did not stand by and let this happen. Black women spoke out about their experiences with rape in public and private spaces, contributing to an increase in awareness about the relationship between racism and sexual violence. In the late 1800s, reports of Black women experiencing rape increased dramatically in Black and white newspapers and reports from the National Association for the Advancement of Colored People (NAACP; McGuire, 2010). However, white newspapers intentionally focused on the rape of Black women by Black men and ignored reports of white men raping Black women, contributing to further protection of "white men's sexual entitlement" (Freedman, 2013, p. 84) and an increasing fear of Black men as predators. Additionally, courts ignored intraracial Black rape (rape perpetuated by Black men on Black women) because the legal system was set up to serve and protect white people. Black women were not considered chaste or moral enough to deserve protection from rape through the white legal system, an extension of the Victorian era seduction laws written to protect white women and their families (Giddings, 1984; McGuire, 2010). Many of the laws written during this time indicated that women who "worked outside the home or whose race had a history of exploitation were outside the realm of 'womanhood' and its prerogatives" (Giddings, 1984, p. 49).

Black women activists challenged the notion that Black women should be excluded from sexual violence laws and addressed unfounded fear about Black men as perpetrators of sexual violence. For example, Ida B. Wells, an activist largely known for her antilynching efforts of the late 1890s, also addressed sexual violence through her work as an activist (Bevacqua, 2000; Giddings, 1984). Mobilized by the lynching of a close friend, Thomas Moss, in Memphis, Tennessee, Wells immediately began collecting information about lynching in the South. She declared, "Lynching was merely an excuse to get rid of Negroes who were acquiring wealth and property and thus keep the race terrorized" (Giddings, 1984, p. 28). She collected information on 728 lynchings that occurred between 1882 and 1892, highlighting the reality that fewer than one third of men who were lynched were accused of rape and even fewer were responsible for it (Giddings, 1984). Wells not only interrupted the myth of Black men as rapists of white women but also uncovered the reality that white women frequently initiated relationships with Black men, further disrupting the myth of Black men as perpetrators and seducers of white women (Giddings, 1984). Wells published the findings of her tracking of lynching patterns in Northern newspapers and in brochures distributed throughout the South. As a result of her work, she was exiled from her home in the South and forced to relocate to the North, where she continued writing about lynchings, the unfounded fear of Black men as rapists, and the minimization of Black women's experiences with sexual violence (Freedman, 2013; Giddings, 1984).

Through her work, Wells also drew attention to the reality that white men raped Black women without fear of repercussion; she wrote, "The rape of helpless Negro girls, which began in slavery days, still continues today without reproof from church, state, or press" (Giddings, 1984, p. 31). As a result of Wells's work, Black women began to speak out publicly about their experiences with sexual violence at the hands of white men, specifically as they worked as domestic laborers in white homes (McGuire, 2010). Wells helped publicize Black women's experiences with rape through Black newspapers throughout the country and white newspapers in the North, resulting in an increase in awareness and attention to the ways racism and sexism intersected to influence Black women's experiences. Wells intended to publish the findings from the lynching investigation independently of a newspaper but lacked the funds to do so. In 1892 Black women's clubs came together to support Wells's work through a testimonial and fund-raiser. The event, which centered on Black women's experiences with sexual violence through testimonials, raised enough money for Wells to publish her work (Giddings, 1984). The Black women's club organizing demonstrated how Black women's experiences with sexual violence could be centered at the same time public consciousness was raised about the ways Black men were harmed by racist ideologies about sexual violence. Civil rights and feminist groups have historically struggled with attempting to engage in activism centering on multiple groups' experiences. For example, feminist groups often center white women's experiences and racial justice groups focus on Black men's experiences (Crenshaw, 1989). The Black feminist organizing of the late 1800s set the stage for a continuation of attention to addressing race and sexual violence throughout the civil rights era of the 1960s.

Civil Rights Era

Although popular rhetoric about the civil rights era in the United States largely focuses on racial justice and legal issues in the 1960s, some historians describe the roots of the civil rights movement as focusing on racial and gender justice (Giddings, 1984; McGuire, 2010). Black activists, and specifically Black women, worked to organize on issues of racism and sexual violence during this time (Freedman, 2013; Giddings, 1984; McGuire, 2010).

In the 1930s nine African American boys from Scottsboro, Alabama, were accused of raping two white women on a train headed to Tennessee. The arrests, trial, and sentencing of these boys happened in two weeks. They were found responsible by an all-white jury and sentenced to death (Freedman, 2013; McGuire, 2010). Black organizations in the South, including the NAACP and Black women's social clubs, quickly organized and raised money for the nine boys' defense. Over the course of 20 years, organizers funded the defense for retrials for all nine of the men, which cleared them of wrongdoing and resulted in their release from jail. This was one of the first cases of successful legal organizing by Black activists and advocacy groups related to sexual violence (McGuire, 2010).

During the same time period, Black women organized to have their cases as sexual violence survivors heard in court. One case in particular garnered national attention. Six white men kidnapped and raped Recy Taylor, a Black woman, as she was walking home from a church function with three of her family members. Taylor survived the assault and reported it to police, who promptly ignored it, claiming they did not have enough evidence to move forward (McGuire, 2010). Rosa Parks, whom historians have painted as the face of the Montgomery, Alabama, bus boycotts, led the movement to get Taylor's case to a jury. Parks formed the Alabama Committee for Equal Justice for Recy Taylor and worked to share the story with as many newspapers as she could. Newspapers in the North took up the case, but the case never made it to a fair trial. However, the court case set the stage for additional organizing related to Black women's experiences with sexual violence and for the Montgomery bus boycotts (McGuire, 2010).

Although "no one has ever called it a women's movement," (McGuire, 2010, p. 39), women were central to the famous bus boycotts in Montgomery. Black women domestics rode buses to work in white homes and were regularly harassed, racially and sexually, by white bus drivers, police officers, and passengers. They were forced to sit in the back of the buses, away from white passengers, and were often subject to lewd comments and groping by white passengers, bus drivers, and police officers as they rode the buses. Because of the voices of Taylor and other Black women who shared their experiences of sexual violence through "testimony and truth-telling" (McGuire, 2010, p. 30), more Black women began to speak out about the racialized sexual violence they experienced. These testimonies by Black women built on the previous work of Wells and helped to shine a light on the "ritual of rape in existence since slavery" (McGuire, 2010, p. 39), which resulted in increased attention to racialized sexual violence and direct action against it.

Similarly, several cases in the 1960s and 1970s highlighted the need for more attention to be given to women killing or severely injuring men in self-defense of sexual violence (Bevacqua, 2000). Further illustrating white men's (especially those in power) entitlement to Black women's bodies, Joan Little, a Black woman, was raped by a white prison warden. Little killed him in self-defense during the assault (Bevacqua, 2000; Davis, 2002; McGuire, 2010). Little was charged with murder and tried in court. Black activist groups organized and raised money for her defense, and she was acquitted in 1975 (Bevacqua, 2000; McGuire, 2010). Additionally, Inez Garcia, a Latina, was raped in her home in California; after the rape, she found and killed her rapist. She was originally convicted of second-degree murder. Activist groups in California raised money for her defense and successfully secured a retrial. She was acquitted of the charges through a self-defense argument (Bevacqua, 2000). These cases further illustrate the ways communities of color engaged in activism related to sexual violence.

Despite the fact that the criminal justice system failed to support and protect Black communities from white violence, Black activists worked within criminal justice systems, as illustrated by activism related to fair trials for Recy Taylor and Joan Little. However, Black activists also worked toward addressing sexual violence through community-based organizations, including rape crisis centers and community accountability processes in the 1970s (Bevacqua, 2000; Bierra et al., 2006; Davis, 1984). Although Black activists worked to draw attention to the intersections of racism, classism, and sexism related to sexual violence, the political climate in the United States shifted to a "tough on crime" mentality rooted in racism (Bevacqua, 2000, p. 116).

Tough-on-Crime Era

The social progress of people of color, specifically African Americans, in the 1960s threatened white patriarchal power, resulting in white male politicians reemploying fear-based strategies similar to those of the early 1900s when white men painted Black men as predators (Alexander, 2010; Allard, 2006). In the 1970s and 1990s, politicians engaged in a tough-on-crime rhetoric rooted in racism, resulting in increased criminalization of people of color (Allard, 2006). Politicians carefully crafted messages about increases in drug use and abuse and drug-related crime in the United States (Alexander, 2010). Their strategies for addressing drug and crime problems included adopting zero-tolerance policies for drug use and creating additional punishments for drug convictions beyond jail time (Allard, 2006). For example, in the 1990s, lawmakers created policies limiting public housing, job opportunities, student loans, and public assistance programs for people with drug convictions. These laws disproportionately affected communities of color, where they were applied most directly, and contributed to skyrocketing rates of unemployment and housing crises (Alexander, 2006; Allard, 2006; Newell, 2013).

A tough-on-crime approach also appealed to white patriarchal values of protecting white women who "belonged" to white men (Bevacqua, 2000, p. 134). White politicians painted Black men as criminals, perpetuating the myth that white women should fear Black men as potential rapists (Bumiller, 2008). White feminist activists capitalized on this tough-on-crime mentality to advocate for the passage of additional legal responses to sexual violence, such as the Violence Against Women Act ([VAWA], 1994). Given that the majority of lawmakers were, and remain to this day, white men, white feminist activists emphasized how sexual violence affected white men through their daughters, wives, and mothers (Bevacqua, 2000; Bumiller, 2008; Corrigan, 2013).

As a result of (white) feminist activism, VAWA passed in 1994, providing new legal attention to issues of violence against women, including sexual violence. Although some hail the passage of the VAWA as a victory for feminist and civil rights groups because the act addresses issues related to immigration and violence (Rivera, 1996), others argue the overreliance on criminal justice systems furthers the criminalization of communities of color and poor communities (Bumiller, 2008). For example, the VAWA requires mandatory arrests for domestic-violence-related calls, which increases chances of women of color being further criminalized through their experiences with violence directed toward them. When police officers arrive on the scene and cannot determine who the primary aggressor is, they frequently arrest both parties, which has a deleterious impact on queer people and people of color (Ritchie, 2006). The VAWA also introduced additional protocols for addressing gender-related violence on college campuses, including sexual violence. Specifically, the VAWA introduced new requirements for college and university officials to engage in specific reporting and response protocols in an effort to protect future victims of sexual violence (American Council on Education, n.d.). Although these policies are designed to reduce rates of sexual violence through enforcement, they likely have effects on campus similar to the mandatory arrest policy in the community. They further silence already marginalized communities who fear and distrust interaction with authority, and they take agency from victims of sexual violence (Freyd, 2016).

Although activists' strategies to increase legal attention to sexual violence were successful, they failed to take into account the significance of racism in the criminal justice system and the ways racism, classism, and sexism intersect to influence the experiences of minoritized communities with sexual violence (Corrigan, 2013; Davis, 1984; Gruber, 2009). The legal system in the United States was built on assumptions of neutrality based on white, patriarchal standards resulting in legal responses to sexual violence perpetuating these norms. For example, lawmakers assume that police and judges will fairly and equitably apply laws to all communities; however, evidence of this is null. As illustrated throughout U.S. history, legal systems frequently fail to protect communities of color from white violence and perpetuate inaccurate presumptions of Black men as criminals (McGuire, 2010; Ritchie, 2006). These traumas are passed down from generation to generation in Black and other minoritized families, resulting in some members of communities not directly experiencing the trauma but experiencing the emotional and psychological toll of these traumas (W. A. Smith, Allen, & Danley, 2007).

Further, the disparate enforcement of drug laws in communities of color and poor communities contributed to additional fear and distrust of police. Some poor women feared losing access to public assistance if they had to interact with legal systems, resulting in their not involving police and legal systems when they were harmed by sexual violence (Allard, 2006; Ritchie, 2006). Further, historic and recent brutalization, rape, and murder of women of color by police officers makes many women of color reluctant to call or rely on police for assistance under any circumstances (Ritchie, 2006).

Because the criminal justice system works from a punitive rather than a reha-bilitative perspective, many women of color who are harmed by men of color are hesitant to send a member of their already minoritized community into a racist system that will not actually result in any change in behavior but may cause additional harm to an entire community (Ritchie, 2006). The failure of white feminists to consider inequities in the criminal and legal justice sys-tem pushed women of color to create separate movements unrelated to legal systems to address sexual violence in their communities (Bevacqua, 2000).

Women of color activists continued organizing independently of white feminist activists because white feminists relied too heavily on a racist and classist criminal justice system as a response to sexual violence (Bierra et al., 2006). For example, since the 1970s, women of color have vocally advocated for prison abolition, highlighting the need for community accountability processes to address sexual violence and additional crime (Davis, 1984; Gid-dings, 1984). By the 1990s, some white feminist voices also began to chal-lenge overreliance on the state for responses to sexual violence (Bumiller, 2008; Corrigan, 2013; Gruber, 2009), albeit for different reasons. Many white feminists (e.g., Bumiller, Corrigan, and Gruber) mention racism as a reason for feminists to consider moving out of traditional legal systems, yet they primarily focus on the incongruence of "feminist goals" of disem-powering women through a patriarchal legal system and advocate for reform rather than abolition (Gruber, 2009, p. 603). Davis (1984) and members of INCITE! (2001) approach prison abolition and community accountability for rape and sexual violence from an intersectional focus, highlighting the ways in which prison systems and the state have historically further harmed already minoritized groups and fail to make any difference in the rates of sexual violence.

Advocating for prison abolition and community accountability, INCITE! (2001) highlights the fact that an increase in imprisoning people has not made communities safer from interpersonal violence. Rates of sexual and domes-tic violence have not changed, despite increases in arrests and imprisonment for violence (Bierra et al., 2006). Considering community accountability practices that transform perpetrators of violence, rather than imprisoning perpetrators, remains significant. Additionally, as antiviolence organizations have seen an increase in the level of funding they receive from state organiza-tions, they have "increased the professionalization of the anti-violence move-ment and alienated it from its community-organizing, social justice roots" (INCITE!, 2001, para. 6). This alienation results in the continued focus on state systems to address sexual violence rather than on community members with the most knowledge and experience in understanding sexual violence directed at poor women and women of color (Bierra et al., 2006).

In spite of antistate and community accountability advocacy by women of color for almost two decades, most white feminist organizations, policy-makers, and educators on college campuses ignore calls to use community accountability processes in lieu of police and state processes. Most feminist-oriented organizations addressing sexual violence on college campuses continue to advocate for policy and police-related responses to sexual violence. Despite a long history of antirape organizing at the intersections of racism and sexism by women of color, today's movements, including those on college campuses, continue to center white women. Failing to consider racism in the history of sexual violence movements results in limited approaches to addressing sexual violence. Implications of this failure are significant for those attempting to address sexual violence on college campuses.

Implications for Campus Sexual Violence Activism and Education

As activism related to sexual violence on college campuses resurges, understanding and acknowledging history remains important. Failure to understand the history of racism as it intersects with sexual violence results in limited and ineffective strategies to address sexual violence. Specifically, overrelying on authoritative (police, state, and legal) responses to sexual violence; engaging in power-evasive, identity-neutral, educational strategies; and organizing parallel rather than intersecting activist movements represent ineffective, ahistorical approaches to sexual violence activism on college campuses. Next, I examine implications for activists and educators to engage in more equitable and effective practices on college campuses.

Overreliance on Legal Issues and Enforcement

Activism related to sexual violence on college campuses today largely centers on responses to sexual violence after it happens (e.g., Know Your IX and End Rape on Campus websites). This is not surprising given that many activists become involved as a result of feeling betrayed by their institutions after they report experiences of sexual violence (Linder & Myers, 2016). Survivors of sexual violence want to feel safe on campus, and that often means they want the perpetrator removed from campus. As a result, they advocate for better responses to sexual violence as their primary forms of activism. Generally, this response focuses on policy and enforcement through campus conduct codes, Title IX compliance, and police intervention. However, the overreliance on policy and enforcement contributes to several limitations in addressing sexual violence on college campuses.

Legal and policy response have historically centered on the issues and concerns of white middle-class women and their families, as shown by the discussion about rape and seduction laws of the Victorian era and the tough-on-crime era of the 1970s through 1990s, and college campuses are no exception to this. A version of this continued mentality was seen in the ways white fathers were overrepresented among the parents interviewed in the documentary *The Hunting Ground* (Linder & Gaspar, 2015). Of the parents featured in the film, most were white fathers, sending the message that sexual violence remains an issue of importance when it negatively affects white men. The lack of understanding of the ways rape and seduction laws were originally written to center on white fathers and their daughters by most activists and policymakers results in continued uncritical centering of wealthy white women and their fathers through legal and policy responses to sexual violence. Legal and policy responses accord privilege to people with access to financial resources and cultural capital in the form of access to knowledge about how systems work (Ritchie, 2006). Campus response systems are no exception. Although many activists advocate for laws written in an objective or neutral manner, the enforcement of these laws and policies is anything but neutral. Further, as discussed throughout this book, power-evasive and identity-neutral actions unconsciously center on dominant groups' experiences.

To address these concerns, activists must consider working outside the legal and policy systems to address sexual violence. Women of color activists have advocated for community accountability processes for interpersonal violence for decades (Bierra et al., 2006; Davis, 1984; INCITE!, 2001). Although it may feel impossible for campus-based activists to work completely outside the systems designed to address sexual violence, activists may consider spending fewer resources (time, energy, and money) advocating for authoritative (legal and police) response to sexual violence.

Women of color from the collective Communities Against Rape and Abuse (CARA) provide 10 accountability principles for addressing sexual violence through communities rather than state and legal systems (Bierra et al., 2006). The principles advocate for the recognition of the humanity of people involved in the situation, including the perpetrator. Members of CARA believe that rehabilitation of perpetrators happens through community accountability for sexual violence, not punitive measures including jail time. Similarly, one of the principles includes "prioritize the self-determination of the survivor" (Bierra et al., 2006, p. 251), which could be directly applied to campus-based activism. Student activists frequently advocate for increased attention to reporting and enforcement (Grinberg, 2014), which often requires faculty and staff to report any instances of survivors disclosing their experiences with sexual violence to a Title IX coordinator. This is directly in conflict with prioritizing the self-determination of survivors. Survivors lose control of what happens in their situations. Further, in some cases, survivors do not want their perpetrators in jail or kicked off campus; they simply want the perpetrator to stop perpetrating. Community accountability processes, including engaging the perpetrator's family and friends in the process of accountability, may assist in meeting the needs of some survivors (Bierra et al., 2006).

Additionally, if activists do choose to continue to engage in policy response to sexual violence, they must intentionally address power and identity in policy responses to sexual violence. As discussed by Iverson in Chapter 11, many current campus policies attempt to address sexual violence through identity-neutral approaches. Identity-neutral approaches unconsciously center dominant perspectives to addressing sexual violence. Activists must advocate for explicit attention to gender identity, sexual orientation, and additional social identities in sexual violence policies.

Additionally, activists must be vocal about the racist approaches to addressing sexual violence through legal and conduct systems. Identifying and tracking identities of survivors and perpetrators held accountable through public processes can assist in this process. Although information about individual cases is confidential in campus conduct processes, it may be possible to gather demographics of students served by the office in an academic year. Further, tracking the identities of people named in campus and community newspapers can also contribute to a more nuanced understanding of the role of racism in current legal and conduct processes. Research indicates that people of color, men, trans*, and queer survivors report their experiences with sexual violence less frequently than their white cisgender straight women counterparts (Banyard et al., 2007; Fisher, Daigle, Cullen, & Turner, 2003; Henry, 2009) and men of color are overrepresented as perpetrators in media stories (Dixon & Linz, 2000). Documenting this on a particular campus can help people to understand that these patterns happen in their own communities in very concrete ways, which may result in more explicit attention to identity and power in policy and response on campuses.

Power-Evasive and Identity-Neutral Approaches to Education

Just as responses to sexual violence are limited through the exclusion of historically marginalized communities in activism and organizing, so are educational responses. Typically, activists involved in educational initiatives related to sexual violence on college campuses attempt to raise awareness about the frequency or dynamics of sexual violence, teach students bystander intervention strategies (Anderson & Whiston, 2005), or direct survivors and their friends to resources for sexual assault survivors. When developed from an ahistoric, power-evasive, identity-neutral lens, each of these programs contributes to inaccurate information about sexual violence, failing to consider a variety of experiences.

Unfortunately, attempts to be more inclusive frequently contribute to identity-neutral and power-evasive educational strategies. For example, many well-intended sexual violence activists and educators choose nongendered language to illustrate that sexual violence can happen to any person. However, this gender-neutral approach negates the reality that the vast majority of perpetrators of sexual violence are men. Further, given that the dominant narrative about sexual violence centers cisgender heterosexual women as victims of sexual violence (see introduction), failing to explicitly name other genders as victims in educational programs perpetuates the uninterrogated ideal that women are victims and men are perpetrators. To interrupt the dominant narrative, activists must explicitly name dynamics of sexual violence not represented in mainstream accounts of sexual violence. Failing to highlight counterstories to the dominant narrative results in uncritical recentering of the dominant narrative because if people do not know another narrative they will continue to picture cisgender white women as victims even when gender-neutral examples are used. Educators must intentionally name power dynamics associated with sexual violence and explicitly provide examples of people from multiple genders experiencing sexual violence.

Similarly, media coverage of sexual violence frequently overrepresents Black men and Latinos as perpetrators of violent crime, including sexual violence, and underrepresents women of color as victims of crime (Dixon & Linz, 2000). An ahistorical approach to sexual violence education fails to connect this current reality with the racist history of white communities creating and perpetuating fear of Black men as perpetrators of sexual violence, thus contributing to a modern-day racist lynch-mob mentality related to sexual violence. In the early twentieth century, white newspapers frequently named Black men as perpetrators of sexual violence and failed to name white men, especially white men raping Black women, as perpetrators of sexual violence (Freedman, 2013; McGuire, 2010). Failing to interrogate the dominant narrative of Black men as perpetrators of sexual violence results in miseducation about sexual violence.

The myth of the Black rapist causes harm not only to Black men who are not perpetrators of sexual violence but also to potential victims socialized only to fear Black men as potential perpetrators of sexual violence and not to fear other men. Although responsibility for preventing sexual violence should never be placed on potential victims, most risk reduction programs are designed to make potential victims aware of the dynamics of sexual violence in an attempt to help them reduce their risk of assault. Failing to interrogate the myth of the Black rapist results in increased risk for potential victims of sexual violence because potential victims are socialized to fear a stereotypical perpetrator. This socialization does not account for the reality that most sexual assaults happen between two people who know each other and often with similar social identities, including the same race (Black et al., 2011). When potential victims only fear a stereotypical perpetrator, they may let down their guard and ignore red flags when they interact with potential perpetrators who do not meet the image of a perpetrator they have been socialized to accept.

Additionally, ignoring or making some perpetrators invisible because they do not meet the definition of a stereotypical perpetrator results in less than effective bystander intervention programs. Bystander intervention programs are designed to teach students to interrupt behavior that may lead to sexual violence. However, when students subscribe to stranger danger myths about sexual violence or believe the myth of the Black rapist, they may not intervene in more common sexual violence situations. Failing to consider ways men who are perceived as good guys may perpetuate sexual violence results in ineffective bystander intervention programs.

Activists must interrupt and call attention to the stereotypes about perpetrators of sexual violence. Specifically, activists may follow Wells's lead with lynching investigations and track the ways sexual violence is represented in the media. How often are perpetrators named? What are the identities of those perpetrators named? Activists engaged in education related to sexual violence must work from a historic, power-conscious perspective. Naming and interrupting the power-evasive, identity-neutral discourse about sexual violence will contribute to more effective educational programs because students will be better informed on the actual dynamics of sexual violence.

Intersecting Versus Parallel Movements

An ahistorical approach to sexual violence activism resulted in continued parallel, rather than intersecting, social movements. Throughout history, white women and women of color frequently worked separately from each other to address issues related to gender, including sexual violence (Giddings, 1984). As previously mentioned, in the late 1800s and early 1900s Black women organized against sexual violence as part of the overall strategies for racial equity. Historians do not document white women's activism related to sexual violence until the 1970s (Bevacqua, 2000). Although some white women engaged with and advocated for Black women's equality during the suffrage movement, and some women of color attempted to engage in white women's organizing in the 1970s, most organizing happened independently of each other. This largely resulted in white feminists' failure to understand and include issues related to multiple forms of oppression in their organizing (Davis, 1981; Giddings, 1984). Similarly, racial justice movements often centered race, ignoring the influences of sexism on Black women's experiences (Crenshaw, 1989).

Centering white women in women's movements and Black men in civil rights movements results in competing "discourses of resistance" (Carbado, Crenshaw, Mays, & Tomlinson, 2013, p. 304) in feminist and civil rights movements. Failing to account for the unique experiences of women of color at the intersection of race and gender contributes to addressing oppression as an additive rather than intersecting experience and results in women of color falling into a chasm. For example, Crenshaw (1989) advanced the concept of intersectionality through an analysis of a legal case in which Black women's experiences were minimized in a discrimination lawsuit. A group of Black women sued General Motors claiming race and sex discrimination. The court would not hear the case because there was no record of discrimination against white women or Black men, therefore making the claims of racism and sexism void. The court failed to intervene at the intersection of the racism and sexism experienced by Black women because it viewed experiences of oppression as additive, rather than intersectional (Crenshaw, 1989).

Similarly, activists in women's movements and racial justice movements frequently ignore the experiences of women of color because the movements include a focus on one issue: racism or sexism (Crenshaw, 1989). This single-issue focus contributes to further marginalizing women of color and separating energies dedicated to addressing oppression with roots in white supremacy and patriarchy. Examining the movements to secure voting rights provides an additional example of these competing discourses.

Black men and white women advocated for the right to vote around the same time in U.S. history. Both groups largely ignored Black women in these struggles. White women intentionally left out Black women in their organizing and advocacy strategies because they believed that including them would limit their opportunities to gain the right to vote (Davis, 1981). Similarly, Black men left Black women out of their advocacy as a way to demonstrate their ability to engage in patriarchy similar to white men, thus hoping for acceptance by white men based on a common experience as men (Giddings, 1984). If the groups had come together and dedicated their energies to challenging white patriarchy, the struggle may have resulted in everyone getting the right to vote at the same time rather than two separate and longer struggles.

The failure to engage in intersectional activist movements continues today. As discussed in Chapter 9, many of today's campus sexual violence organizers minimize issues related to oppression in sexual violence activism. Even some activists who identify as people of color or queer minimize their experiences with racism and homophobia because they fear it would distract from the larger issue of sexual violence they were attempting to address. Similarly, women of color involved in racial justice activism frequently minimize their experiences with sexism to maintain attention on racism. A recent discussion about sexual violence at historically Black colleges and universities illustrated how Black women felt like they needed to be silent about their experiences with sexual violence to maintain a focus on addressing racism (Badejo, 2016). These examples illustrate the invasive nature of racism, sexism, and heterosexism on the psyches of all people, even members of those groups. Failing to understand how oppressions are interconnected results in less than effective movements because strategies for addressing oppression are incomplete.

To address these incomplete strategies, activists must center the experiences of the most marginalized groups in society in their work (Crenshaw, 1989). Addressing sexual violence at the intersection of multiple forms of oppression increases the likelihood that oppression will be addressed more completely. As Crenshaw (1989) stated,

> If their efforts instead began with addressing the needs and problems of those who are most disadvantaged and with restructuring and remaking the world where necessary then others who are singularly disadvantaged would also benefit. In addition, it seems that placing those who currently are marginalized in the center is the most effective way to resist efforts to compartmentalize experiences and undermine potential collective action. (p. 73)

Sexual violence activists would do well to consider this strategy. By highlighting the ways sexual violence affects different people based on the intersection, rather than on additions, of their identities, activists will be more effective in their work.

Some activists with salient subordinated identities (e.g., women of color, trans* activists, activists with disabilities) may be hesitant to build coalitions across identities because of their previous painful experiences with oppression. Activists with mostly dominant salient identities (e.g., white cisgender heterosexual activists) must understand and deal with this hesitation. For example, because women of color have been ignored or harmed by white feminists for decades, they may be hesitant to participate in coalition building. White feminists must work to address the wrongs of the past that created this harm rather than being defensive or declaring that they are different from "those feminists." Actions speaks louder than words. White feminists must do the work of educating themselves, showing up, stepping back, and admitting their mistakes.

A both/and approach may also assist in coalition building. For example, interacting in community with people with similar experiences with oppression is important for healing. Similarly, people must also be educated in their dominant identities about experiences different from their own, without relying on people with subordinated identities to educate them. This education may need to take place in spaces with people who share dominant identities.

Coalitions that consist of affinity groups for people with shared subordinated identities to come together and discuss those experiences and caucus groups for people in dominant identities to educate each other may result in more effective coalitions. Once people participate in their own processes of healing and education, they may be ready to engage across difference to build coalitions. This is ongoing work. People who experience oppression are never completely healed, nor are people ever completely educated in their dominant identities, but people can begin to do self-work and cautiously enter coalitions and partnerships with people who have previously harmed them.

Concluding Thoughts

Ida B. Wells provided an illustration of a both/and strategy for addressing racism and sexism in sexual violence work. Wells drew attention to the ways white people targeted Black men as alleged rapists. In doing this, she also created space for Black women to speak out about their experiences with sexual violence. As I reflect on this, I cannot help but think of the many parallels between the Black Lives Matter movement and Wells's antilynching campaign. Black Lives Matter activism originated to draw attention to police brutality directed toward Black individuals, primarily Black men, similar to the antilynching activism centering on brutality directed toward Black men. Further, Black Lives Matter activism was initiated by three queer Black women, similar to the ways Wells's antilynching work was primarily organized and supported by Black women. Finally, the Black Lives Matter movement has largely relied on social media and informal networks of information sharing to gain momentum similar to how Wells's antilynching campaigns relied on Black-owned newspapers and fund-raising by Black communities to effectively share her message. Wells's campaign created a space for Black women to share their stories about sexual violence at the same time they challenged racism directed toward Black communities by white, patriarchal power. Similarly, the Black Lives Matter movement has resulted in some increased attention to violence directed toward Black trans* people and women.

I also reflect on the ways white feminists allowed their own racism to get in the way of coalition building with Black feminists throughout history, especially in the period immediately following Wells's work on antilynching. White women's fear of losing the little power they had prevented them from engaging completely with Black women who advocated for similar changes. We are at a crossroads yet again. Can it be different? What if white feminists reflected on this history? What if white feminists considered how their focus on a single-issue struggle may result in limited strategies for addressing sexual violence? What if white feminists opened their minds, considered ways racism intersects with sexism to create a climate in which sexual violence thrives? What if white feminists gave up their fear of losing power?

Racism and sexual violence have always intersected. White men have always used rape as a tool of power and control directed toward communities of color and women and non-gender-binary people. Racial justice and antisexual violence activists will benefit from examining our collective histories, better understanding ways movements for equity share common roots. If white women followed the lead of women of color in approaching sexual violence from an intersectional lens in our history, we might be in a different place today. It is not too late. Paying attention to each other's and our collective histories may allow us to move forward in a more power-conscious manner, resulting in more effective strategies for addressing sexual violence on college campuses and in society at large.

References

Alexander, M. (2010). *The new Jim Crow: Mass incarceration in the age of colorblindness.* New York, NY: The New Press.

Allard, P. (2006). Crime, punishment, and economic violence. In INCITE! Women of Color Against Violence (Ed.), *Color of violence: The INCITE! anthology* (pp. 158–163). Cambridge, MA: South End Press.

American Council on Education. (n.d.). *New requirements imposed by the Violence Against Women Reauthorization Act.* Retrieved from www.acenet.edu/news-room/Documents/VAWA-Summary.pdf

Anderson, L. A., & Whiston, S. C. (2005). Sexual assault education programs: A meta-analytic examination of their effectiveness. *Psychology of Women Quarterly, 29*, 374–388.

Badejo, A. (2016, January 21). *"Our hands are tied because of this damn brotherhood-sisterhood thing."* Retrieved from www.buzzfeed.com/anitabadejo/where-is-that-narrative#.jlLeN4605

Banyard, V. L., Ward, S., Cohn, E. S., Plante, E. G., Moorhead, C., & Walsh, W. (2007). Unwanted sexual contact on campus: A comparison of women's and men's experiences. *Violence and Victims, 22*, 52–70.

Bevacqua, M. (2000). *Rape on the public agenda: Feminism and the politics of sexual assault.* Boston, MA: Northeastern University Press.

Bierra, A., Carrillo, O., Colbert, E., Ibarra, X., Kigvamasud'Vashti, T., & Maulana, S. (2006). Taking risks: Implementing grassroots community accountability strategies. In INCITE! Women of Color Against Violence (Ed.), *Color of violence: The INCITE! anthology* (pp. 250–266). Cambridge, MA: South End Press.

Black, M. C., Basile, K. C., Breiding, M. J., Smith, S. G., Walters, M. L., Merrick, M. T., . . . Stevens, M. R. (2011). *The National Intimate Partner and Sexual Violence survey: 2010 summary report.* Retrieved from www.cdc.gov/violenceprevention/pdf/nisvs_executive_summary-a.pdf

Bohmer, C., & Parrot, A. (1993). *Sexual assault on campus: The problem and the solution.* New York, NY: Maxwell Macmillan.

Bumiller, K. (2008). *In an abusive state: How neoliberalism appropriated the feminist movement against sexual violence.* Durham, NC: Duke University Press.

Carbado, D. W., Crenshaw, K. W., Mays, V. M., & Tomlinson, B. (2013). Intersectionality: Mapping the movements of a theory. *Du Bois Review, 10,* 303–312.

Corrigan, R. (2013). *Up against a wall: Rape reform and the failure of success.* New York, NY: New York University Press.

Crenshaw, K. (1989). Demarginalizing the intersection of race and sex: A Black feminist critique of antidiscrimination doctrine, feminist theory, and anti-racist politics. *University of Chicago Legal Forum, 1,* 139–167.

Davis, A. (1971). Reflections on the Black woman's role in the community of slaves. *Black Scholar, 3*(4), 2–15.

Davis, A. (1981). *Women, race, & class.* New York, NY: Random House.

Davis, A. (1984). *Women, culture, & politics.* New York, NY: Random House.

Davis, A. (2002). Joan Little: The dialectics of rape (1975). *Ms. Magazine.* Retrieved from www.msmagazine.com/spring2002/davis.asp

Dixon, T. L., & Linz, D. (2000). Overrepresentation and underrepresentation of African Americans and Latinos as lawbreakers on television news. *Journal of Communication, 50,* 131–154.

Donat, P. L., & D'Emilio, J. (1992). A feminist redefinition of rape and sexual assault: Historical foundations and change. *Journal of Social Issues, 48*(1), 9–22.

Fisher, B. S., Daigle, L. E., Cullen, F. T., & Turner, M. G. (2003). Reporting sexual victimization to the police and others: Results from a national-level study of college women. *Criminal Justice and Behavior, 30*(1), 6–38.

Freedman, E. B. (2013). *Redefining rape: Sexual violence in the era of suffrage and segregation.* Cambridge, MA: Harvard University Press.

Freyd, J. J. (2016). *The problem with "required reporting" rules for sexual violence on campus.* Retrieved from www.huffingtonpost.com/jennifer-j-freyd/the-problem-with-required_b_9766016.html

Giddings, P. (1984). *When and where I enter: The impact of Black women on race and sex in America.* New York, NY: HarperCollins.

Grinberg, E. (2014, February 12). *Ending rape on campus: Activism takes many forms.* Retrieved from www.cnn.com/2014/02/09/living/campus-sexual-violence-students-schools

Gruber, A. (2009). Rape, feminism, and the war on crime. *Washington Law Review,* *84,* 581–660.

Henry, W. J. (2009). The effects of sexual assault on the identity development of Black college women. *Michigan Journal of Counseling, 36*(2), 17–23.

INCITE! (2001). *INCITE! Critical resistance statement: Gender violence and the prison industrial complex (2001).* Retrieved from www.incite-national.org/page/incite-critical-resistance-statement

Lindemann, B. S. (1984). "To ravish and carnally know": Rape in eighteenth-century Massachusetts. *Signs, 10,* 63–82.

Linder, C., & Gaspar, E. (2015). Media review: *The Hunting Ground. Journal of Student Affairs Research and Practice, 52,* 452–454. doi:10.1080/19496591.2015.1081602

Linder, C., & Myers, J. S. (2016). Institutional betrayal as a motivator for campus sexual assault activism. *NASPA Journal About Women in Higher Education.* Manuscript submitted for publication.

McGuire, D. L. (2010). *At the dark end of the street: Black women, rape, and resistance—a new history of the Civil Rights Movement from Rosa Parks to the rise of Black power.* New York, NY: Knopf.

Newell, W. (2013). The legacy of Nixon, Reagan, and Horton: How the tough on crime movement enabled a new regime of race-influenced employment discrimination. *Berkeley Journal of African-American Law & Policy, 15,* 3–36.

Ritchie, A. J. (2006). Law enforcement against women of color. In INCITE! Women of Color Against Violence (Ed.), *Color of violence: The INCITE! anthology* (pp. 138–156). Cambridge, MA: South End Press.

Rivera, J. (1996). The Violence Against Women Act and the construction of multiple consciousness in the civil rights and feminists movements. *Journal of Law & Policy, 4,* 463–511.

Smith, A. (2005). *Conquest: Sexual violence and American Indian genocide.* Cambridge, MA: South End Press.

Smith, W. A., Allen, W. R., & Danley, L. L. (2007). "Assume the position . . . you fit the description": Psychosocial experiences and racial battle fatigue among African American male college students. *American Behavioral Scientist, 51*(4), 551–578. doi:10.1177/0002764207307742

Trask, H. K. (2006). The color of violence. In INCITE! Women of Color Against Violence (Ed.), *Color of violence: The INCITE! anthology* (pp. 81–87). Cambridge, MA: South End Press.

Violence Against Women Act, 42 U.S.C. §§13701–14040 (1994).

PART TWO

CONTEMPORARY CONTEXT

4

FOR BRANDON, FOR JUSTICE

Naming and Ending Sexual Violence Against Trans* College Students

Susan B. Marine

As trans* individuals and communities grow in visibility, presence, and societal recognition, a troubling trend is becoming increasingly clear. Violence, and particularly sexual violence, against *trans* and gender nonconforming individuals is alarmingly common (Lombardi, Wilchins, Priesing, & Malouf, 2001; Stotzer, 2009). In this chapter I define *trans* as a person whose gender identity does not correspond with the sex and gender identity assigned to them at birth. While data continue to emerge, it is becoming clear that sexual violence rates among trans* individuals are as high or higher than those of cisgender populations, and yet the media continues to tell us that rape is something that (only) cisgender men do to (only) cisgender women.

Despite significant efforts to name and interrupt its occurrence, rates of sexual violence on college campuses have remained relatively stable for the past 40 years (Fisher, Cullen, & Turner, 2000; Koss, Gidycz, & Wisniewski, 1987). And although we know that trans* folk are frequently targeted by perpetrators of sexual violence, what is less understood is the degree to which these statistics represent the experiences of those in college who identify as trans*. The number of trans* students attending college has grown significantly on college campuses in recent years (Nicolazzo, 2015), and some colleges are heeding the call of their specific needs and concerns (Marine, 2011). Colleges in the United States have been historically constructed in ways that enforce genderism (Bilodeau, 2009), a system by which two binary, mutually exclusive genders (and sexes) are centered in daily operations, institutional practices, and policies. One aspect of correcting this injustice is attending to the needs of trans* survivors of violence. Campus administrators who wish to be fully inclusive and supportive of trans* students must understand and respond effectively to trans* survivors of sexual violence, despite the fact that sexual violence against trans* students is rarely explored in research. Taking a critical lens on this issue means starting with survivors and centering understanding of trans* survivors' experiences. From there, campus administrators and educators must work to address unmet needs trans* students have on campus, including appropriate support and accountability and effective prevention approaches. Inclusion means trans*-ing the barriers to competent and compassionate response and is a critical aspect of working to end genderism on campuses in all its forms.

Is Trans* Sexual Violence Unimaginable?

Sexual violence in the cultural imaginary is typically invoked by the figure of a (white cisgender) woman accosted by a stranger (a man of color) in a dark place, violated against her will, terrorized by the act and the vulnerability she experiences. In the nearly five decades since the antirape activist movement was born, activist educators have come to better understand a different cultural imaginary, one in which a college-age woman is lured into a dangerously constructed social setting, incapacitated (either willfully or accidentally) by alcohol or other drugs, taken back to the assailant's dorm room or fraternity house, and raped. Although this progression has given voice and visibility to millions of survivors, the near ubiquity of these scenarios leaves little room for considering the experiences of survivors who are not cisgender women assaulted by those who may or may not be cisgender men. Similarly, the system designed to serve survivors of sexual violence is not equipped to take gender diversity into full account, and as a result, responses to campus rape have been unfailingly genderist in their incarnations.

Arguably, genderism suffuses every aspect of the current discourse about campus rape. Hill (2003) defined *genderism* as a "system of beliefs that reinforces a negative evaluation based on gender nonconformity. . . . [It includes] the cultural notion that gender is an important basis by which to judge people, and that nonbinary genders are anomalies" (p. 119). One aspect of genderism particular to sexual violence on campus is the way it erases the voices and experiences of trans* survivors of violence, even as the voices of sexual violence survivors generally have become amplified in recent years (Gillibrand, 2015). What does it mean when trans* survivors cannot see themselves reflected in these narratives? What will it mean for their healing, for accountability, for the goal of eradicating genderism on college campuses?

Although these questions elide easy responses, understanding sexual violence prevalence and incidence among trans* communities, and the effect of sexual violence on trans* lives, is a crucial first step in pointing the way to a more holistic vision of ending violence for people of all genders. While sexual violence against trans* people may be currently unimaginable, understanding it is the first step to making it unthinkable.

The Scope of the Problem

Scarce data exist about the prevalence of sexual violence happening to trans* people, and most studies examine incidence and prevalence in relatively small convenience samples. Researchers are also careful to note that studies of one segment of the trans* population, such as trans* women, trans* sex workers, or trans* elders, are not representative of the entirety of the trans* community (Cook-Daniels & Munson, 2010; Mizock & Lewis, 2008). It is vitally important to understand the diversity within the group alongside the putative unity encompassed in trans*-ing gender and sex norms (Bornstein, 1994). Prevalence rates among the various studies indicate that between 14% and 58% of trans* individuals have experienced some kind of forced sexual contact, ranging from sexual touch to rape, in the course of their adult lives (Heintz & Melendez, 2006; Kenagy, 2005; Lombardi et al., 2001; Xavier, Honnold, & Bradford, 2007). Certain factors such as identifying as transsexual, being involved in sex work, being young (under 35), and being in a physically abusive relationship appeared to elevate one's risk of experiencing sexual violence. Economic discrimination, depression, and isolation were often cited effects of the trauma, as were negative coping behaviors such as substance abuse and self-harm.

A study conducted by FORGE, a Minneapolis-based trans* advocacy group (Cook-Daniels & Munson, 2010), revealed that repeated sexual assault was common, and that for the majority, "the abuser's perception of [their] gender/gender presentation/gender expression was a contributing factor in the abuse/assault(s)" (p. 147). Sexual violence happening between women has been historically silenced or ignored in movements to end sexual violence, and likewise sexual violence between trans* women has also been disregarded in the literature. Not a single study to date has examined sexual violence among lesbian-identified trans* women. This returns us to the question of what is actually imaginable. As Girshick (2002a) noted, "To say, 'my rapist was a woman' brings no image to mind for most people. Instead, the questions of 'how could that be?' and 'what did she actually do?' reflect people's disbelief" (p. 1502).

Until quite recently, expansive data about the incidence of sexual violence among college students were nonexistent. However, in 2015 the Association of America Universities conducted a large national sample study on 27 member campuses, exploring the total incidence and prevalence of sexual violence, harassment, stalking, and interpersonal violence (Cantor et al., 2015). The researchers found that college students who identify as trans*, genderqueer, questioning their gender identity, or gender nonconforming (TGQN) experience sexual violence on campus at greater rates than cisgender women; 12.4% of TGQN students in the survey experienced penetration by force or incapacitation, and 29.5% of TGQN students experienced unwanted sexual contact of some kind while in college. These figures are alarming and further support the need to shift educators' attention to the TGQN student community for prevention and intervention efforts.

Additionally, research on student attitudes about violence in intimate partnerships sheds some meaningful light on how students in same-sex relationships (including trans* students) perceive violence as a function of their gender identity/expression. One study found that among lesbian, gay, bisexual, transgender, and queer (LGBTQ) students, those who expressed a more masculine gender identity, whether assigned a male or female sex at birth, were more likely to perpetrate intimate partner violence and survive it than those who perform their gender in ways that are more typically perceived to be feminine (Jacobson, Daire, Abel, & Lambie, 2015). It is surprising to learn that in this study, masculine-of-center trans* individuals were more likely to accept being victimized by their partners, troubling the assumption that *masculinity* is defined as never being vulnerable or victimized.

Singh and McKleroy's work (2010) showed that different markers of privileged or oppressed identities demonstrably place trans* individuals at greater or lesser risk of significant trauma and its aftereffects. Gender expression in particular appears to pay a significant role: Trans* women and those who do not identify as women but who express their gender on the feminine end of the gender spectrum are at significantly greater risk of experiencing gender-based violence and abuse, including sexual violence. The aftereffects appear to be compounded for trans* women also. According to Nuttbrock and colleagues (2014), "The lives of transgender women are seemingly complicated by the fact that earning an economic livelihood, legally or illegally, presents the prospects of exposure to gender abuse and perhaps depression" (p. 2197). Trans* people of color, particularly trans* women of color, are at much greater risk of harm, and in fact an epidemic of murders against trans* women of color in the past decade, escalating to 35 in the past two years ("These Are the Trans People Killed in 2016," 2016), has prompted urgent calls for action from the trans* community and its allies (Blake, 2015; Ring, 2015).

These studies suggest that violence happening to trans* people occurs under a variety of conditions with a variety of effects. That being said, when we look at rates across such studies, it appears that an average of

50% of trans* people experience sexual violence at some point in their lives (Munson & Cook-Daniels, 2015; Stotzer, 2009), which is a much higher percentage of victimization than in the cisgender population. Doubtlessly, rates of sexual victimization among trans* individuals in college require further study and exploration. Turning our attention to the compelling story of one college-age survivor provides important signposts of where the work to improve prevention and response can begin.

Brandon's Story

In 1993 Brandon Teena,[1] a young trans* man living in rural Nebraska, was brutally murdered at the hands of two local men who became enraged when they learned that Brandon was assigned a female sex at birth (Mizock & Lewis, 2008). A documentary film capturing the aftermath of the rape and its effects on Brandon offers important insights about surviving rape as a trans* person, and the ways that service systems are structurally under-equipped to empower trans* survivors (Muska & Olafsdóttir, 1998). In the days leading up to the murder, the men who murdered Brandon confronted him about his gender identity, dragged him into a truck, and brutally raped him. Brandon was interrogated by the sheriff about the incident and was asked a number of egregious questions, including if he had *really* never had vaginal sex before at age 21, if he helped his assailants "get it up," and "why he ran around pretending he was a boy." Brandon's small, defeated voice in the audio recording is barely audible, but the impact of this retraumatization is clear. After the rapes subsided, Brandon was ordered that he was never to tell anyone it happened, just before he was brutally attacked again. The assailants ended the attack by asking him, "We're still friends, right?" (Muska & Olafsdóttir, 1998).

Discussing the rapes in the film, Brandon's friend Joann commented that "Brandon's greatest fear was to be touched by a man, to be raped by a man. . . . [Brandon] said 'I would be just sick if a man kissed me or touched me. And it happened.'" Others in the film reported that Brandon did not initially want to report the rapes to the police, even when implored by his girlfriend's mother "that no one deserves to be raped." After questioning the assailants at length, the police chief affirmed that he thought a crime had been committed but that he wanted to "investigate further" before pressing charges. When questioned by the police, Brandon said he did want to file charges and make a complaint. Three days passed before the assailants were questioned; one of them admitted raping Brandon but was not taken into custody. Brandon left town to begin to heal from the trauma. Three days later, the two assailants who raped Brandon Teena found and murdered him (Muska & Olafsdóttir, 1998).

More than 20 years after it took place, Brandon's rape and the aftermath continues to accurately reflect the horror faced by trans* survivors of rape. Their gender identities, always under surveillance and policing by others, are never more so than in the aftermath of sexual violation. Their gender identities are contested and ultimately negated in the act of rape. They are targeted by assailants for whom instability of gender categories causes fury and violent rage. They are dehumanized in the rape act, not only in the violation itself but also in the obliteration of their gender identity, in this case, their masculinity. The trauma of this violation is deeply intense and may cause fragmentation of identity as reflected in Brandon's words in the film, when he said, "I have a sexual identity crisis. . . . I don't even know if I can even talk about it" (Muska & Olafsdóttir, 1998).

Brandon's violation was further magnified by the way it was treated in the mainstream LGBT press. Gay journalists were hostile to Brandon's identity as a trans* man, with one referring to him as a "woman who lived and loved as a man, and was killed for carrying it off" (Califia, 2003, p. 41). Additionally, Brandon's case was "a prime example of police negligence and society's ignorance toward transgendered [sic] people" (Davies, 2002, p. 209).[2]

There is no question that the incredulous response of the police, those entrusted with providing accountability for the crime, amplified the trauma Brandon experienced, a phenomenon known as institutional betrayal (Smith & Freyd, 2013). We will never know if Brandon's attackers might have been held accountable solely for the rape, as the criminality of the act was eclipsed by the murder they committed days later. And so the perfect storm of a dehumanized and otherized victim, coupled with a transphobic community and support systems, proved to be literally fatal. Although Brandon was not a college student at the time of his rape, his story points to important lessons about how rape has an impact on young adult trans* survivors and the urgency of the work that needs to be done to ensure that compassionate, skilled care is available while we work to end sexual violence in all its forms.

Providing Compassionate, Skilled Care for Trans* Survivors of Sexual Assault

The story of the rape of Brandon Teena, and the failure of the systems he turned to for help and support, is a cautionary tale that cannot be repaired but must instead serve as a catalyst for change as we work toward centering the needs of trans* survivors in current service systems. In the following sections, I review what is known about the effects of sexual violence on trans* individuals and communities, some of the obstacles to compassionate care in traditional service systems, and ways those service systems and prevention approaches can be transformed to be critically inclusive of the needs of trans* survivors. The goal of eliminating sexual violence on the college campus requires expansive thinking and a willingness to engage with long-held beliefs about the nature of victimization and perpetration, and to reframe the work of ending violence so that the needs of trans* survivors are part of the frameworks of support and social change.

Effects of Sexual Violence in Trans* Individuals

The trauma associated with surviving sexual violence has been well documented and includes many different symptoms, including depression, anxiety, isolation, hypervigilance, and adoption of maladaptive coping mechanisms (e.g., excessive alcohol use and suicide or self-harm; Herman, 1997). These responses may be magnified in trans* individuals as a result of societal transphobia, which may manifest itself in familial rejection, peer isolation, and lack of available resources for post-traumatic healing and support (Mizock & Lewis, 2008; Munson & Cook-Daniels, 2015). Trans* survivors may also face additional challenges as a result of economic marginalization; this may be especially pronounced among trans* survivors engaged in sex work, trans* survivors of color, and trans* survivors living with a disability, among others who are multiply marginalized. Trans* survivors' needs for competent support are thus the same and in some ways different from the needs of cisgender survivors.

Trans* survivors often experience self-blame after an experience with assault, particularly amplified by the fact that most are assaulted by an intimate partner or other known perpetrator. The trauma experienced during an assault often leads to a sense of paralysis, followed by persistent memories and flashbacks once the survivor escapes the immediate threat of harm. Post-traumatic stress disorder (PTSD) and its attendant symptoms—inability to eat and sleep, dissociation, recurrent nightmares, persistent negative thoughts and beliefs, self-blame, overwhelming emotions or numbness—is a common experience of trans* survivors. Feeling vigilant, hyperaroused, and unable to participate in normal life activities or relationships is another common experience. Survivors often describe a sense of being out of control in their bodies and feelings with respect to traumatic responses, largely because they can be triggered at any time, because of stimuli that remind them of the experience (sights, sounds, people, or any predictable or unpredictable reminders of the event). Because sexual violence is rarely given productive airtime in the media, these feelings and reactions can often cause survivors to turn inward and experience shame. Research suggests that the shame and guilt experienced by survivors of violence may often be compounded among trans* survivors who have survived transphobia in society; as if it is not alarming enough that 41% of trans* individuals in one national study have attempted suicide, a staggering 64% of trans* sexual assault survivors have done so (Munson & Cook-Daniels, 2015).

Given the impact that sexual violence has on trans* survivors' lives, it is crucial for response services to be maximally inclusive and responsive to the needs of this population. However, there are genderist obstacles to obtaining trans*-competent services that must first be named in order to be addressed.

Troubling Crisis Response Services

The rape crisis movement was founded on the feminist theoretical premise that men's violence perpetrated against women is a form of social control that upholds the patriarchal social order (Brownmiller, 1993). Although this theory has helped explain the socially stratified realities of who perpetrates and who survives sexual violence to a large extent, it does not fully explain the experiences of trans* individuals of varying genders, sometimes victimized by other trans* individuals, sometimes by cisgender perpetrators. The assumptions inherent in feminist sexual violence theories do not cohere in all cases, such as when a masculine-presenting trans* individual is assaulted by hir feminine-presenting cisgender partner. It also does not account for the motivations or thought processes of those who perpetrate violence against trans* individuals, nor the impact such violence has on the life experiences of trans* survivors whose gender performance and expression are always under surveillance, judgment, and often erasure by the world at large (Feinberg, 1996). This perspective has contributed to the failure of various systems in providing adequate care for trans* survivors.

   Failed rape crisis center response. In documentation of their experiences, trans* survivors rarely seek formal services after an assault, citing perceived lack of credibility, and when doing so, they often wait years to seek this support. In the words of one survivor from the Cook-Daniels and Munson (2010) study, "For rape . . . I was considered a male at the time; no one would have believed I was raped by a female." Recent studies suggest that among rape response service providers, knowledge, competence, and familiarity with LGBTQ issues broadly is low; providers as well as those who access their services agree that significant training is needed (National Center for Victims of Crime and National Coalition of Anti-Violence Programs, 2010). The feminist movement's success in establishing responsive and well-coordinated rape crisis services for cisgender white women is without dispute; however, the models employed by such centers lack inclusiveness that would ensure they are beneficial to many, including trans* survivors, especially those with additional subordinated social identities. For example, Seelman (2015) found that being low income, a non-U.S. citizen, or identifying on the male or masculine end of the gender spectrum resulted in receiving substandard services from rape crisis centers.

Trans*-identified survivors of rape and sexual assault have thus rarely found suitable support, including medical advocacy and crisis counseling, from traditional rape crisis service providers, and have been left out of efforts to build feminist coalitions with cisgender women to combat rape. This was made abundantly clear in the case of *Vancouver Rape Relief v. Nixon*, a case in which a trans* woman who volunteered at a rape crisis service in Canada was terminated from her position. The training coordinator stated that "only a woman, born so, and who grew up understanding what it means to be a girl and a woman in an oppressive society, could understand Rape Reliefs political view of male violence and, therefore qualify as a 'peer' for Rape Reliefs purposes" (Mayeda, 2005, p. 454)

Failed health care response. Health care systems are also often clearly ineffective in responding to the health care needs of trans* individuals (Mizock & Lewis, 2008) and have been characterized by some researchers as cisnormative (Bauer et al., 2009). Providers are generally not familiarized with the health care needs of trans* people, and the stigma associated with presenting as trans* in a clinical care setting is often prohibitive (Poteat, German, & Kerrigan, 2013). Sexual assault survivors need (and should expect to receive) specialized care in emergency settings following an experience with sexual violence; such care is designed not only to treat any injuries that occur in the course of the assault but also to preserve forensic evidence for the potential of a future criminal prosecution. One of the most challenging aspects of seeking treatment and evidence collection following an assault is the often weighty decision to disclose one's trans* status to health care providers. To conduct the most appropriate forms of sexually transmitted infection testing and evidence collection after an experience with sexual violence, trans* survivors must be willing to describe not only the trauma they endured but also the aspects of their bodily morphology (including in some cases their genital configuration, reproductive organ status, hormone use, and other aspects of their bodies' composition).

In these cases, it is impossible to predict whether a trans* survivor will encounter a knowledgeable and compassionate professional. More often than not, the trans* survivor will encounter unfamiliarity and subsequent maltreatment. As one trans* patient stated, "Once they found out I was transsexual, oh my god, everything changed. They made me wait; they put me in a different bed" (Bauer et al., 2009, p. 355). Trans* survivors are also reluctant to press charges after experiencing rape owing to the persistent mistreatment they have experienced at the hands of law enforcement, citing the very real possibility of revictimization in the criminal justice system (Xavier et al., 2004).

Research with survivors has thus indicated that appropriate medical support, posttrauma counseling, and skilled advocacy has the potential to either magnify or ameliorate the trauma associated with an experience with rape (Campbell, 2005); it stands to reason that given the general lack of attention paid to tailoring these processes to trans* survivor needs, the possibility of a negative outcome to this experience is very real. It is abundantly clear that systems, as well as individuals, can do grave harm to trans* survivors, and thus solutions to these harms must be addressed systemically.

Trans Student and Survivor Resilience*

As demonstrated, trans* survivors of sexual violence, whether on campus or in society at large, face an uphill battle in accessing appropriate, responsive, and culturally competent services to support them in recovering from the assault. Despite these challenges, evidence suggests that trans* students exhibit significant resilience in managing the daily effects of genderism on campus, and this may in fact aid them in surviving violence. In hir study of nine trans* students on a midwestern public campus, Nicolazzo (2015) found that trans* students faced multiple and varied forms of genderist behavior in their daily lives and, to cope, drew on support within "a constellation of kinship networks" (p. 131), while also making conscious choices about whether (and if) to be out about being trans* or to challenge genderist behaviors as a means for preserving their energy. These strategies render *resilience* as a verb, something participants in Nicolazzo's study practiced or performed depending on the day, place, or other contextual factors. Race and experiences with disability figured into this process as well, as students of color and those with various mental and physical health differences in hir study recognized their resilience as intimately tied up with these subordinated identities in ways that were not reflected in the narratives of more privileged students. Coupled with the previously discussed and extensive evidence of greater risk for violence among these subgroups within the trans* population, the formation of more responsive support services on college campuses must be centered on serving those whose risk for violence, and likelihood of genderist mistreatment, are the greatest.

The resiliency of trans* survivors of sexual violence is also inherently clear, given the paucity of resources available to them. Acknowledging this, trans* advocacy organization FORGE developed a comprehensive resource guide to self-help and healing following an experience with sexual violence (Munson & Cook-Daniels, 2015). The guide provides concrete strategies for coping with strong emotions, using technology to access virtual and in-person support, and developing standard operating procedures for self-soothing and grounding during a time of intense emotions and triggering. These strategies provide trans* survivors with tried-and-true methods to advance their healing from trauma and to build resilience within themselves and their communities.

New Directions: Advocacy for Change

Fostering trans* survivor resilience is an important aspect of healing, yet a commitment to making systemic change is essential. Although trans* survivors' concerns have been largely overlooked in the provision of response services to date, the increasing number of trans* students on college campuses means that renewed attention to all aspects of their needs, including their needs following an experience with violence, is imperative. Enormous strides have been made to advance the inclusion of trans* students on some campuses, but researchers have documented that 90% of U.S. colleges and universities still do not offer gender-inclusive nondiscrimination policies, trans*-inclusive housing or bathroom facilities, and other important markers of trans* student inclusion (Rankin & Beemyn, 2012). The following recommendations are intended to advance campuses in creating cultures and support services that will support trans* survivors in healing, reduce genderism, and ultimately promote an end to the experience of sexual violence for trans* students.

Recommendation 1: All campus professionals should be familiar with trans student needs and concerns, and committed to ending genderism.* To create a culture where sexual violence against trans* students is unthinkable is to know and relate authentically to trans* students' needs and concerns. Given that the vast majority of faculty and student affairs administrators identify as cisgender, it is imperative for those of us who do not claim a trans* identity to work to educate ourselves about the experiences of trans* students and work to actively meet the needs of trans* students to ensure their persistence in college (Marine, 2011). Because genderism typifies the experiences of trans* students, noting and working to correct genderist practice is another critical role of student affairs professionals. Specific to sexual violence, genderist practice may include prevention efforts that disregard the unique risk and protective factors facing trans* students in their relationships, response services that require students to identify on the binary to access treatment, and representations of students as uniformly cisgender in publications depicting sexual assault scenarios. Avoiding singular use of binary gender pronouns in marketing materials, using names in scenarios that are not associated with one gender or another (e.g., Chris), and stating, "Students of any gender may experience violence; services and programs are open to students of all genders" are important ways to communicate inclusion and defy and redefine *normativity*.

Recommendation 2: Analyses of the causes and conditions that lead to sexual violence must include attention to the realities of trans* lives and specifically to transphobic oppression. Inarguably, feminist movements have led the charge for improved response services, and feminists have tirelessly advocated for individual and systemic change in response to rape. However, as Girshick (2002a) noted, "One of the major challenges to the antiviolence movement today is to reevaluate our feminist analysis in order to be more inclusive" (p. 1518). Naming and analyzing violence directed at cisgender women by cisgender men as a result of patriarchal oppression does not fully capture the cultural conditions that perpetuate violence against those who do not identify as cisgender women or who are not perpetrated against by cisgender men. Rather than abandoning existing analyses, it will prove more fruitful to retain the aspects of feminist theories that pertain to all enactments of oppression through violence. Regardless of the genders of the survivor or perpetrator, sexual violence is an act of *power over*, and while the particulars vary, the effects appear to be essentially the same. The silencing of survivors, the potential for encountering culturally insufficient support services, and the miniscule chance of having one's perpetrator held responsible for the crime of violence are common themes in the aftermath of all sexual violence. Expanding understanding of how trans* survivors are specifically harmed by sexual violence means improvement on, rather than abandonment of, feminist theoretical contributions. Feminists and trans* rights activists, as well as all of us who are both, can and must find common ground in building this expanded analysis together. As Julia Serano (2013) noted, "We all have a mutual goal: to find a support network outside of the hetero male-centric mainstream where we can finally feel empowered" (p. 206).

Suggesting that these theories are deficient in some respects is not a new proposition. Feminist theories developed to respond to violence have been transformed over time to become more inclusive, as exemplified by the addition of intersectional analysis. Black feminist theorists (e.g., Collins, 1999; Crenshaw, 1995) recognized and corrected the limitations inherent in theories about violence that were developed by white women in response to the violence perpetrated by white men. Because they name and deconstruct the burdens of experiencing violent oppression through the lens of multiple, overlapping social identities, intersectional theorists provide a meaningful way to understand and respond to this victimization, especially as it pertains to those who are oppressed in multiple ways (e.g., by being in minoritized racial or ethnic groups, living with a disability, or experiencing economic marginalization). Importantly, these theories continue to reveal the deficits present in the ways that most antiviolence organizing and service provision are suffused with white supremacy.

These theories bring additional clarity when applied to analyses of violence perpetrated against trans* individuals and communities. As captured poignantly in a study of trans* survivors (Munson & Cook-Daniels, 2015),

> Theories just don't work to make sense of a lot of abusive relationships that seem to contradict social hierarchies, e.g. where the victim is a man or where the abuser is a person of colour. It's so much harder when you feel you need to protect a whole community, or that people might not believe you. (pp. 34–35)

Intersectional theory provides an essential foundation for understanding the different facets of multiple oppressions, and devising creative and effective strategies to resist these oppressions (Collins, 2009).

Recommendation 3: All prevention and response efforts related to sexual violence on campus must center trans* survivor needs and concerns. Survivors of violence, particularly those who identify on the LGBTQ spectrum, want to see services and programs geared to them and to their specific identities (Girshick, 2002b). This includes indicating through visual symbols, language, and other tangible aspects of care provision that trans* individuals and identities are welcome. This can ideally be accomplished by ensuring that trans* individuals are members of care provider staff at organizations offering postassault services, including campus-based services. Empowering sexual assault survivors is a universal mandate; care providers should focus on allowing all survivors to tell their stories and support them in seeking whatever avenues of accountability and healing are most appropriate to their needs. Student affairs professionals, health providers, counselors, and adjudication officers on college campuses constitute the front line of response for survivors on campus and should approach their work through an empowerment stance. Ensuring survivors can speak for themselves whenever possible, can make fully informed choices, and can refuse services or accommodations as desired is also an important part of this approach.

Sexual violence prevention educators have adopted numerous strategies, including prevention seminars/workshops, peer education, and bystander prevention techniques, to reduce the prevalence of sexual violence. However, best practice guidance for sexual violence prevention education on college campuses often indicates that it should be conducted in *separate gender* groups (Banyard, Plante, & Moynihan, 2003), reinforcing heterosexism and genderism.[3] This practice should be discontinued, as it assumes that students identify on the binary and thus defaults to genderist assumptions. Instead, educators should focus on aspects of prevention education that are common to all acts of sexual violence, helping students to understand how sexual violence is used to forcefully disempower survivors, and what steps they can take to change their communities to promote intolerance of violence. Inclusion of examples of students of nonbinary genders who experience sexual violence is key to crafting inclusive education, as is engaging trans* students in conducting education prevention work. Currently, research on the perspectives of prevention educators on issues of gender-inclusive sexual violence work is under way and will provide insight as to the complexities and rewards of making such efforts.

In summary, each campus constituency—medical care providers, counselors, campus police, and adjudication officers, particularly—must take the initiative to learn about trans* sexual violence. Each must understand the specific impact that transphobia has on help-seeking behaviors and on barriers to appropriate, compassionate care (Mizock & Lewis, 2008). Rather than treating trans* survivor students that professionals work with as opportunities for skill and competence development, it is vital for all college officers, particularly cisgender professionals, to learn about trans* lives and experiences by reading relevant literature and attending structured professional development opportunities. It is also crucial for people to reflect on their own paths to knowing and living their gender identities as well. The growing body of literature on trans* student experiences and trans* experiences with sexual violence, although not yet integrated, is a good place to start and will provide professionals with increased knowledge for developing trans*-inclusive services and protocols. Building ongoing evaluative mechanisms for trans* survivors to provide feedback will ensure continuous improvement in the way these services are designed and delivered. Not surprisingly, evidence suggests that trans* students may invest time and energy in particular campus spaces deemed to be safer, such as LGBTQ/women's/gender centers, multicultural and other social justice centers, and academic departments related to the study of gender (Nicolazzo, 2015; Pryor, 2015). The personnel of these spaces should be especially well trained to respond sensitively to disclosures of sexual assault from trans* students.

Conclusion

Sexual violence changes lives, and this is especially true when an experience with sexual violence interrupts a college student's life and future. Trans* individuals experience violence in significantly greater numbers than cisgender people; the recent rise in the visibility of trans* college students means that attending to this reality is urgent. Specifically, as colleges and universities must be for *all* students, these institutions must be prepared to educate trans* students about their risks of experiencing sexual violence, offer trans*-inclusive and culturally competent services to those who experience violence, and provide clear and responsive avenues for holding perpetrators accountable.

Promising signs of renewed attention to the concerns and needs of queer students on college campuses was symbolized in the recent release of Wimberly's (2016) *LGBTQ Issues in Education: Advancing a Research Agenda*, yet there was no mention in any part of this foundational text that sexual violence among queer and trans* students is a priority for study, policy development, or prevention efforts. More remains to be done not only to attend to the positive, growth-fostering aspects of trans* student experience but also to prevent (and ultimately eliminate) trans* student experiences with sexual violence and related trauma. The aftermath of the rape at the near end of Brandon Teena's too brief life exemplifies the devastation that poorly designed and delivered responses to sexual violence can mean and the ways they exacerbate suffering needlessly. Brandon's life chances were foreclosed by the horror of transphobic violence and the culture of complicity it created. His is a cautionary tale of what happens when trans* lives are not valued, and when violence against trans* people is considered permissible even as it may be considered unimaginable. Colleges and universities that do nothing to expand their survivor response protocols to become trans* centered or to ensure that campus and community health care and rape crisis service responders are trans* competent in their orientations are quite simply complicit in retraumatizing trans* survivors. Ending violence against trans* individuals in all its forms is a moral imperative that is the responsibility of all on college campuses and a shared mandate whose time has come to enact.

Notes

1. It should be noted that scholarly explorations of the Brandon Teena case suggest that while he consistently referred to himself using both he/him pronouns, Brandon also described himself variously as a hermaphrodite, as a person born of both sexes, and as a male in a woman's body. Though clearly transcending gender norms, Brandon likely did not have available knowledge of the term *transgender* to refer to himself. Others who have written about the case have speculatively decided and assigned Brandon's "true gender and sex," an act of violence in and of itself. For more on this discussion, see Sloop (2000) and Hale (1998).

2. It is important to note that the term *transgendered* is not generally considered appropriate when referring to trans* people. All people are gendered in different ways; trans* people are not more or less gendered than cisgender people.

3. The concept of there being two separate and easily distinguishable genders (and sexes) has been disproven by many, including biologist Anne Fausto-Sterling (2008). Thus, it is quite limiting to separate group participants in this manner and runs the risk of erasing those whose identities fall outside the binary.

References

Banyard, V., Plante, E., & Moynihan, M. (2003). Bystander education: Bringing a broader community perspective to sexual violence prevention. *Journal of Community Psychology, 32*(1), 67–79.

Bauer, G. R., Hammond, R., Travers, R., Kaay, M., Hohenadel, K. M., & Boyce, M. (2009). "I don't think this is theoretical: This is our lives": How erasure impacts health care for transgender people. *Journal of the Association of Nurses in AIDS Care, 20*, 348–361.

Bilodeau, B. L. (2009). *Genderism: Transgender students, binary systems and higher education.* Saarbrucken, Germany: VDM Verlag.

Blake, A. (2015, July 23). 10 transgender women killed so far in 2015. *Washington Times.* Retrieved from www.washingtontimes.com/news/2015/jul/23/ten-transgender-women-killed-so-far-2015

Bornstein, K. (1994). *Gender outlaws: On men, women, and the rest of us.* New York, NY: Routledge.

Brownmiller, S. (1993). *Against our will: Men, women, and rape* (2nd ed.). New York, NY: Fawcett Books.

Califia, P. (2003). *Sex changes: The politics of transgenderism* (2nd ed.). San Francisco, CA: Cleis.

Campbell, R. (2005). What really happened? A validation study of rape survivors' help-seeking experiences with the legal and medical systems. *Violence and Victims, 20*, 55–68.

Cantor, D., Fisher, B., Chibnall, S., Townsend, R., Lee, H., Bruce, C., & Thomas, G. (2015). *Report on the AAU Campus Climate Survey on Sexual Assault and Sexual Misconduct.* Retrieved from www.aau.edu/uploadedFiles/AAU_Publications/AAU_Reports/Sexual_Assault_Campus_Survey/AAU_Campus_Climate_Survey_12_14_15.pdf

Collins, P. H. (1999). *Black feminist thought: Knowledge, consciousness, and the politics of empowerment* (2nd ed.). New York, NY: Routledge.

Collins, P. H. (2009). Forward: Emerging intersections—building knowledge and transforming institutions. In B. T. Dill & R. E. Zambrana (Eds.), *Emerging intersections: Race, class, and gender in theory, policy, and practice* (pp. vii–xiii). New Brunswick, NJ: Rutgers University Press.

Cook-Daniels, L., & Munson, M. (2010). Sexual violence, elder abuse, and sexuality of transgender adults, age 50+: Results of three surveys. *Journal of GLBT Family Studies, 6*, 142–177.

Crenshaw, K. W. (1995). Mapping the margins: Intersectionality, identity politics, and violence against women of color. In K. Crenshaw, N. Gotanda, G. Peller, & K. Thomas (Eds.), *Critical race theory: The key writings that formed the movement* (pp. 357–383). New York, NY: The New Press.

Davies, M. (2002). Male sexual assault victims: A selective review of the literature and implications for support services. *Aggression and Violent Behavior, 7*, 203–214.

Fausto-Sterling, A. (2008). *Myths of gender: Biological theories about women and men.* New York, NY: Basic Books.

Feinberg, L. (1996). *Transgender warriors: Making history from Joan of Arc to Dennis Rodman.* Boston, MA: Beacon Press.

Fisher, B., Cullen, F. T., & Turner, M. G. (2000). *The sexual victimization of college women.* Washington, DC: Bureau of Justice Statistics.

Gillibrand, K. G. (2015, January 21). Carrying their weight: Giving voice to survivors of campus sexual assault. *Huffington Post.* Retrieved from post.com/rep-kirsten-gillibrand/carrying-their-weight-giv_b_6516630.html

Girshick, L. B. (2002a). No sugar, no spice: Reflections on research on woman-to-woman sexual violence. *Violence Against Women, 8,* 1500–1520. doi:10.1177/107780102237967

Girshick, L. B. (2002b). *Woman-to-woman sexual violence: Does she call it rape?* Boston, MA: Northeastern University Press.

Hale, C. J. (1998). Consuming the living, dis-remembering the dead in the Butch FTM, Borderlands. *GLQ, 4*(2), 311–348.

Heintz, A. J., & Melendez, R. M. (2006). Intimate partner violence and HIV/STD risk among lesbian, gay, bisexual, and transgender individuals. *Journal of Interpersonal Violence, 21,* 193–208.

Herman, J. (1997). *Trauma and recovery: The aftermath of violence—from domestic abuse to political terror.* New York, NY: Basic Books.

Hill, D. B. (2003). Genderism, transphobia, and gender bashing: A framework for interpreting anti-transgender violence. In B. C. Wallace & R. T. Carter (Eds.), *Understanding and dealing with violence: A multicultural approach* (pp. 113–136). Thousand Oaks, CA: SAGE.

Jacobson, L. E., Daire, A. P., Abel, E. M., & Lambie, G. (2015). Gender expression differences in same-sex intimate partner violence victimization, perpetration, and attitudes among LGBTQ college students. *Journal of LGBT Issues in Counseling, 9,* 100–216. doi:10.1080/15538605.2015.1068144

Kenagy, G. P. (2005). Transgender health: Findings from two needs assessment studies in Philadelphia. *Health & Social Work, 30,* 19–26.

Koss, M. P., Gidycz, C. J., & Wisniewski, N. (1987). The scope of rape: Incidence and prevalence of sexual aggression and victimization among a national sample of students in higher education. *Journal of Consulting and Clinical Psychology, 55,* 162–170. doi:10.1037/0022-006X.55.2.162

Lombardi, E. L., Wilchins, R. A., Priesing, D., & Malouf, D. (2001). Gender violence: Transgender experiences with violence and discrimination. *Journal of Homosexuality, 42*(1), 89–101.

Marine, S. B. (2011). *Stonewall's legacy: Bisexual, gay, lesbian, and transgender students in higher education.* San Francisco, CA: Jossey-Bass.

Mayeda, G. (2005). Re-imagining feminist theory: Transgender identity, feminism, and the law. *Canadian Journal of Women & the Law, 17,* 424–471.

Mizock, L., & Lewis, T. K. (2008). Trauma in transgender populations: Risk, resilience, and clinical care. *Journal of Emotional Abuse, 8,* 335–354.

Munson, M., & Cook-Daniels, L. (2015). *Transgender sexual violence survivors: A self-help guide to healing and understanding.* Retrieved from forge-forward.org/2015/09/trans-sa-survivors-self-help-guide

Muska, S. (Director), & Olafsdóttir, G. (Director). (1998). *The Brandon Teena story* [Documentary film]. United States: Bless Bless Productions.

National Center for Victims of Crime & National Coalition of Anti-Violence Programs. (2010). *Why it matters: Rethinking victim assistance for lesbian, gay, bisexual, transgender, and queer victims of hate violence & intimate partner violence.* Retrieved from http://ncdsv.org/images/NCVC_Whyitmatters_LGBTQreport_3-2010.pdf

Nicolazzo, Z. (2015). *"Just go in looking good": The resilience, resistance, and kinship-building of trans* college students* (Doctoral dissertation). Retrieved from www.ohiolink.edu/etd

Nuttbrock, L., Bockting, W., Rosenblum, A., Hwahng, S., Mason, M., Macri, M., & Becker, J. (2014). Gender abuse and major depression among transgender women: A prospective study of vulnerability and resilience. *American Journal of Public Health, 104,* 2191–2199.

Poteat, T., German, D., & Kerrigan, D. (2013). Managing uncertainty: A grounded theory of stigma in transgender health care encounters. *Social Science in Medicine, 84,* 22–29.

Pryor, J. T. (2015). Out in the classroom: Transgender student experiences at a large public university. *Journal of College Student Development, 56,* 440–455.

Rankin, S., & Beemyn, G. (2012). Beyond a binary: The lives of gender nonconforming youth. *About Campus, 17*(4), 2–10.

Ring, T. (2015, August 16). Three more Black trans* women reported murdered. *Advocate.* Retrieved from www.advocate.com/transgender/2015/08/16/three-more-black-trans-women-reported-murdered

Seelman, K. L. (2015). Unequal treatment of transgender individuals in domestic violence and rape crisis programs. *Journal of Social Service Research, 41,* 307–325.

Serano, J. (2013). *Excluded: Making feminist and queer movements more inclusive.* Berkeley, CA: Seal Press.

Singh, A. A., & McKleroy, V. S. (2010). "Just getting out of bed is a revolutionary act": The resilience of transgender people of color who have survived traumatic life events. *Traumatology, 17*(2), 34–44.

Smith, C. P., & Freyd, J. J. (2013). Dangerous safe havens: Institutional betrayal exacerbates sexual trauma. *Journal of Traumatic Stress, 26,* 119–124.

Sloop, J. M. (2000). Disciplining the transgendered: Brandon Teena, public representation and normativity. *Western Journal of Communication, 64*(2), 165–189.

Stotzer, R. L. (2009). Violence against transgender people: A review of United States data. *Aggression and Violent Behavior, 14,* 170–179. doi:10.1016/j.avb.2009.01.006

These are the trans people killed in 2016. (2016). Retrieved from www.advocate.com/transgender/2016/7/19/these-are-trans-people-killed-2016

Wimberly, G. L. (Ed.). (2016). *LGBTQ issues in education: Advancing a research agenda.* Washington, DC: American Education Research Association.

Xavier, J. M., Hitchcock, D., Hollinshead, S., Keisling, M., Lewis, Y., Lombardi, E., . . . Williams, B. (2004). *An overview of U.S. trans health priorities: A report by the Eliminating Disparities Working Group.* Retrieved from www.researchgate.net/publication/237290410_An_Overview_of_US_Trans_Health_Priorities_A_Report_by_the_Eliminating_Disparities_Working_Group_August_2004_Update

Xavier, J. M., Honnold, J. A., & Bradford, J. B. (2007). *The health, health-related needs, and lifecourse experiences of transgender Virginians.* Retrieved from www.vdh.virginia.gov/epidemiology/diseaseprevention/documents/pdf/THISFINALREPORTVol1.pdf

5

"THE WOUNDS OF OUR EXPERIENCE"

College Men Who Experienced Sexual Violence

Daniel Tillapaugh

I think that I am still struggling to validate myself as a survivor. I think I still feel kind of weird, like the language doesn't feel right in my mouth. Rape doesn't [sound] right in my mouth. Really, none of it does. And I think part of that is the narrative that we're used to seeing in terms of what rape is and the fact that my story isn't really in line with that. But I think that I am slowly getting there. (Aidan)

For many professionals working in higher education, the statistic that one in five women have survived an experience of rape or sexual assault (Black et al., 2011) is commonly recalled and incorporated into their campus's sexual violence prevention efforts. However, far less often included are statistics of men who are survivors of sexual violence (MSSV).[1] In this chapter, *sexual violence* is defined as any unwanted sexual experiences. These experiences could include rape and other forms of sexual coercion, which can include "an experience of being pressured or forced by another person to have contact which involved touching of sexual parts or sexual intercourse—oral, anal, or vaginal" (Struckman-Johnson & Struckman-Johnson, 1994, p. 96). In this chapter, I situate the current literature on men who have survived sexual violence in the context of higher education. Additionally, I offer the counternarratives of four cisgender or transgender men who survived sexual violence during college within the past five years. Their stories provide compelling insights and implications for higher education professionals on how to critically serve and support other men who experience sexual violence during their time as students on campus.

Men and Sexual Violence

One in five men are survivors of sexual violence beyond rape (Black et al., 2011). Only 29% sought help after their experience of sexual assault; furthermore, only 12% of these men reported their experience to the police (Light & Monk-Turner, 2009). Because of the rates and complexities of violence against individuals from historically underrepresented communities, these statistics become even more of a problem when disaggregating by race and sexual orientation.

Sexual Violence Among Men of Color and Gay, Bisexual, Queer, or Transgender Men

Men who have identities that are underrepresented along dimensions of race, gender identity, or sexual orientation are at increased risk for sexual violence. For instance, Black and colleagues (2011) found that approximately 33% of multiracial men and 22.6% of Black men had survived an experience of sexual violence beyond rape in their lifetime. Additionally, Johnson and Sigler (2001) found that up to 32% of men with developmental disabilities experienced sexual assault. The rates for sexual violence increase drastically for those who identify as gay, bisexual, or queer (as a marker of sexuality). Gay, bisexual, and queer men are three times more likely to report experiences of sexual violence than their heterosexual peers (National Coalition of Anti-Violence Programs, 2011).

Fifty percent of transgender individuals experience sexual violence over their life span (Stotzer, 2009), challenging the predominant views of society and popular culture that reinforce the fallacy that sexual violence happens only to heterosexual cisgender women who are assaulted by heterosexual cisgender men (Scarce, 1997). Additionally, the overall statistics of MSSVs are typically skewed given that men are less likely to report sexual violence than women, even in surveys (Turchik & Edwards, 2012). As a result of this fallacy, the experiences of MSSVs have often been silenced and ignored, which further adds to survivors' trauma.

Physiological and Psychological Impact on MSSVs

Sexual violence has an impact on each MSSV's emotional and physiological well-being, which can vary widely (Scarce, 1997). Compared to males who had not reported experiences of sexual violence, MSSVs were more likely to be diagnosed with anxiety or depression (Choudhary, Smith, & Bossarte, 2012; Tewksbury, 2007). Additionally, MSSVs are more likely to report concerns of mental health, including feelings of aggression or failure, lack of appetite, insomnia or excessive sleeping, and lethargy (Gilbody, Richards,

Brealey, & Hewitt, 2007). Relatedly, MSSVs often express feelings of self-blame, low self-esteem, and guilt about their experiences of sexual violence (Isley, 1998; Mezey & King, 1989; Struckman-Johnson & Struckman-Johnson, 1994; Tewksbury, 2007).

Connected to feelings of depression or anxiety, many MSSVs experience forms of post-traumatic stress following their experiences, which has consequences for their interpersonal interactions (Aosved, Long, & Voller, 2011). In their study involving 12 males who were sexually coerced by their female partners, Platt and Busby (2009) found that MSSVs reported increased negative feelings about intimate relationships and feelings of loss. Some MSSVs in college have also reported increased challenges with their academic functioning as well as a reduction in being involved in social interactions and activities on campus (Banyard et al., 2007). MSSVs have reported greater sexual problems following their experiences; these challenges included an avoidance of sexual activity or engaging in high-risk sexual promiscuity (Plant, Plant, & Miller, 2005; Tewksbury, 2007). For MSSVs, their experiences of sexual violence have a tremendous impact. Yet, the reality is that many MSSVs are struggling on their own in silence and often feel isolated.

MSSVs in Colleges and Universities

Scholars on MSSVs have looked at the issue of sexual violence over the life span (Light & Monk-Turner, 2009; Stermac, Del Bove, & Addison, 2004). Few studies have investigated the experience of MSSVs confined solely to colleges and universities. Yet some scholars (Struckman-Johnson, 1988; Tewksbury, 2007; Tewksbury & Mustaine, 2001) have found that "between one in five and one in eleven males" are victims of sexual violations during college (Tewksbury, 2007, p. 24). In one study, 23 college males were asked to provide more detail about their forced sex experience (Struckman-Johnson, 1988). Fifty-two percent of those males were coerced through psychological pressure to have sex, 28% experienced psychological pressure and physical restraint, 10% were physically forced to engage in sex, and 10% were assaulted while intoxicated and were unable to provide consent (Struckman-Johnson, 1988). Additionally, college men who survived childhood sexual abuse are at greater risk for revictimization and adult sexual assault than their nonvictimized peers (Aosved et al., 2011). All this information points to the need for increased attention and education among higher education professionals to understand that men are experiencing sexual violence in our institutions yet often remain silent.

One third of college men who experience sexual victimization told no one (Banyard et al., 2007). They did not tell a friend, a family member, a faculty member, or a staff member; instead, they kept their experience hidden and a secret. This statistic is not surprising given the socialization of hegemonic masculinity among men in Western society (Donaldson, 1993; Kimmel, 2004), particularly men in college (Kimmel, 2008). Hegemonic masculinity socializes men to believe that they must be "a man in power, a man *with* power, and a man of power" (Kimmel, 2004, p. 184). Yet, this becomes a problem given that hegemonic masculinity reinforces the need for men to socially construct norms that reinforce being macho or masculine and avoid anything that could be perceived as feminine (Kilmartin & Berkowitz, 2005). This notion, rooted in sexism and homophobia, reinforces men's behaviors to be dominant and aggressive, particularly regarding sex and intimacy, and often leads to men victimizing women and other men (Kilmartin & Berkowitz, 2005).

For many college men, this perception of being viewed as feminine by others creates a culture of silence among them (Kimmel, 2008) and serves as an impediment to reporting sexual violence (Sable, Danis, Mauzy, & Gallagher, 2006). Sable and colleagues (2006) stated that college men "may fail to report because reporting is perceived to jeopardize their masculine self-identity" as it relates to the stigma of sexual violence or coercion against men (p. 160). Many MSSVs decide not to report their experiences out of fear that they will not be believed (Isely, 1998; Mezey & King, 1987). As a result, campus administrators, law enforcement, counselors, and medical professionals often lack sympathy for and have misunderstandings about MSSVs (Banyard et al., 2007; Mezey & King, 1989; Turchik & Edwards, 2012).

One of the critiques of the extant literature on MSSVs inside and outside higher education is that almost all the studies on this topic and population are quantitative in nature. Although it is helpful to understand the statistics involved in the sexual violence experiences of men, the voices of survivors themselves are missing. As a result, this chapter highlights the counternarratives of MSSVs to challenge the commonly held assumptions of sexual violence in higher education.

Counternarratives as Critical Lens

Many of the sexual violence prevention efforts at colleges and universities in the United States have reinforced a false binary that sexual violence typically includes heterosexual cisgender women assaulted by heterosexual cisgender men (Kilmartin & Berkowitz, 2005). This belief has been reinforced by a unilateral focus on statistics, which has created a master narrative of sexual violence on campus. Media images of sexual violence survivors often reinforce the master narrative that sexual violence is a problem or concern only for women. An article in *Time* magazine explored campus-based statistics on sexual assault and other forms of violence from various universities and national studies (Gray, 2015). The article mentioned only statistics based on cisgender college women's experiences of sexual violence with no discussion of other survivors (Gray, 2015). This discussion perpetuates a master narrative of sexual violence that negates sexism, heterosexism, genderism, and racism, and erases other survivors of sexual violence and their lived experiences who are not cisgender college women. As a result, counternarratives become an important contribution to challenging dominant thought.

Critical scholars often use counternarratives, or counterstories, "to challenge, displace, or mock . . . pernicious narratives and beliefs" (Delgado & Stefancic, 2001, p. 43). Counternarratives are the act "of telling the stories of those people whose experiences are not often told" (Solórzano & Yosso, 2009, p. 138). Most often, these counternarratives center on the experiences of people of color to challenge the master narrative or the commonly held universal truths that reinforce power and privilege for those in dominant groups (Solórzano & Yosso, 2009).

In the following sections, I present counternarratives of four cisgender and transgender men who are survivors of sexual violence. I have chosen to use counternarrative as a theoretical framework to discuss MSSVs to center on four men's experiences as a marginalized group within the discourse of sexual violence in higher education. In this chapter, I introduce Aaron, Aidan, Micah, and Sam; each became an MSSV during his undergraduate or graduate school experience.

Aaron

As a first-year student at his undergraduate institution on the East Coast, Aaron, a white cisgender man from an upper-middle-class background, experienced sexual coercion. Identifying as "either straight or bi-curious," he was stalked by a fellow student in his residence hall, who (on at least two occasions) entered Aaron's residence hall room without his consent while Aaron was sleeping. During the first experience, Aaron woke up and "suspected someone was in the room . . . so [he] called out [his] roommate's name." Immediately, "this dark outline" of a person "disappeared out [his] door." Shaken by the experience, Aaron and his roommate agreed to keep their door locked at all times. The second experience happened one night when Aaron's roommate left the room unlocked when he went to take a shower down the hallway. During that brief time, Aaron awoke to find a man standing over him with his hand outstretched touching the sheets covering Aaron. Immediately, he confronted the man about what he was doing, and the man ran from the room. Aaron ran after him, demanding to know why he was in his room. A campus sexual violence prevention peer educator himself, Aaron was traumatized by this event, particularly in light of his campus administrators' unhelpful responses to his situation.

Aidan

A Black gay cisgender man, Aidan experienced sexual assault and intimate partner violence during his time at his institution in the Mountain States region where he received his undergraduate and graduate degrees. In his first semester of graduate school, he hooked up with a man he had met who disclosed that he had a girlfriend and was just interested in having no-strings-attached nonreciprocal sex. Throughout the semester, Aidan kept in touch with the man every once in a while. The man engaged in some manipulative behavior, asking for money or telling Aidan, "All of this stuff that he wanted to do to me, and [that] he wanted to be with me." After a period of not being in touch, the man contacted Aidan and asked for money. Aidan was unable to provide him with money and accused him of being interested only because of the monetary component of the relationship. The man "assured [him] that that wasn't the case," and as a result, Aidan invited the man over to his house, promising that they could have penetrative sex. He said that after the man arrived, an hour and a half late, "the kisses that he promised and the cuddling and all of that very quickly turned [away]." In an attempt to show his feelings for the man, Aidan allowed the man to have anal sex with him; however, the experience was "incredibly painful" and when he asked him to stop, "He told me 'No.'" Aidan's experiences were then complicated because of his work as a graduate assistant on his campus and because his coworkers and closest friends were mandated reporters legally required by Title IX of the 1972 Education Amendments to report observed or suspected violence, leaving him without many other people with whom he could disclose and process his experiences.

Micah

Micah, a white queer, transmasculine man, attended the same large private university in the Mid-Atlantic region for his undergraduate and graduate degrees. He was actively involved as a student leader on campus, particularly with the campus's LGBT (lesbian, gay, bisexual, and transgender) Resource Center. Micah came out as trans* during his first year of college, and early in his gender identity development, he claimed that he operated in "an assimilationist sort of perspective on my trans*-ness. Just sort of wanted to be just a dude—a straight guy." But during his second year of college, he "reconnected . . . back to a sort of queer framework" and started dating men. In his third year of undergraduate school, Micah was using Grindr, a social media application for men who have sex with men, and set up a meeting with a man who lived in the surrounding area. After meeting up for drinks at a local gay bar, they went back to Micah's apartment and started to hook up, but they stopped because the man had had too much to drink. Micah awoke during the night to discover "[they] were having sex." The next morning, Micah drove the guy home and afterward wondered if it had all been a dream or not and questioned "if it had really happened." Two years later, he attended a session on sexual trauma survivors at a conference, and while listening to others share their stories, "it really started to sink in about what had happened two years prior." His experience at this conference brought up his past sexual violence experience and led to a challenging time in his life processing through the experience.

Sam

A white cisgender queer-identified man, Sam grew up in the mid-Atlantic region and attended the flagship public university in his home state for undergraduate and graduate school. Throughout his life, Sam experienced multiple incidents of sexual violence and coercion. Growing up in a physically, verbally, and emotionally abusive household, he struggled with his nascent queer identity in his rural home. In college, his first sexual experience with another man was with his boyfriend, who had told him, "If you don't do this, you don't love me." During that experience, his boyfriend was "very aggressive," and as a result, Sam dealt with torn skin and "bled for days afterwards." Based upon that experience, Sam was left thinking "it was just normal interaction" and assumed that was just how "gay men interacted." This type of "normal" behavior in Sam's mind also included experiences of sexual coercion, including being groped by other men—often strangers—while out dancing at gay clubs. Throughout college, he used alcohol and drugs as a coping mechanism. He said that he would smoke large amounts of marijuana, go on Grindr, look for available sex partners, and "coerce myself into those encounters on a daily basis for months." Prior to starting work on his master's degree, Sam connected with a mentor in his professional field in a nearby city. The mentor invited Sam to have brunch with him and meet him at his house. After arriving, the mentor asked Sam to have sex with him. Sam recounted, "I convinced myself that I, in fact, want[ed] to join him and, because of what I thought he could provide and the role that I thought I would play, I allowed us to have a sexual encounter that I didn't want to have." Following this experience, Sam was distraught, naming it "the worst college experience in my life." These experiences continued to play a major role in Sam's life, including affecting his health and well-being as well as his ability to engage in healthy intimate relationships, in either platonic or romantic ways.

Finding Commonality

One commonality among Aaron, Aidan, Micah, and Sam is their identity as men who survived sexual violence or coercion during college. The preceding passages allow the reader to hear their voices, gain insight on their salient identities, and learn more about their particular stories as survivors. In the following sections, I discuss three common patterns from their collective counternarratives: negotiating fear and shame, problematizing sexual violence responses, and reflecting on sexual violence and masculinity.

Negotiating Fear and Shame

Following their sexual violence experiences, each of the men felt shame and fear, which were manifested in various ways. For Micah and Aidan, part of the shame they felt was connected to aspects of their salient social identities. Micah said, "I would say there was a lot of shame in, with the statistics of, especially around trans* folks who are survivors, trying to grapple with being one of those numbers." He mentioned how his safety was one of his mother's biggest worries when Micah decided to transition, and after his experience, he said, "I was sort of coming to terms with what it meant to be a survivor, [and] thinking, 'Well, does that just reinforce her fear of what it means for me to be trans*?'" Relatedly, Aidan stated that aspects of his shame were connected to how others in the LGBTQ community might perceive him because of the decisions he had made. He recounted:

> While I don't blame myself for what happened, I think that there's still other elements of the situation that I am trying to figure out how to hold myself accountable for—like sleeping with a man who is in a relationship. . . . And I think that part of that shame also has to do with my identity as a gay man, and the things I've tried to stand for, and the things that I, you know, tried to be for my people and the folks that I know and the folks that are impacted by the same things.

This fear of perception is deeply connected to how shame and fear also creates challenges in negotiating interpersonal relationships.

The negotiation of fear and shame often resulted in changes in their personal behavior in connecting with other people. For example, Aaron stated how following his experiences of sexual coercion he was riddled with self-doubt and blamed himself by wondering what he had done to lead on his fellow resident. He stated that he came to the realization that "maybe I needed to be a little more guarded in how I show affection with people because it's sending the wrong message." Similarly, following his sexual assault by his older mentor, Sam said,

I think it has contributed to a mistrust of older gay men. . . . And since the assault, every time one of those men makes a comment that is directed at me in a sexual nature, that I used to just laugh off and treat as a friend, now is seen as a threat. I can't not see them as threats. And so my trust for them is now broken, and they haven't done a thing.

This sense of broken trust was particularly consequential for intimate future experiences with others. Micah discussed his need to be very clear about boundaries with others, particularly when beginning a relationship with another person, saying,

> Like what does disclosure mean around telling them [about my experience of sexual violence] or making sure that they know that I'm trans* and certain things about consent and expectations for sexual encounters and really coming to a point of, there are certain things that I want to make sure are said before any encounter happens.

For Micah, this type of boundary setting was important to reestablish a sense of control and negotiate healthy interpersonal connections. However, for some, the intrapersonal connection was more difficult to face.

Feelings of fear and shame among the MSSVs in this study also led many of the men to use coping mechanisms that were often unhealthy. For example, Sam commented, "I feel like the emotional distress that I felt from the incident has become so normal to me that it's hard even to separate out what it looks like anymore. That it just has become kind of like a dull ache." This inability to process one's feelings or emotions was often discussed in the form of "numbing." In our conversation, Micah discussed Brene Brown's work on vulnerability, saying Brown talks about the ways that individuals numb themselves, but that "you can't . . . selectively numb emotion. And that when you do that for the negative, you also do it for the positive." Micah shared how he experienced difficulty during a recent training session when asked to name emotions. He stated how he could "name the sort of umbrella emotions" and used anger as an example, but how hard it was for him to "really narrow it down between frustrated or anguish or rage." Feeling frustrated by this, Micah reflected, "And so I think those two years of pushing that [being sexually assaulted] away, that impacted the ways in which I'm able to articulate what's going on, feelings wise. I think it's really hindered my emotional intelligence."

For Sam, the experience of numbing was accomplished via alcohol and drug abuse. He said that "within a four-hour period, I needed to have 7 to 10 drinks in my system." After his experiences of sexual violence, this pattern continued even further because "I was able to just bury and split from the emotional experience of it, so I think what unfortunately happened is because it offered . . . the false sense of satisfaction and validation because I felt that with the numbing." Sam said that following his sexual assaults, he would

> start smoking marijuana in large amounts . . . you know, copious amounts of marijuana and then go on an app like Grindr and looking for someone who didn't even meet a standard for me, but just was available. And then meeting people that I was not interested in at all, and forcing myself to have sex that was, I would coerce myself into those encounters on a daily basis, for months.

Sam's pattern of alcohol abuse, drug abuse, and high-risk sexual encounters served as a coping mechanism to numb the feelings he had as a result of his experience of sexual violence. All the men said their experiences resulted in challenges emotionally. Among the participants, their interactions with campus administrators brought about a whole different set of challenges.

Problematizing Sexual Violence Responses

The decision to (not) report their experience of sexual violence was an individual one. Of the four men, only Aaron reported his experience to campus administrators, an encounter which he characterized as "horrible." The day he went to his campus police, Aaron's mother had called ahead and given an officer information about the incident.

> I remember like one police officer had me give the story standing up in the middle of this police station lobby area where people are sitting around, having coffee, or just waiting . . . to get their lost bike helmet or some shit, and it was just awful. I felt so self-conscious and weird about it.

He continued to describe his encounter, saying, "This very unsympathetic guy who's just standing there with his arms folded, and just didn't bother to try to figure out what happened from whoever answered my mom's phone call, and was a total dick about it." After finding out that he would have no influence on the outcome of submitting an official report, Aaron walked out, but as he was leaving, the officer encouraged him to contact the dean on call.

Aaron called the dean and shared his experience. He recalled that the dean said, "You know, most of the time people can just settle this. You know, you can just tell him that . . . you don't want him in your room." To which Aaron responded, "I was asleep. I thought it just kind of went without saying that I didn't want people there." As a sexual violence peer educator, Aaron was frustrated by the dean's reaction and asked him, "Do you tell people . . . who have just gone through sexual assault that you should have just told them you didn't want it?" The dean replied hastily, "Oh well, you know, in the more severe cases that we get, of course we react . . . in appropriate ways." But in reflecting on that, Aaron noted, "It just added to the feeling that I was not . . . what he considered a 'severe case' or really an important one. So it was just total bullshit." In the end, Aaron returned to the police station and spoke to a detective who specialized in sexual violence cases. However, he chose not to file an official report because the officer confirmed to him that "you can't really control the outcome of the committee on discipline because they decide, not you." The officer did call the perpetrator and told him that he should stay away from Aaron, advised him to seek professional help, and said that what he did was not appropriate.

The other three men made the choice not to report their experiences of sexual violence. However, in some cases, that decision felt predetermined. For example, Aidan held a dual role on his campus: He was a graduate student as well as a university employee in a graduate assistantship role. He told me that his institution's review of the Title IX legislation, in light of the Dear Colleague letter from the U.S. Department of Education (2011) that strongly reminded federally funded higher education institutions of their responsibility to comply with Title IX, changed matters tremendously when it came to sexual violence on campus. Campus administrators increased their vigilance as mandated reporters, and there seemed to be a climate of fear and concern about sexual violence. Because of his dual role, Aidan felt restricted from telling any of his close mentors, colleagues, or even fellow students given their roles as mandated reporters. This only increased his feelings of isolation in the aftermath of his sexual assault. He recalled, "I think I partially felt robbed of some of that [lack of support] through the indirect consequences of some of the Title IX conversation on campus." Other participants also mentioned Title IX and its influence on increasing conversations and training on sexual violence.

For Aidan and Micah, who were also university employees, their awareness of Title IX as well as their direct experiences in sexual violence trainings and conversations on campus presented certain challenges. As Micah stated,

That one in five statistic was sort of one of the opening points [of a sexual violence training he attended]. And so I struggle with the compulsion to interject and add the 1 in 16 or the 50% of trans* folks as a means to assert visibility, I guess I would call it. And so that compulsion to say, "You know, hold on. You're missing folks, including myself," runs up against "Will that impact how I'm viewed in the space?"

Aidan experienced a similar tension. He reflected on conversations with higher education colleagues on sexual violence, saying,

I think it's always interesting to note that whenever we're talking about survivors and folks that have been impacted or assaulted, it's always, they're always referred to as women. . . . That . . . has indirectly caused a lot of weirdness for me. . . . I think, on the one hand, it sort of speaks to me and says, "Oh, we're invisible." Right? Like we, like the things that have happened to us [as MSSVs] aren't as important.

Aidan and Micah experienced feelings of erasure as men who were survivors themselves in conversations on sexual violence. They never advocated for ignoring the very real dangers present for women around sexual violence, yet they expressed a need for a more inclusive discussion of who survivors of sexual violence and coercion actually are. This need for inclusive discussions on survivors of sexual violence creates an opportunity to present information on the experiences of men and how their experiences are connected to ideas of masculinity in society.

Reflecting on Sexual Violence and Masculinity

Another pattern that emerged among the men was their reflections of survivorship as men and how that connects to the concept of masculinity. Micah astutely discussed this issue in critiquing current programming on sexual violence prevention geared to men:

On issues of masculinity, it's almost always explicitly engrained in preventative programming. And how "Oh, we have to teach men not to rape." Right? And then it's about masculinity and all of that. But it's not on the opposite end about survivor support when it comes to men.

This lack of survivor support as it relates to masculinity was keenly felt by many of the MSSVs in this study. Reflecting on his own view of masculinity, Aaron expressed feeling conflicted, saying,

I felt like I shouldn't be this upset by like what had happened to me. . . . I should be a little stronger about this. And I should not be very affected, and . . . I should have been able to defend myself a little better because I'm physically larger than this person. And . . . he shouldn't be like a threat to me, and I shouldn't be a victim.

For Aaron, his feelings of self-blame were deeply rooted in the performativity of his masculinity, given his thoughts that his physicality should have protected him from such violence. Similarly, Sam expressed feeling "emasculated by the sexual assault." Yet, at the same time, he said "that expression of sexuality, that even being a part of coerced sexuality is still the reinforcement of some weird hypermasculinity. And so . . . even though I was the victim . . . it still was a reinforcement of my own masculinity."

Critiquing socially constructed (and often implicitly accepted) notions of masculinity was common among the men, yet they were often complicit in reifying masculinity. Looping back to his experiences in the sexual violence training session, Micah reflected on the tensions he felt between his transmasculine identity, which is largely informed by dominant power, and his identity as a survivor of sexual violence:

> Part of this contention between preserving my masculinity, of what feels like preserving my masculinity, and naming my survivorship is around, like, the intersection of my whiteness in masculinity. And feeling like, so in that, in the sexual assault training, in that moment, it felt as if I would be taking up too much space. And that wasn't the space in which it was needed or worth taking that space in that moment. And so part of that decision around when [to disclose] is also trying to keep in check that dominance.

Connected to this critique of masculinity, Aaron shared his frustration over how masculinity creates conditions that lead men to restrict their emotions:

> I have my own difficulty really opening up to people, partially as a result of having experienced sexual violence, and so I have to prove myself, like I have to prove that I'm not someone who's, you know, this . . . sex-driven mindless thing that like masculinity is kind of made out to be is pretty frustrating.

For the men, negotiating societal norms of masculinity in conjunction with their identities as survivors of sexual violence provided them with opportunities to challenge hegemonic ideals, rooted in heterosexism, sexism, and genderism, and adopt healthy masculinities. At the same time, the men continued to do this largely in isolation and through self-reflection given that the majority of the men were not connected to other men who were survivors of sexual violence.

Discussion and Concluding Thoughts

For Aaron, Aidan, Micah, and Sam, their experiences of sexual violence had a significant impact on their lives. Their counternarratives provide implications for higher education professionals to consider as they engage in professional practice. First, college student educators must acknowledge that cisgender women are not the only survivors of sexual violence in higher education. Dialogues and training sessions on campus must be more inclusive and include other vital statistics and narratives that reflect the experiences of all survivors rather than reinforce a single narrative (that of cisgender women as survivor). By including this information, higher education professionals can begin to disrupt the dominant discourse on sexual violence in higher education and perhaps reduce the fear and shame that MSSVs may have, given that they can see representations of themselves within these dialogues, training sessions, and other spaces and places on campus.

Second, there is a strong need to review policies, brochures, websites, and other campus-based materials and ensure that the language we are using regarding sexual violence is inclusive of all genders. If men who have survived sexual violence do not see themselves and their experiences included in campus policies and procedures, then they will likely not report or seek those resources. Third, college administrators are encouraged to consider the ways that the campus disciplinary process allows survivors the opportunity to minimize the number of times survivors must recite their narrative and ensure that individuals hearing their statements (i.e., campus police, conduct officers) are trained effectively to be able to be compassionate and respectful of victims' experiences. Additionally, MSSVs have a strong need to feel in control of who knows their story and the outcome of the process to avoid feeling revictimized by the disciplinary process itself. Yet, knowing the outcome of the process is impossible given due process and the campus judicial system; therefore, this becomes a deterrent to some survivors in coming forward to report their experiences.

Fourth, campus-based sexual violence prevention efforts must grapple with the ways masculinity, particularly hegemonic masculinity, has an influence not only on prevention programming but also on survivor support. This may mean that counselors and campus health and wellness administrators need to reach out to MSSVs through social norms campaigns and one-on-one and group counseling opportunities in the hope that these men can process their feelings, which may include shame and fear. Violence prevention administrators may need to review hotline volunteer trainings to ensure proper available resources for MSSVs and include men in their marketing efforts. Peer educator groups should include messages related to MSSVs in their programs and be prepared to share resources with MSSVs.

Helping MSSVs process their survivorship is important yet often difficult. For the MSSVs discussed in this chapter, their feelings of fear and shame compelled them to either avoid disclosure of their trauma to others (Aidan and Sam) or only share it with close friends or family (Aaron and Micah). Given that many MSSVs tend to avoid disclosure, it is important for higher education professionals to be affirming to MSSVs who do decide to disclose their experiences to them. Professionals should commit themselves, in word and deed, to be strong advocates for all sexual violence survivors, and they should be knowledgeable about available resources, including MSSV survivor groups or organizations and counselors who specialize in sexual violence and trauma. Additionally, given that some MSSVs do disclose what happened to them to others, higher education professionals should work to educate students and families on how to best support their loved ones who experience sexual violence or coercion and educate them on available resources as well.

Professional associations have a responsibility to educate their members on the experiences of MSSVs as well. Umbrella student affairs and higher education organizations, such as ACPA—College Student Educators International and NASPA—Student Affairs Administrators in Higher Education, as well as functional area-based organizations, such as the Association of College and University Housing Officers-International, Association of College Unions International, and American School Counselor Association, often play a role in helping provide resources to their members about sexual violence prevention. Yet, much of the conference programs, webinars, and other materials provided focus largely on the experiences and statistics of cisgender women as survivors. There may be some mentions of MSSVs, but these are fleeting and few. These professional organizations have a duty to help their members understand that sexual violence survivors are represented among all genders, not just women.

Finally, campus administrators must balance the need for reporting sexual violence on their campuses and demonstrating care and compassion for survivors themselves. As in the case of Micah's institution, the tipping point on Title IX mandates and legislation can create campus climates that reinforce a compliance-only attitude when discussing sexual violence. If students feel constrained contacting campus administrators out of fear that the individual they are speaking with will have to report the details obtained in that conversation, administrators risk violating survivors once again. Campus officials must continue to follow mandates and regulations while also centering on the immediate and long-term needs of our students who have survived sexual violence.

In my last interview with Sam, I asked him to reflect on the process of discussing his experiences of sexual violence with me. He discussed the "catharsis" involved from sharing his story, and he paraphrased a few lines from a poem by Persian poet Rumi, saying, "Don't look away. Keep your gaze upon the bandaged place. It's where the light shines through you." He continued with the following:

I think that there is a lot of liberation in examining our wounds. . . . I really feel like it is this process of unpacking and applying a critical lens and a reflective lens to the wounds of our experience . . . because while we cannot build a foundation on top of a wound, I think that by examining the wound and making that effort to heal, and allow, because what is that pain a response to? Right? Pain just doesn't exist in a vacuum. The pain comes out of your relationship to yourself.

In sharing their stories, Aaron, Aidan, Micah, and Sam all engaged in an act of liberation, one that challenged and problematized the larger dominant ideology on sexual violence in higher education and allowed them the time and space to "gaze upon the bandaged place" as a way to continue to heal. Higher education professionals must engage in the act of helping all sexual violence survivors to be seen and heard to then begin to heal from their experiences. To not do this is an incredible failure of our mission and purpose as educators.

Note

1. I use the term *men* as an inclusive signifier of one's gender, whether one is cisgender or transgender, rather than *male*, which describes one's sex (Lev, 2004). Yet, many scholars often use male and man interchangeably. In this chapter, when I use *man*, I am being specific in describing participants' gender identity, not necessarily their sex. Yet, when citing other scholars' scholarship, I use their terminology, which may have different meanings.

References

Aosved, A. C., Long, P. J., & Voller, E. K. (2011). Sexual revictimization and adjustment in college men. *Psychology of Men & Masculinity, 12,* 285–296.

Banyard, V. L., Ward, S., Cohn, E. S., Plante, E. G., Moorhead, C., & Walsh, W. (2007). Unwanted sexual contact on campus: A comparison of women's and men's experiences. *Violence and Victims, 22,* 52–70.

Black, M. C., Basile, K. C., Breiding, M. J., Smith, S. G., Walters, M. L., Merrick, M. T., . . . Stevens, M. R. (2011). *The National Intimate Partner and Sexual Violence Survey (NIVIS): 2010 summary report.* Atlanta, GA: National Center for Injury Prevention and Control, Centers for Disease Control and Prevention.

Choudhary, E., Smith, M., & Bossarte, R. M. (2012). Depression, anxiety, and symptom profiles among female and male victims of sexual violence. *American Journal of Men's Health, 6*(1), 28–36.

Delgado, R., & Stefancic, J. (2001). *Critical race theory: An introduction.* New York: New York University Press.

Donaldson, M. (1993). What is hegemonic masculinity? *Theory and Society, 22,* 643–657.

Gilbody, S., Richards, D., Brealey, S., & Hewitt, C. (2007). Screening for depression in medical settings with the Patient Health Questionnaire (PHQ): A diagnostic meta-analysis. *Journal of General Internal Medicine, 22,* 1596–1602.

Gray, E. (2015, June 25). University survey highlights role of "verbal coercion" in sexual assault. *Time.* Retrieved from time.com/topic/campus-sexual-assault/

Isley, P. J. (1998). Sexual assault of men: College-age victims. *NASPA Journal, 35,* 305–317. doi:10.2202/1949-6605.1063

Johnson, I., & Sigler, R. (2001). Forced sexual intercourse among intimates. *Journal of Interpersonal Violence, 15,* 95–108.

Kilmartin, C., & Berkowitz, A. (2005). *Sexual assault in context: Teaching college men about gender.* Mahwah, NJ: Erlbaum.

Kimmel, M. S. (2004). Masculinity as homophobia: Fear, shame, and silence in the construction of gender identity. In P. F. Murphy (Ed.), *Oxford readings in feminism: Feminism and masculinities* (pp. 182–199). New York, NY: Oxford University Press.

Kimmel, M. S. (2008). *Guyland: The perilous world where boys become men.* New York, NY: Harper.

Lev, A. I. (2004). *Transgender emergence: Therapeutic guidelines for working with gender-variant people and their families.* New York, NY: Routledge.

Light, D., & Monk-Turner, E. (2009). Circumstances surrounding male sexual assault and rape: Findings from the National Violence Against Women Survey. *Journal of Interpersonal Violence, 24,* 1849–1858.

Mezey, G., & King, M. (1987). Male victims of sexual assault. *Medicine, Science, and the Law, 27,* 122–124.

Mezey, G., & King, M. (1989). The effects of sexual assault on men: A survey of 22 victims. *Psychological Medicine, 19,* 205–209.

National Coalition of Anti-Violence Programs. (2011). *Hate violence against lesbian, gay, bisexual, transgender, queer, and HIV-affected communities in the United States in 2010.* Retrieved from www.avp.org/storage/documents/Reports/2012_NCAVP_2011_HV_Report.pdf

Plant, M., Plant, M., & Miller, P. (2005). Childhood and adult sexual abuse: Relationships with "addictive" or "problem" behaviours and health. *Journal of Addictive Diseases, 21,* 25–38.

Platt, J. J., & Busby, D. M. (2009). Male victims: The nature and meaning of sexual coercion. *American Journal of Family Therapy, 37,* 217–226. doi:10.1080/01926180802403302

Sable, M. R., Danis, F., Mauzy, D. L., & Gallagher, S. K. (2006). Barriers to reporting sexual assault for women and men: Perspectives of college students. *Journal of American College Health, 55,* 157–162.

Scarce, M. (1997). Same-sex rape of male college students. *Journal of American College Health, 45*(1), 171–173.

Solórzano, D. G., & Yosso, T. J. (2009). Critical race methodology: Counterstorytelling as an analytical framework for educational research. In E. Taylor,

D. Gillborn, & G. Ladson-Billings (Eds.), *Foundations of critical race theory in education* (pp. 131–147). New York, NY: Routledge.

Stermac, L., Del Bove, G., & Addison, M. (2004). Stranger and acquaintance sexual assault of adult males. *Journal of Interpersonal Violence, 19*, 901–915.

Stotzer, R. (2009). Violence against transgender people: A review of United States data. *Aggression and Violent Behavior, 14*, 170–179.

Struckman-Johnson, C. (1988). Forced sex on date: It happens to men, too. *Journal of Sex Research, 24*, 234–241.

Struckman-Johnson, C., & Struckman-Johnson, D. (1994). Men pressured and forced into sexual experience. *Archives of Sexual Behavior, 23*(1), 93–114.

Tewksbury, R. (2007). Effects of sexual assaults on men: Physical, mental and sexual consequences. *International Journal of Men's Health, 6*(1), 22–35.

Tewksbury, R., & Mustaine, E. E. (2001). Lifestyle factors associated with the sexual assault of men: A routine activity theory analysis. *Journal of Men's Studies, 9*, 153–182.

Title IX of the Education Amendments, 20 U.S.C. §1681 et seq. (1972).

Turchik, J. A., & Edwards, K. M. (2012). Myths about male rape: A literature review. *Psychology of Men & Masculinity, 13*, 211–226.

U.S. Department of Education. (2011). *Dear colleague letter: Sexual violence.* Retrieved from https://www2.ed.gov/about/offices/list/ocr/letters/colleague-201104.html

6

THE INTERSECTIONS OF LIVED OPPRESSION AND RESILIENCE

Sexual Violence Prevention for Women of Color on College Campuses

Ciera V. Scott, Anneliese A. Singh, and Jessica C. Harris

Women students of color experience sexual violence at the intersections of sexism, racism, classism, homophobia, religious xenophobia, and other forms of oppression, thus confounding their experiences with trauma and resilience (see Abbey & Jacques-Tiura, 2010; Olive, 2012; Smith, 2005; West, 1995). For example, an African American woman who is sexually assaulted may find herself experiencing physical and emotional distress in response to her sexual trauma in addition to the overt, racially charged hate crimes (e.g., nooses drawn on whiteboards, Black student leadership being treated with derogatory racial epithets by white students) that were co-occurring on her campus during the time of her sexual trauma (Izadi, 2015). Moreover, sexual violence is not solely about gender; it is also often about race, class, religion, ability, and much more.

In this chapter, we explore the experiences of women of color and sexual violence on college campuses. First, we describe how trauma theory may be applied to women of color survivors of sexual violence and the common challenges that women of color students experience on college campuses—including the intersections of racism and sexism. Second, we review the ways that women of color college students resist and are resilient to multiple oppressions and nurture their own liberation and healing as survivors. Third, we discuss implications for mental health providers and student affairs professionals working with women of color survivors. When used in

119

this chapter, the term *women* refers to cisgender and transgender women, although we recognize that the majority of research on college women and sexual violence, as well as college women of color and sexual violence (what little research exists), centers on cisgender women. The term *women of color* refers to all individuals who identify their gender as women; do not benefit from white privilege; and are discriminated against on the bases of their race, gender identity, and intersecting identities.

Trauma Theory and Women of Color Survivors of Sexual Violence

The present-day conceptualization of trauma theory includes the development of psychological research and literature across the span of several decades (Briere, Hodges, & Godbout, 2010; Brown, 2008; Herman, 1997; Tolin & Foa, 2008), yet researchers give little attention to the unique experiences of women of color survivors on college campuses. Mental health professionals and social justice advocates have worked to shift society's attitudes toward trauma from the imposition of severe pathology to a more in-depth understanding of how experiencing trauma may elicit behavioral and emotional responses that can have a long-term impact on a survivor's daily functioning, mental health, and interpersonal relationships (Herman, 1997). Trauma theory as a framework provides connections between a trauma survivor's symptomology and the identified traumatic incident, rather than attributing one's symptomology to perceived character flaws (Herman, 1997). In addition, service providers using trauma theory in their practice often consider the role that white patriarchal, socially dictated and regulated stereotypes play in victim blaming, depression, and lower self-esteem among women of color survivors (Neville, Heppner, Oh, Spanierman, & Clark, 2004).

Employing tenets of Herman's (1997) trauma theory such as establishing safety and trust, reconfiguring the survivor's trauma narrative, and rebuilding the survivor's connection to her community can prove beneficial in the healing of female sexual violence survivors (Fahs, 2011). Judith Herman's (1997) foundational work provides a comprehensive framework that helping professionals may use to explore the trauma experiences of sexual violence survivors. Herman asserted that a trauma survivor's recovery process starts with a safe and nonjudgmental healing relationship with the survivors themselves, as well as between the survivors and helping professionals involved in their healing. Additionally, sexual violence survivors may decide to undergo remembrance and mourning, whereby survivors recount their trauma incident to decrease the emotional intensity attached to memories of the trauma and their perpetrator(s). Remembrance and mourning also encompasses grieving the negative physical, emotional, and interpersonal challenges that the trauma experience has inflicted on the survivor's life. Finally, individuals who have survived sexual violence may benefit from intentional reconnection to positive social support systems, engaging life activities, and meaning-making actions, for example, volunteering as a sexual violence advocate with organizations such as the National Organization of Sisters of Color Ending Sexual Assault (2013; sisterslead.org) or the National Alliance to End Sexual Violence (endsexualviolence.org; Herman, 1997).

Through the lens of trauma theory (Herman, 1997), educators working with women of color survivors on the college campus may refer survivors to service providers who facilitate safe, nonjudgmental spaces of healing wherein they validate the lived experiences of survivors. Furthermore, mental health clinicians who serve women of color sexual violence survivors may employ aspects of narrative therapy (M. White & Epston, 1990), providing survivors with an opportunity to write down their sexual assault story, via a vignette, a poem, a play, or other penned account, to confront their perpetrators through the safety of their written words and begin the journey to decrease the emotional latency attached to their sexual violence experience. Women of color sexual violence survivors could also be encouraged to connect with student organizations and program initiatives on their campuses and in their communities that celebrate women of diverse backgrounds as a source of social support, validation, and connection.

Women of color sexual violence survivors are only half to one third as likely as their white counterparts to seek mental health services following trauma (Amstadter, McCauley, Ruggiero, Resnick, & Kilpatrick, 2008). Cultural mistrust of white-centered health service systems in general (Suite, La Bril, Primm, & Harrison-Ross, 2007) coupled with cultural stigma regarding usage of mental health facilities (Das, Olfson, McCurtis, & Weissman, 2006) may deter women of color sexual violence survivors from seeking treatment. It is imperative for university officials working with women of color sexual violence survivors to consider the varying ways a survivor's intersecting, historically minoritized identities may have an impact on her trauma experience as well as her coping and healing journey (Brown, 2008). For example, women of color survivors may experience feelings of isolation, hopelessness, self-blame, and confusion resulting from their experiences of sexual trauma that are further compounded by possible feelings of exclusion and prejudice stemming from sexism, racism, and other forms of oppression that are embedded in the college environment. Moreover, the very act of sexual violence against women of color is heavily influenced by intersecting systems of patriarchy and white supremacy—including sexism and racism (see Chapter 2). Other identities, beyond race and gender, intersect and inform the survivor's experiences and responses to sexual violence. Social identities, identity-specific experiences, and systems of domination influence the experiences of women of color sexual violence survivors and must be accounted for in sexual violence prevention efforts on the college campus.

In working with sexual violence survivors, trauma theory (Herman, 1997) can be used to empower and model self-compassion as women of color process long-term effects of sexual violence such as self-blame and diminished self-worth (Littleton & Breitkopf, 2006), challenges with intimacy (Blain, Gavolski, & Peterson, 2011), and interpersonal difficulties following disclosure of sexual violence (Ahrens & Aldana, 2012). Women of color sexual violence survivors typically report higher rates of depression, substance abuse, suicide, and post-traumatic stress disorder (PTSD) than their white counterparts following an experience of sexual violence (Bryant-Davis, Chung, & Tillman, 2009). We must stress that these responses to sexual violence are influenced by systems of domination that work to further minoritize, isolate, and oppress women of color survivors; these responses are not (solely) attributable to the individual. Mental health professionals serving women of color sexual violence survivors must consider the cultural stigma surrounding sexual violence, how this may impair a survivor's ability to disclose the experience to close family members or acquaintances in their community, and the impact of cultural silence regarding sexual violence on the psychological health and ability to experience self-compassion for sexual violence survivors in historically minoritized populations (Bryant-Davis et al., 2009).

Influence of Sexism and Racism on Reporting Sexual Violence

Mental health practitioners and student affairs professionals who provide services for college students must understand how the intersections of male and white supremacy influence women of color survivors' experiences with and responses to sexual violence. Survivors of all genders report feelings of guilt or shame, unease regarding confidentiality, and apprehension about others believing their story as major barriers to reporting an incident of sexual violence (Littleton & Breitkopf, 2006; Ullman, Peter-Hagene, & Relyea, 2014). Women survivors may feel hesitant to report sexual violence for fear of others' retaliation or a desire to protect a perpetrator who was a family member or close friend (Sable, Danis, Mauzy, & Gallagher, 2006). Society often imposes self-blame and guilt on women through sexist beliefs and rape myths concerning sexual violence, significantly decreasing the probability that they will report their assault or seek mental health services to assist with their healing process (Starzynski, Ullman, Filipas, & Townsend, 2005; Yamawaki, 2007). We explore several of these sexist beliefs in the following paragraphs.

Sexism. The perceived "sexiness" of survivors' attire at the time of assault is often used to place blame on victims of sexual violence (Whatley, 2005).

Students from all gender identities may believe women wear revealing attire to feel sexy and attractive. However, in one study, only 3% of women respondents stated that they intentionally wore revealing clothing to sexually seduce other individuals of another gender (Moor, 2010). Society perpetuates sexist attitudes that support victim blaming of women survivors of sexual violence and preserve the false assertion that women who wear revealing clothing are inviting sexual violence (Burn, 2009).

College students frequently report believing that women bear more responsibility for encounters with sexual violence and that women who survived acts of sexual violence used poor judgment in their interactions with their sexual violence perpetrators (Untied, Orchowski, Mastroleo, & Gidycz, 2012; Zinzow & Thompson, 2011). The sexist attitudes that fuel victim blaming, shaming, and discrediting the lived experiences of women survivors of sexual violence contribute to deterring survivors from reporting their sexual trauma and maintain society's silencing of women related to this trauma (Edwards et al., 2014; Miller, Canales, Amacker, Backstrom, & Gidycz, 2011). These myths and unsubstantiated beliefs exist at the intersections of sexism, patriarchy, and the imbalance of power and privilege as they relate to gender and historical blaming and shaming of women survivors of sexual violence (Freedman, 2007; Gerber & Cherneski, 2006; Stewart, 2014).

Racism. Racism intersects with sexism to influence women of color survivors' experiences with sexual violence response, prevention, and healing. Next, we examine ways Black, Latina, Asian, indigenous, and multiracial women are constructed and dehumanized at the intersections of race and gender. We do not outline these stereotypes to perpetuate them or to detail how to work with or work around them. Instead, we outline these racist and sexist stereotypes to ensure that educators understand how macrolevel systems of domination intersect to influence women's microlevel experiences with sexual violence. For example, systems of domination construct several populations of women of color as hypersexualized and promiscuous, which influences women's everyday decisions to report sexual violence and others' perceptions of women of color survivors who speak out about sexual violence.

Racist stereotypes about women of color underpin the perceived credibility of women of color when reporting incidents of sexual violence (George & Martínez, 2002). White patriarchal norms rooted in the institution of U.S. slavery continue to confine Black women's sexuality to objectifying stereotypes that portray Black women in a negative and dehumanizing manner (Griffin, 2013). During U.S. slavery, Black women were objectified as the physical property of their slave owners, with their owners employing white male privilege and power to force Black women slaves, who were labeled as sexually promiscuous, to submit to their owners' sexual advances (Bell, 2004). The historical objectification of Black women is perpetuated in modern-day culture through the Jezebel and Sapphire stereotypes (hooks, 1981). The Jezebel stereotype describes Black women as hypersexualized and seductive temptresses, whereas the Sapphire stereotype demonizes Black women as angry, vindictive, and opportunistic (hooks, 1981). For more information on the history of women of color and sexual violence, see Chapter 2.

Further objectification of Black women as gold diggers, welfare queens, and freaks maintains racist views that Black women continuously crave sex and will use sex for material gain (Collins, 2009). The existence of racist stereotypes regarding Black women's sexuality justifies sexual violence against Black women, with Black women being viewed as yearning sexual attention and deserving of physical mistreatment. These racist and sexist stereotypes may deter Black women college students who experience sexual violence from reporting their traumatic experience because of fear they may be labeled as or seen through a demeaning stereotype, resulting in others blaming them for the sexual violence.

Additionally, the lack of response and care from police officers often negatively affects Black women college students' trust in the police. In one study, Black women student survivors often disclosed their sexual assault to friends but rarely reported the sexual violation to law enforcement agencies (Lindquist, Crosby, Barrick, Krebs, & Settles-Reaves, 2016). The publicized deaths of Black women such as Sandra Bland, Ralkina Jones, and Raynett Turner, who all died while in police custody in July 2015, could possibly influence Black women's decisions whether to report incidents of sexual violence to law enforcement or seek additional help for their sexual trauma (Tanis, 2015; Wheeler & George, 2005). In fact, 17% of Black women report instances of sexual violence to police, compared to 44% of white women (Krebs, Lindquist, & Barrick, 2010). In December 2015, former Oklahoma City police officer Daniel Holtzclaw was found guilty of 18 criminal charges of sexual violence against 13 Black women whom he sexually violated following traffic stops (Martinez & Mullen, 2015). Holtzclaw used his male, white-passing (Holtzclaw is Asian and white biracial but passes and identifies as white), and law enforcement privilege to not only sexually violate but also forcibly silence Black women. This violence, as well as the aftereffects of women's experiences with this violence, occurred at the intersection of race, sex, and class and was entangled in male privilege, power, and domination.

Finally, in the Black community, Black women may be confined and silenced by politics of respectability (Collins, 2005; E. F. White, 2001). Respectability politics aim to create a unified (imagined) Black community through detailing and enforcing ideological notions of ideal standards of Blackness (E. F. White, 2001). The politics of respectability are grounded in the belief that Black women must be clean, pious, sexually pure, and self-restrained (Higginbotham, 1993). This ideology may constrain Black women's reporting of sexual violence as it compromises their respectability. Politics of respectability for Black women students who are sexually violated by Black men are further nuanced. This is because Black women may be hesitant to tarnish the reputation of Black men, as well as their own reputation, threatening the unity of the Black campus community through politics of respectability (see Badejo, 2016). For example, Spelman College, a historically Black institution, mishandled several Black women students' reports that Black men at Morehouse College, a historically Black institution and Spelman's brother institution, sexually violated them. Women students suggested that the mishandling of the cases by both institutions was tied up in "this damn brotherhood-sisterhood thing" (Badejo, 2016), a reference to the politics of respectability in the Black community. Additionally, women were hesitant to report their assault for fear it would tarnish the reputation of their assailant; the historically Black colleges and universities; and, ultimately, the Black community (Badejo, 2016).

Latinas in the United States have also been labeled with racist stereotypes that commodify their sexuality and increase their risk of sexual victimization (Merskin, 2007). Latinas are portrayed throughout U.S. media as the cantina girl; the faithful, self-sacrificing señorita; and the vamp (Keller, 1994). The cantina girl depicts a hypersexualized Latina who is "a naughty lady of easy virtue" (Keller, 1994, p. 40), whereas the faithful, self-sacrificing señorita is portrayed as willing to protect her white male romantic interest no matter the threat of physical harm to herself (Keller, 1994). Latinas pictured as vamps use their intellectual capacity for devious means, often manipulating men to fulfill their desires (Keller, 1994). These stereotypes are dominant in mainstream media and are often coupled with the cultural construct of *marianismo*, which characterizes Latinas as submissive, religious, and self-sacrificing women who maintain their sexual virginity until marriage (Castillo & Cano, 2007). The collectivist nature of Latina/o culture places great value on the interdependence of Latinas within their family (*familismo*), obedience and reverence of Latinas based on their status in their family (*respecto*), and Latinas' preservation of harmony (*simpatía*) in their interpersonal relationships by maintaining a pleasant demeanor (Castillo, Perez, Castillo, & Ghosheh, 2010). Latina college students who experience social pressure to adhere to the tenets of *marianismo* may not disclose incidents of sexual violence to close acquaintances, family members, or law enforcement because of perceptions that reporting their sexual trauma may disrupt the emotional well-being of others or bring shame to their families.

Asian/Pacific Islander American (APIA) women are frequently depicted as submissive sexual objects (Koo, Nyugen, George, & Andrasik, 2015). APIA women may experience greater social pressure to conform to traditional Western and Christian gender roles related to expected abstinence behaviors for women by refraining from sex and alcohol before marriage (Koo et al., 2015). Women of Asian descent may attempt to adhere to a conservative portrayal of women to counteract societal stereotypes of APIA women as "exotic and hypersexual" (Koo et al., 2015). APIA women students who survive acts of sexual violence may not disclose their trauma because of feelings of shame or embarrassment related to failing to meet these restrictive cultural standards related to their sexuality (Koo et al., 2015). Additionally, women of Asian descent are constructed as upholding collectivist and interdependent cultural views in which the in-group's desires and sense of harmony are valued higher than those of the individual (Lui, 2015). APIA survivors of college sexual violence may choose not to disclose their sexual trauma to close friends or family members to avoid causing discord in the lives of their loved ones (Koo et al., 2015).

One in three American Indian and Alaska Native women experience sexual violence during their lifetime, as opposed to the national average of one in five women overall (Tjaden & Thoennes, 2000). Non-Native men perpetrate nearly 90% of the sexual violence committed against American Indian and Alaska Native women (Owens, 2012). Historically, American Indian and Alaska Native women were sexually victimized as a "tool of war" during the colonization of the Unites States (Owens, 2012, p. 513). White settlers used sexual violence against Native women as a means of conquest and control during the forced removal of Native American tribal nations from the eastern and southern United States during the infamous Trail of Tears in the early 1800s (Amnesty International USA, 2007). The historical oppression of American Indian and Alaska Native women in the United States may deter college women from this minority group from disclosing sexual violence because of the marginalization they experience at predominantly white college campuses.

Sixty-four percent of multiracial women will experience some form of sexual violence other than rape in their lifetime, and more than 32% of multiracial women will experience rape in their lifetime (Breiding et al., 2011). These rates of violence are higher than those of any other racial group of men or women. Multiracial women also experience sexist and racist stereotypes that portray them as vulnerable, hypersexual, and tragic (Nakashima, 1992). Moreover, historically, mixed-race individuals are often the product of sexual violence (Nakashima, 1992). Although multiracial individuals experience sexual violence at disproportionate rates, little to no research or practice has inquired into this population's experiences with violence on the college campus.

We stress that we do not explore these stereotypes to encourage educators and researchers to work around them or work with them. Instead, we encourage all those working on the college campus and in community health organizations to challenge these stereotypes in their work. How can we work against the belief that women of color are hypersexual, promiscuous, or submissive? How can we deconstruct these stereotypes in all aspects and forms and not just as they relate to sexual violence on the college campus? It is critical that we, as educators and scholars, do not negate white supremacist, patriarchal, and other dominant structures that are ingrained in our institutions; in our minds; and subsequently; in approaches to sexual violence prevention, response, and healing for women of color survivors.

Lesbian, gay, bisexual, queer, and/or transgender (LGBQ and/or T) women of color survivors of sexual violence. A review of how other identities intersect to inform more nuanced experiences within the community of women of color is beyond the scope of this chapter. Here, we offer a glimpse into two intersecting identities and how this further informs women of color's experiences with sexual violence on the college campus. Women of color college students who identify as LGBQ and/or T have reported experiencing verbal abuse, physical violence, or sexual objectification as a result of their sexual orientation or gender identity (Friedman & Leaper, 2010). LGBQ and/or T women of color on college campuses may be discriminated against because of one or all of their minority statuses (Friedman & Leaper, 2010). Moreover, Balsam and colleagues (2015) demonstrated that women of color who identify as LGBQ and/or T report alarmingly high rates of sexual violence during adulthood (43.5% of African Americans, 56% of Latina Americans, and 60.5% of Asian Americans).

Additionally, LGBQ and/or T minority college women are more likely not to disclose their sexual minority status to family members, creating an additional barrier to reporting incidents of sexual violence (Acosta, 2010; Rothblum, 2014). LGBQ and/or T women of color sexual violence survivors may feel hesitant about disclosing their sexual orientation or gender identity to loved ones because of cultural stigma, lack of awareness, and perceived lack of acceptance of sexual minorities among communities of color (Aranda et al., 2015; Zimmerman, Darnell, Rhew, Lee, & Kaysen, 2015). These feelings of exclusion or rejection, as well as valid experiences of prejudice and oppression based on their sexual orientation or gender identity, may be an additional obstacle for survivors to overcome in experiencing safety, nonjudgment, and validation when disclosing their trauma to loved ones. Additionally, African American LGBQ and/or T young adults have reported less access to health insurance and fewer months of full-time employment in comparison to their white counterparts (Balsam et al., 2015). These socioeconomic factors and lack of resources may hinder LGBQ and/or T students of color from seeking adequate medical care and behavioral health services following sexual violence incidents. Finally, interlocking systems of domination construct and maintain intersections of racism, sexism, genderism, and transphobia that inform the experiences of transgender women of color who may feel hesitant to report sexual violence to law enforcement or university officials for fear of being retaliated against or physically harmed as a result of the pervasive cultural stigma and documented hate crimes against transgender women (Dalton, 2015).

Implications

Resiliency to Multiple Oppressions

Although women of color survivors of sexual violence on college campuses experience multiple oppressions as detailed in the previous sections, it is also important to recognize the resiliency they hold. *Resilience* has been defined as a person's ability to heal and return from adversity and challenging times (Masten, 2010). Although resilience has typically been studied as a white and Western construct related to individualism (Singh, 2012), additional sources of resilience, such as community and collective resilience, are relevant to the lives of women of color survivors of sexual violence. Research on the resilience of women of color who have survived some type of sexual trauma has increased over the past decade. For instance, in a qualitative study of the resilience strategies Black survivors of sexual abuse used in their healing, participants noted the following aspects: (a) understanding their traumatic symptoms, (b) externalizing racist and sexist stereotypes of Black women, (c) negotiating family relationships and accessing community support, (d) transforming religion and spirituality into a source of healing, (e) reclaiming sexuality, and (f) integrating multiple identities as a survivor (Singh, Garnett, & Williams, 2012). For South Asian women survivors of child sexual abuse, resilience and healing included cultivating hope, accessing social support in the South Asian community, engaging in social advocacy, and engaging in intentional self-care (Singh, Hays, Chung, & Watson, 2010). Although resilience and healing from sexual trauma may look different in and across the racial/ethnic communities of women of color, providers working with women of color survivors of sexual violence should seek to ensure services enhance, not detract from, resilience and coping.

Liberation Movements Led by Women of Color Survivors

In addition to interrogating how college campus responses to sexual violence account for multiple sources of oppression and resilience that women of color survivors experience, providers should be aware of the liberation movements led by women of color survivors. The organization INCITE! is a voice of the women of color movement against sexual trauma and has sought to centralize the concerns of colonization, racism, intersectional oppressions, police militarization and injustice, and other issues that contextualize women of color and their experiences of trauma as demonstrated in the following:

> Movements against sexual and domestic violence have been critical in breaking the silence around violence against women. But as these movements are increasingly professionalized and de-politicized, they're often reluctant to address how violence operates in institutionalized ways and against oppressed people. INCITE! recognizes that it is *impossible* to seriously address sexual and intimate partner violence within communities of color without addressing these larger structures of violence (including militarism, attacks on immigrants' rights and Indigenous treaty rights, the proliferation of prisons, economic neo-colonialism, the medical industry, and more). So our organizing is focused on places where state violence and sexual/intimate partner violence intersect. (INCITE!, 2014, para. 5)

Resources from organizations such as INCITE! may be found online, and women of color survivors of sexual violence may benefit from having resources about in-person meetings and conferences as they move through the healing process. Because community-based organizations can change rapidly, evolving in their goals and efforts, providers should seek to make sure the resources they share with survivors are up to date, relevant, and culturally responsive to the lives of women of color sexual violence survivors on college campuses.

Implications for Working With Women of Color Survivors of Sexual Violence

Mental health providers and student affairs professionals on college campuses should commit themselves to creating affirmative spaces for women of color sexual violence survivors to feel physically and emotionally safe enough to disclose their stories to close friends, classmates, professors, fellow sorority or fraternity members, or other acquaintances who could encourage the survivors to report their sexual trauma to medical practitioners, educators, therapists, or law enforcement. The development of a positive environment for women of color sexual violence survivors in the university system may begin with the intentional engagement of college students in didactic and experiential opportunities related to diversity as well as visible institutional support of diversity-related student initiatives on campus (Denson & Chang, 2009). Student support offices or university departments that host campaigns to create awareness about sexual violence against women, such as the Clothesline Project and Take Back the Night rallies (Lee, Caruso, Goins, & Southerland, 2003), should be purposeful in integrating women of color speakers, presenters, and institutional allies into these events to validate the lived experiences of minority sexual violence survivors on college campuses. Organizers cannot stop at integrating women of color speakers; these events must also explicitly interrogate the impact of racism, classism, homophobia, and additional forms of oppression on women of color's experiences of sexual violence. Additionally, it may be advantageous to create new campaigns and prevention programs that address sexual violence initiatives that have historically excluded, or have not explicitly included, women of color. New programs must address sexism, racism, and other systems of domination that influence the lived realities of women students of color broadly and women of color and sexual violence survivors specifically. These programs could be grounded in academic curricula and consist of required courses that focus on sexism, racism, genderism, and classism in the lives of marginalized populations on the college campus. Additionally, women of color collectives should be started across college campuses as a liberatory (physical and mental) space in which women of color faculty, administrators, and students come together to empower and coalesce with one another. Campus outreach should be held at university orientation sessions, health fairs, student organization general body meetings, or events hosted by athletic departments and Greek life that serve women of color. It is also important to talk about intersectionality within communities of color, so that these communities, and the members within them, are provided with information about intersecting systems of domination as well as how these systems often work to stifle liberation and coalition building and influence oppressive experiences on campus. In essence, educators can provide new tools to communities of color, and women of color, to destabilize the "master's house."

Women of color sexual violence survivors may have a steadfast mistrust of campus agencies' or law enforcement's ability or willingness to positively support them if they choose to disclose their experience with sexual violence. As a result, mental health providers and student affairs professionals should be proactive in educating themselves on the realities of the intersections of multiple identities and on conducting outreach with student organizations that serve women of color across intersecting identities (i.e., sexual orientation and religion or spirituality). This knowledge should aim to ensure that campus health care providers, police officers, residential life employees, and other university personnel will respond in an affirming and positive way if a woman of color survivor reports an incident of sexual violence to campus staff (Orchowski, Meyer, & Gidycz, 2009).

When designing sexual violence campaigns, there are important ways to not only include but also centralize the experiences of women of color survivors. For example, images used in campaigns must not solely feature white women as victims and people of color as perpetrators (Olive, 2012). In addition, educators must ask at the beginning of campaigning and programming how tacit understandings of racist and sexist stereotypes inevitably influence their approach and the outcomes of campaigns and programs (Jenny, 2009). Once this question is asked, those same educators must plan how to destabilize, not work around, these stereotypes. The University of Michigan Sexual Assault Prevention and Awareness Center (2016) includes a statement that challenges the deleterious stereotypes and myths concerning women of color and sexual violence on its website:

> Myths and stereotypes result in a society that often denies or seeks to minimize the impact of sexual violence on women of color. In order to both prevent the sexual victimization of women of color and to better help women of color who are survivors, it is imperative that our society recognize that sexual violence affects not only White women, but women of all races, and that an act of sexual violence is never the victim's fault. In order to do this, we must challenge both the racist and sexist beliefs that we hold, and that we see in the society around us. (para. 5)

Just as this example from the University of Michigan Sexual Assault Prevention and Awareness Center proactively addresses myths, beliefs, concerns, and the experiences women of color may have with sexual violence, interventions with sexual violence must centralize the experiences of women of color. Health care and student affairs staff across campuses should have diverse practitioners in terms of race, ethnicity, and gender. All staff and practitioners should have strong multicultural and social justice training in the intersections of oppressions that women of color survivors of sexual violence may face when seeking services.

In addition, because of the complexities that women of color survivors face when seeking services for sexual violence, providers should be prepared to discuss new, more appropriate ideas concerning sexual violence reporting and services. For instance, because of the experiences women of color have with police in their home and campus communities, they may not want to interact with traditional systems of police and campus intervention (Tanis, 2015; Wheeler & George, 2005). Understanding the complexities in such cases, providers should be prepared to refer to culturally competent, power-conscious, community-based organizations. For example, although discounted and framed as inadequate by the professionalization of the field of sexual violence response by white women, restorative justice initiatives in people of color communities are important resources for addressing sexual violence. The Centre for Justice and Reconciliation (2016) defined *restorative justice* as the following:

> Restorative Justice is a theory of justice that emphasizes repairing the harm caused by criminal behavior. It is best accomplished through cooperative processes that allow all willing stakeholders to meet, although other approaches are available when that is impossible. This can lead to transformation of people, relationships, and communities. (para. 3)

Restorative justice initiatives seek to create an environment between a person who has been harmed and the person who has harmed that individual—cases that would typically move through the criminal justice system (Stubbs, 2010). Restorative justice initiatives used to address the wrongs committed against women of color sexual violence survivors include harm reduction through sexual crime prevention programming, sexual violence perpetrators being held accountable for their crimes and the harm inflicted on their survivors, and compensation granted by perpetrators to the survivors, while reintegrating both into their communities through collaborative efforts among all involved communities, the government, and university officials (Centre for Justice and Reconciliation, 2016). Sexual violence advocacy rooted in restorative justice demands that sexual violence perpetrators visibly own responsibility for their crimes committed against women of color survivors. This assertion could prove to be a corrective healing experience for communities of color, given our nation's history of enforcing white male privilege and power by minimizing, discrediting, or wholly ignoring incidents of sexual violence committed against women of color.

Although these alternatives to traditional campus sexual violence reporting may be rare in and around college contexts in the United States, there have been examples of restorative justice with sexual violence in other areas. Restorative justice interventions may involve the facilitation of dialogue between sexual violence survivors and their perpetrator, in which the perpetrator may be asked to issue a verbal or written apology to the survivor (Bletzer & Koss, 2012). Restorative justice also emphasizes the transformative power of surrounding the survivor with a validating social support system, including family, friends, and legal support who positively affirm the survivor and may join the survivor at any remediation dialogues that occur between the survivor and the perpetrator (Koss, Wilgus, & Williamsen, 2014). Restorative justice initiatives provide opportunities for healing among the survivor, the perpetrator, and their shared community at large, given this approach's emphasis on the rehabilitation of all parties involved in the sexual violence incident prior to their reintegration into their communities (Koss, Bachar, & Hopkins, 2003; Marsh & Wager, 2015).

Particularly with women of color survivors of sexual violence, restorative justice initiatives should be carefully considered as these initiatives may perpetuate systemic inequities for women of color. Restorative justice processes entail survivors and perpetrators sharing their stories of the sexual violence experience. However, the extent to which survivors are able to share their full story is not always effectively interrogated in the process and may be further complicated by histories of racism and colonization (Stubbs, 2010). For example, in working with a Japanese American sexual violence survivor, it is crucial to remember how the U.S. government oppressed Japanese Americans by treating them as enemies of the United States during World War II, resulting in the forced internment of 120,000 Japanese Americans in American concentration camps (Hastings, 2011). It is also important to consider how gendered and racialized stereotypes that depict Asian American women as exotic and hypersexual (Koo et al., 2015) may affect this Japanese woman student's experience of sexual violence. University and community partners that may integrate restorative justice practices in their work with Japanese American and other women of color survivors must challenge the historical status quo of silence and oppression imposed on individuals of this shared heritage by ensuring the survivor was provided with a safe, nonjudgmental, and egalitarian space for her to voice her story.

In this chapter, we describe how women of color survivors may navigate their experiences of sexual violence within systems of domination and access campus services for support and healing. Understanding that women of color survivors experience the multiplicative stressors of racism and sexism, among other oppressions, is a starting point for designing culturally responsive services for this group. In addition, staff and practitioners must have a comprehensive approach to designing services for women of color survivors of sexual violence that seeks not only to understand their experiences but also to empower women of color survivors to take the next steps in coping with and healing from their experiences with sexual violence.

References

Abbey, A. D., & Jacques-Tiura, A. J. (2010). Sexual assault among diverse populations of women: Common ground, distinctive features, and unanswered questions. In H. Landrine & N. F. Russo (Eds.), *Handbook of diversity in feminist psychology* (pp. 391–425). New York, NY: Springer.

Acosta, K. (2010). How could you do this to me? How lesbian, bisexual, and queer Latinas negotiate sexual identity with their families. *Black Women, Gender, and Families, 4*(1), 63–85.

Ahrens, C., & Aldana, E. (2012). The ties that bind: Understanding the impact of sexual assault disclosure on survivors' relationships with friends, family, and partners. *Journal of Trauma and Dissociation, 13,* 226–243. doi:10.1080/152997 32.2012.642738

Amnesty International USA. (2007). *Maze of injustice: The failure to protect Indigenous women from sexual violence in the USA.* New York, NY: Amnesty International Publications.

Amstadter, A., McCauley, J., Ruggiero, K., Resnick, H., & Kilpatrick, D. (2008). Service utilization and help seeking in a national sample of female rape victims. *Psychiatric Services, 59,* 1450–1457. doi:10.1176/appi.ps.59.12.1450

Aranda, F., Matthews, A., Hughes, T., Muramatsu, N., Wilsnack, S., Johnson, T., & Riley, B. (2015). Coming out in color: Racial/ethnic differences in the relationship between level of sexual identity disclosure and depression among lesbians. *Cultural Diversity and Ethnic Minority Psychology, 21,* 247–257. doi:10.1037/a0037644

Badejo, A. (2016). *What happens when women at historically Black colleges report their assaults?* Retrieved from www.buzzfeed.com/anitabadejo/where-is-that-narrative?utm_term=.lwXw5lVq6#.dwWLeA07q

Balsam, K., Molina, Y., Blayney, J., Dillworth, T., Zimmerman, L., & Kaysen, D. (2015). Racial/ethnic differences in identity and mental health outcomes among young sexual minority women. *Cultural Diversity and Ethnic Minority Psychology, 21,* 380–390. doi:10.1037/a0038680

Bell, E. (2004). Myths, stereotypes, and realities of Black women. *Journal of Applied Behavioral Science, 40,* 146–159. doi:10.1177/0021886304263852

Blain, L., Gavolski, T., & Peterson, Z. (2011). Female sexual self-schema after interpersonal trauma: Relationship to psychiatric and cognitive functioning in a clinical treatment-seeking sample. *Journal of Traumatic Stress, 24,* 222–225. doi:10.1002/jts.20616

Bletzer, K. V., & Koss, M. P. (2012). From parallel to intersecting narratives in cases of sexual assault. *Qualitative Health Research, 22,* 291–303. doi:10.1177/1090820X11430948

Breiding, M. J., Smith, S. G., Basile, K. C., Walters, M. L., Chen, J., & Merrick, M. T. (2011). *Prevalence and characteristics of sexual violence, stalking, and intimate partner violence victimization—National Intimate Partner Violence Survey, United States, 2011.* Retrieved from www.cdc.gov/mmwr/preview/mmwrhtml/ss6308a1.htm

Briere, J., Hodges, M., & Godbout, N. (2010). Traumatic stress, affect dysregulation, and dysfunctional avoidance: A structural equation model. *Journal of Traumatic Stress, 23,* 767–774. doi:10.1002/jts.20578

Brown, L. (2008). *Cultural competence in trauma therapy: Beyond the flashback.* Washington, DC: American Psychological Association.

Bryant-Davis, T., Chung, H., Tillman, S., & Belcourt, A. (2009). From the margins to the center: Ethnic minority women and the mental health effects of sexual assault. *Trauma, Violence, & Abuse, 10,* 330–357.

Burn, S. (2009). A situational model of sexual assault prevention through bystander prevention. *Sex Roles, 60,* 779–792. doi:10.1007/s11199-008-9581-5

Castillo, L., & Cano, M. (2007). Mexican American psychology: Theory and clinical application. In C. Negy (Ed.), *Cross-cultural psychotherapy: Toward a critical understanding of diverse client populations* (2nd ed., pp. 85–102). Reno, NV: Bent Tree Press.

Castillo, L., Perez, F., Castillo, R., & Ghosheh, M. (2010). Construction and initial validation of the Marianismo Beliefs Scale. *Counseling Psychology Quarterly, 23,* 163–175. doi:10.1080/ 09515071003776036

Centre for Justice and Reconciliation. (2016). *Lesson 1: What is restorative justice?* Retrieved from http://restorativejustice.org/restorative-justice/about-restorative-justice/tutorial-intro-to-restorative-justice/lesson-1-what-is-restorative-justice/

Collins, P. H. (2005). *Black sexual politics: African Americans, gender, and the new racism.* New York: NY. Routledge.

Collins, P. H. (2009). *Black feminist thought: Knowledge, consciousness, and the politics of empowerment* (3rd ed.). New York, NY: Routledge.

Dalton, D. (2015, October 15). The 22 trans women murdered in 2015. *Daily Dot.* Retrieved from www.dailydot.com/politics/trans-women-of-color-murdered

Das, A., Olfson, M., McCurtis, H., & Weissman, M. (2006). Depression in African Americans: Breaking barriers to detection and treatment. *Journal of Family Practice, 55,* 30–39.

Denson, N., & Chang, M. (2009). Racial diversity matters: The impact of diversity-related student engagement and institutional context. *American Educational Research Journal, 46,* 322–353. doi:10.3102/0002831208323278

Edwards, K., Probst, D., Tansill, E., Dixon, K., Bennett, S., & Gidycz, C. (2014). In their own words: A content-analytic study of college women's resistance to sexual assault. *Journal of Interpersonal Violence, 29,* 2527–2547. doi:10.1177/0886260513520470

Fahs, B. (2011). Sexual violence, disidentification, and long-term trauma recovery: A process-oriented case study analysis. *Journal of Aggression, Maltreatment, and Trauma, 20,* 556–578. doi:10.1080/10926771.2011.586400

Freedman, E. (2007). Patriarchy revisited: Gender, race, and sexual violence. *Journal of Women's History, 19*(4), 154–162. doi:10.1353/jowh.2007.0071

Friedman, C., & Leaper, C. (2010). Sexual-minority college women's experiences with discrimination: Relations with identity and collective action. *Psychology of Women Quarterly, 34,* 152–164. doi:10.1111/j.1471-6402.2010.01558.x

George, W., & Martínez, L. (2002). Victim blaming in rape: Effects of victim and perpetrator race, type of rape, and participant racism. *Psychology of Women Quarterly, 26,* 110–119. doi:10.1111/1471-6402.00049

Gerber, G., & Cherneski, L. (2006). Sexual aggression toward women. *Annals of the New York Academy of Sciences, 1087,* 35–46. doi:10.1196/annals.1385.007

Griffin, R. (2013). Gender violence and the Black female body: The enduring significance of "crazy" Mike Tyson. *Howard Journal of Communications, 24,* 71–94. doi:10.1080/10646175.2013.748602

Hastings, E. (2011). "No longer a silent victim of history": Repurposing the documents of Japanese American interment. *Archival Science, 11*, 25–46. doi:10.1007/s10502-010-9113-2

Herman, J. (1997). *Trauma and recovery: The aftermath of violence—from domestic violence to political terror.* New York, NY: Basic Books.

Higginbotham, E. (1993). *Righteous discontent: The women's movement in the Black Baptist church, 1880–1920.* Cambridge, MA: Harvard University Press.

hooks, b. (1981). *Ain't I a woman? Black women and feminism.* Boston, MA: South End Press.

INCITE! (2014). *Analysis: INCITE!'s dangerous intersections.* Retrieved from http://incite-national.org/page/analysis

Izadi, E. (2015, November 9). The incidents that led to the University of Missouri president's resignation. *Washington Post.* Retrieved from www.washingtonpost.com/news/grade-point/wp/2015/11/09/the-incidents-that-led-to-the-university-of-missouri-presidents-resignation/enny

Jenny, X. (2009). *Race and rape: Keeping racism out of your campaign.* Retrieved from www.safercampus.org/blog/2009/10/race-and-rape-keeping-racism-out-of-your-campaign/

Keller, G. D. (1994). *Hispanics and United States film: An overview and handbook.* Tempe, AZ: Bilingual Review/Press.

Koo, K., Nguyen, H., George, W., & Andrasik, M. (2015). The cultural context of nondisclosure of alcohol-involved acquaintance rape among Asian American college women: A qualitative study. *Journal of Sex Research, 52*, 55–68. doi:10.1080/00224499.2013.826168

Koss, M., Bachar, K., & Hopkins, C. (2003). Restorative justice for sexual violence: Repairing victims, building community, and holding offenders accountable. *Annals of the New York Academy of Sciences, 989*, 384–396.

Koss, M., Wilgus, J., & Williamsen, K. (2014). Campus sexual misconduct: Restorative justice approaches to enhance compliance to Title IX guidance. *Trauma, Violence, & Abuse, 15*, 242–257. doi:10.1177/1524838014521500

Krebs, C. P., Lindquist, C. H., & Barrick, K. (2010). *The Historically Black College and University Campus Sexual Assault (HBCU-CSA) Study.* Retrieved from www.ncjrs.gov/pdffiles1/nij/grants/233614.pdf

Lee, R., Caruso, M., Goins, S., & Southerland, J. (2003). Addressing sexual assault on college campuses: Guidelines for a prevention/awareness week. *Journal of College Counseling, 6*(1), 14–23. doi:10.1002/j.2161-1882.2003.tb00223.x

Lindquist, C. H., Crosby, C. M., Barrick, K., Krebs, C. P., & Settles-Reaves, B. (2016). Disclosure of sexual assault experience among undergraduate women at Historically Black Colleges and Universities. *Journal of American College Health.* Advance online publication. doi:10.1080/07448481.2016.1181635

Littleton, H., & Breitkopf, C. (2006). Coping with the experience of rape. *Psychology of Women Quarterly, 30*, 106–116. doi:10.1111/j.1471-6402.2006.00267.x

Lui, P. (2015). Intergenerational cultural conflict, mental health, and educational outcomes Among Asian and Latino/a Americans: Qualitative and meta-analytic review. *Psychological Bulletin, 141*, 404–446. Retrieved from http://dx.doi.org/10.1037/a0038449

Marsh, F., & Wager, N. (2015). Restorative justice in cases of sexual violence. *Probation Journal, 62*, 336–356. doi:10.1177/0264550515619571

Martinez, M., & Mullen, J. (2015). *Victims describe assaults by convicted ex-Oklahoma City cop Daniel Holtzclaw*. Retrieved from www.cnn.com/2015/12/11/us/oklahoma-daniel-holtzclaw-verdict/index.html

Masten, A. S. (2001). Ordinary magic: Resilience processes in development. *American Psychologist, 56*(3), 227–238.

Merskin, D. (2007). Three faces of Eva: Perpetuation of the hot-Latina stereotype in *Desperate Housewives*. *Howard Journal of Communications, 18*, 133–151. doi:10.1080/10646170701309890

Miller, A., Canales, E., Amacker, A., Backstrom, T., & Gidycz, C. (2011). Stigma-threat motivated nondisclosure of sexual assault and sexual revictimization: A prospective analysis. *Psychology of Women Quarterly, 35*, 119–128. doi:10.1177/0361684310384104

Moor, A. (2010). She dresses to attract, he perceives seduction: A gender gap in attribution of intent to women's revealing style of dress and its relation to blaming the victims of sexual violence. *Journal of International Women's Studies, 11*(4), 115–127.

Nakashima, C. (1992). An invisible monster: The creation and denial of mixed-race people in America. In M. P. P. Root (Ed.), *Racially mixed people in America* (pp. 162–180). Newbury Park, CA: SAGE.

Neville, H., Heppner, M., Oh, E., Spanierman, L., & Clark, M. (2004). General and culturally specific factors influencing Black and White rape survivors' self-esteem. *Psychology of Women Quarterly, 28*, 83–94. doi:10.1111/j.1471-6402.2004.00125.x

Olive, V. C. (2012). Sexual assault against women of color. *Journal of Student Research, 1*, 1–9.

Orchowski, L., Meyer, D., & Gidycz, C. (2009). College women's likelihood to report unwanted sexual experiences to campus agencies: Trends and correlates. *Journal of Aggression, Maltreatment, and Trauma, 18*, 839–858. doi:10.1080/10926770903291779

Owens, J. (2012). Historic in a bad way: How the Tribal Law and Order Act continues the American tradition of providing inadequate protection to American Indian and Alaska Native rape victims. *Journal of Criminal Law and Criminology, 102*, 497–524.

Perales, C. (2014, February 12). *The misrepresented and hypersexualized Latina*. Retrieved from http://thestripesblog.com/2014/02/12/the-misrepresented-and-hypersexualized-latina/

Rothblum, E. (2014). Mars to Venus or Earth to Earth? How do families of origin fit into GLBTQ lives? *Journal of GLBT Family Studies, 10*, 231–241. doi:10.1080/1550428X.2014.857235

Sable, M., Danis, F., Mauzy, D., & Gallagher, S. (2006). Barriers to reporting sexual assault for women and men: Perspectives of college students. *Journal of American College Health, 55*, 157–162. doi:10.3200/JACH.55.3.157-162

Singh, A. A. (2012). Transgender youth of color and resilience: Negotiating oppression, finding support. *Sex Roles, 68*, 1–13. doi:10.1007/s11199-012-0149-z

Singh, A. A., Garnett, A., & Williams, D. (2012). Resilience strategies of African American women survivors of child sexual abuse: A qualitative inquiry. *Counseling Psychologist, 41*, 1093–1124. doi:10.1177/0011000012469413

Singh, A. A., Hays, D., Chung, B., & Watson, L. (2010). South Asian immigrant women who have survived child sexual abuse: Resilience and healing. *Violence Against Women, 16*, 444–458. doi:10.1177/1077801210363976

Smith, A. (2005). *Conquest: Sexual violence and American Indian genocide.* Cambridge, MA: South End Press.

Starzynski, L., Ullman, S., Filipas, H., & Townsend, S. (2005). Correlates of women's sexual assault disclosure to informal and formal support sources. *Violence and Victims, 20*, 417–432. http://dx.doi.org/10.1891/0886-6708.20.4.417

Stewart, A. (2014). The Men's Project: A sexual assault prevention program targeting college men. *Psychology of Men and Masculinity, 15*, 481–485. Retrieved from http://dx.doi.org/10.1037/a0033947

Stubbs, J. (2010). Restorative justice, gendered violence, and indigenous women. In J. Ptacket (Ed.), *Restorative justice and violence against women* (pp. 103–122). New York, NY: Oxford University Press.

Suite, D., La Bril, R., Primm, A., & Harrison-Ross, P. (2007). Beyond misdiagnosis, misunderstanding and mistrust: Relevance of the historical perspective in the medical and mental health treatment of people of color. *Journal of the National Medical Association, 99*, 879–885.

Tanis, F. (2015, August 4). Blood on the leaves: Black women and the new lynching [Web log post]. Retrieved from www.forharriet.com/2015/08/blood-on-leaves-black-women-and-new.html

Tjaden, P., & Thoennes, N. (2000). *Findings from the National Violence Against Women Survey.* Washington, DC: U.S. Department of Justice and Centers for Disease Control and Prevention.

Tolin, D., & Foa, E. (2008). Sex differences in trauma and posttraumatic stress disorder: A quantitative review of 25 years of research. *Psychological Trauma: Theory, Research, Practice, and Policy, S*(1), 37–85. doi:10.1037/1942-9681.S.1.37

Ullman, S., Peter-Hagene, L., & Relyea, M. (2014). Coping, emotion regulation, and self-blame as mediators of sexual abuse and psychological symptoms in adult sexual assault. *Journal of Child Sexual Abuse, 23*, 74–93. doi:10.1080/10538712.2014.864747

University of Michigan Sexual Assault Prevention and Awareness Center. (2016). *Sexual assault and women of color.* Retrieved from http://sapac.umich.edu/article/57

Untied, A., Orchowski, L., Mastroleo, N., & Gidycz, C. (2012). College students' social reactions to the victim in a hypothetical sexual assault scenario: The role of victim and perpetrator. *Violence and Victims, 27*, 957–972.

West, C. M. (1995). Mammy, Sapphire, and Jezebel: Historical images of Black women and their implications for psychotherapy. *Psychotherapy, 32*, 458–466.

Whatley, M. A. (2005). The effect of participant sex, victim dress, and traditional attitudes on causal judgments for marital rape and victims. *Journal of Family Violence, 20*, 191–200. doi:10.1007/s10896-005-3655-8

Wheeler, J. G., & George, W. H. (2005). Rape and race: An overview. In K. H. Barrett & W. H. George (Eds.), *Race, culture, psychology, and law* (pp. 391–402). Thousand Oaks, CA: SAGE.

White, E. F. (2001). *Dark continent of our bodies: Black feminism & politics of respectability*. Philadelphia, PA: Temple University Press.

White, M., & Epston, D. (1990). *Narrative means to therapeutic ends*. New York, NY: Norton.

Yamawaki, N. (2007). Rape perception and the function of ambivalent sexism and gender-role traditionality. *Journal of Interpersonal Violence, 22*, 406–423. doi: 10.1177/0886260506297210

Zimmerman, L., Darnell, D., Rhew, I., Lee, C., & Kaysen, D. (2015). Resilience in community: A social ecological development model for young adult sexual minority women. *American Journal of Community Psychology, 55*, 179–190. doi:10.1007/s10464-015-9702-6

Zinzow, H., & Thompson, M. (2011). Barriers to reporting sexual victimization: Prevalence and correlates among undergraduate women. *Journal of Aggression, Maltreatment, and Trauma, 20*, 711–725.

7

SEXUAL VICTIMIZATION OF DEAF AND HARD-OF-HEARING COLLEGE STUDENTS

LaVerne McQuiller Williams

Sexual violence is a common occurrence on college campuses and universities. Studies find that between 27% and 40% of college women (Banyard et al., 2007; Fisher, Cullen, & Turner, 2000; Hines, 2007; Hines & Saudino, 2003) and 7% to 8% of college men (Banyard et al., 2007; Hines, 2007; Hines & Saudino, 2003) reported some form of sexual violence victimization over the course of an academic year. Another reality is the growing number of students with disabilities enrolling in college. Between 1999 and 2003, there was about a 69% increase in the number of undergraduate students with disabilities enrolled at degree-granting institutions (1,508,000 in 1999 to 2,156,000 in 2003; Hamblet, 2009). According to the latest data, 11.1% of undergraduate college students report having a disability (National Center for Education Statistics, 2015).

Despite the increasing numbers of college students with disabilities and the prevalence of sexual violence on campus, the experiences of sexual violence in this population have largely been ignored. In most cases, this neglect has prevented the adoption of adequate policies and services for sexual violence that support this student group on college campuses. Moreover, this neglect is compounded by the societal devaluation of those with disabilities in general and the stereotypes that people with disabilities are asexual and dependent (Curry et al., 2009).

A limited body of research has examined sexual violence among college populations with disabilities. In this chapter, I review this extant literature on college students' experiences with sexual violence, centered on Deaf and hard-of-hearing college students in the hopes of a better understanding of sexual violence among this population and how best to respond. To accomplish this, I provide an overview of sexual violence among people with disabilities and information on sexual violence in the Deaf community. Next, I examine the literature on sexual violence among Deaf and hard-of-hearing college students, including the intersectionality of sexual orientation and auditory status. The chapter concludes with recommendations and directions for future research.

Sexual Violence Among People With Disabilities

People with disabilities are at an elevated risk for sexual violence (Haydon, McRee, & Halpern, 2011; Powers et al., 2002; Powers et al., 2009). Furthermore, research suggests that compared to people without disabilities, people with disabilities report longer durations of abuse (Nosek, Howland, & Young, 1997). Women with disabilities experience sexual violence at similar or increased rates compared to the general population (Brownlie, Jabbar, Beitchman, Vida, & Atkinson, 2007; Martin et al., 2006; Mitra, Lu, & Manning, 2012; Mitra, Mouradian, & Diamond, 2011; Obinna, Krueger, Osterbaan, Sadusky, & DeVore, 2006; Powers et al., 2009; Sullivan, Vernon, & Scanlan, 1987). In a comparison of women with and without disabilities, women with disabilities were four times more likely to experience sexual violence than women without disabilities (Casteel, Martin, Smith, Gurka, & Kupper, 2008; Martin et al., 2006). The few studies that have examined sexual violence among men with disabilities have found that men with disabilities are more likely to experience sexual violence than men without disabilities (Haydon et al., 2011; Mitra et al., 2011; Mitra & Mouradian, 2014).

Risk factors that contribute to abuse against people with disabilities have also been identified. For example, Andrews and Veronen (1993) cited the following reasons for increased vulnerability to victimization among people with disabilities: increased dependency on others for long-term care, denial of human rights that results in perceptions of powerlessness, less risk of discovery as perceived by the perpetrator, difficulty in being believed, less education about appropriate and inappropriate sexuality, social isolation and increased risk of manipulation, physical helplessness and vulnerability in public places, and "values and attitudes within the field of disabilities toward mainstreaming and integration without consideration for each individual's capacity for self-protection" (p. 148). Additionally, isolation, cultural barriers, and the lack of identification of the abuse contribute to high rates of abuse for people with disabilities (Plummer & Findley, 2012).

Sexual Violence in the Deaf Community

Statistics from the National Institutes of Health estimate that about 15% of American adults have hearing loss (National Institute on Deafness and Other Communication Disorders, 2014). In the United States, Deaf people do not see themselves as having a disability but rather have a culture and way of communication that is denied or not recognized by the dominate hearing culture (Holcomb, 2012; Sadusky & Obinna, 2002). The capital *D* is used to acknowledge the unique cultural identity of Deaf individuals (Anderson, Leigh, & Samar, 2011) and "signifies that a person is attached to a community, which uses ASL [American Sign Language] and Deaf culture as part of their everyday lives" (Chin et al., 2013, p. 1). Similar to other cultures, Deaf culture is characterized by learned behaviors of a group that has its own language, norms, values, and traditions (Nomeland & Nomeland, 2012).

Deaf individuals, particularly children, are more likely to experience sexual violence than the general population (Anderson & Leigh, 2011; Sullivan et al., 1987; Westcott & Jones, 1999). Fifty percent of Deaf individuals have experienced sexual violence in their lifetime, compared to 25% of hearing females and 10% of hearing males (Sullivan et al., 1987). Additionally, children who are Deaf or hard of hearing are at an increased risk of sexual violence when compared to hearing children (Burnash, Rothman-Marshall, & Schenkel, 2010). Deaf females experience sexual violence at higher rates than Deaf males (Sullivan et al., 1987; Westcott & Jones, 1999).

Similar to Deaf children, recent research suggests that Deaf adults are more likely to experience sexual violence than hearing adults. For example, Johnston-McCabe, Levi-Minzi, Van Hassely, and Vanderbeek (2011) using a sample of 46 Deaf and hard-of-hearing women concluded that women who were Deaf and hard of hearing were at a greater risk of psychological, physical, and sexual abuse than hearing women. In a later study examining intimate partner violence (IPV) among Deaf adults, Pollard, Sutter, and Cerulli (2014) found that forced sex and emotional abuse were more prevalent among Deaf adults than in the general population and that differences between men and women in abuse experiences among Deaf adults were smaller than those found in IPV studies in the general population.

Sexual Violence Among College Students With Disabilities

To date, few studies have examined sexual violence against college (or college-age) students with disabilities. Comparing sexual violence rates of Canadian college students with the general population, DuMont and colleagues (2012) found that students were almost 60% less likely than nonstudent victims to report a disability (i.e., cognitive, physical, or sensory). In a cross-sectional study of 101 students with disabilities from a large northeastern university, 5% of the sample reported experiencing sexual violence within the past year, whereas 27% reported experiencing sexual violence before age 17 (Findley, Plummer, & McMahon, 2015). Using a national probability sample of almost 27,000 college students that included males and females, Scherer, Snyder, and Fisher (2013) reported that students with disabilities (physical, mental, or learning) were almost twice as likely to experience intimate partner victimization (physical, psychological, and/or sexual abuse) than students without disabilities. Specifically, the researchers found that 3.3% of participants with disabilities reported experiencing sexual abuse within the past year, compared to 1.2% of students without disabilities.

Sexual Violence Among Deaf and Hard-of-Hearing College Students

Collectively, the few studies examining sexual violence among college students with disabilities reveal that students with disabilities are at a higher risk for sexual violence compared to students without disabilities (DuMont et al., 2012; Findley et al., 2015; Scherer et al., 2013). Although these studies are informative, they are limited in that specific disabilities are not discerned. It is crucial for each type of disability to be examined separately because the risk factors for sexual violence associated with specific disabilities (e.g., deafness, physical mobility) as well as the barriers to access services may be quite different depending on the specific type of disability.

Similar to the general population, there is great heterogeneity in the experiences of sexual violence for rape survivors. However, one unique characteristic of violence in the Deaf community is communication abuse, which can prevent victims from being able to seek help and compounds their isolation. Communication abuse includes controlling the victim's communications with others or damaging or destroying communication devices to prevent a Deaf "victim from 'having a voice' and communicating with others" (Mastrocinque et al., 2015, p. 17). Examples of communication abuse may include damaging hearing aids, refusing to communicate or relay conversations to the victim, tracking the victim's messages, or tying the victim's hands to prevent the victim from signing (Mastrocinque et al., 2015; Packota, 2000). Communication abuse can also manifest itself as a result of the hearing status of the perpetrator. In this regard, a power imbalance can occur in hearing-Deaf relationships when value is placed on English over ASL as a preferred communication method, or when the victim does not have equal access to the majority language (Anderson & Kobek Pezzarossi, 2014). Accordingly, if the perpetrator is hearing, he or she can exert control over communications with others, including the police, family, and friends, with or without the victim's knowledge (Mastrocinque et al., 2015).

Understanding sexual violence against Deaf and hard-of-hearing individuals also requires consideration of the social context of disability. One theoretical framework that can contribute to this understanding is disability theory. Disability perspectives have been shown to be influential in the context of disability as a framework "for resisting the conventional assumption that disabilities are inherent impairments subject to scientific diagnoses" (Benedet & Grant, 2014, p. 134). Moreover, understanding the social construction of disability in relation to sexual violence rightly avoids locating the particular vulnerability of people with disabilities to sexual violence in something inherent in the victims themselves (Benedet & Grant, 2014.). As Ballan and Freyer (2012) have noted, this equates to saying that people with disabilities are vulnerable to sexual violence because they are vulnerable. Shifting the focus from individuals with disabilities and their vulnerability for violence to the larger context, the social disability framework seeks to address the barriers and discriminatory attitudes that may have an impact on seeking help.

Through the lens of the disability framework, Deaf survivors of sexual violence experience unique issues that may serve as barriers to seeking help including issues of stereotypes, language, and confidentiality (Anderson & Kobek Pezzarossi, 2014). When Deaf individuals report sexual violence, they face stereotypes about not only being a victim of sexual violence but also being Deaf (Obinna et al., 2006). A model of these stereotypes or "seven myth conceptions" was proposed by Job (2004) for examining the sexuality of Deaf individuals:

1. Deaf individuals are eternal children and asexual.
2. Deaf individuals need to live in environments that restrict and inhibit their sexuality, to protect themselves and others.
3. Deaf individuals should not be provided with sex education, as it will only encourage inappropriate behavior.
4. Deaf individuals should be sterilized because they will give birth to children who are also disabled.

5. Deaf individuals are sexually different from other people and are more likely to develop diverse, unusual, or deviant sexual behavior.
6. Deaf individuals are oversexed, promiscuous, sexually indiscriminate, and dangerous, and you have to watch your children around them.
7. Deaf individuals cannot benefit from sexual counseling or treatment.

These stereotypes and misperceptions of Deaf and hard-of-hearing individuals are still prevalent (Joharchi & Clark, 2014) and may have implications for survivors of sexual violence. For example, service providers often do not pay attention to sexual trauma experiences and sexual histories of individuals with disabilities because of the misperception that individuals with disabilities are often not referred to in a sexual manner (Anderson, 2014).

Additionally, survivors often have feelings of guilt and embarrassment because of the social stigma attached to sexual violence, these feelings can be compounded in the Deaf community because of its small, close-knit nature. Because the Deaf community places high value on group unity and face saving, Deaf victims are often reluctant to report because of concerns that revealing sexual violence particularly in the Deaf community would "disclose that such problems existed within the community" (Lightfoot & Williams, 2009, p. 142). The close-knit nature of the Deaf community may also affect the Deaf victim's willingness to report in that it may compromise anonymity and erode privacy. The problems of confidentiality are compounded by the fact that anonymity is almost nonexistent in the Deaf community because of its size and structure (Obinna et al., 2006); therefore, revealing experiences of sexual violence is a serious concern for many Deaf individuals who fear that their identity will not remain hidden from the community (Mastrocinque et al., 2015). Describing how the insular nature of the Deaf community can have an impact on survivors, Barber, Wills, and Smith (2010) stated,

> The community tends to be very tight knit and small enough that Deaf people not only know local community members, but also Deaf people throughout the United States. This often results in the inability of victims to maintain privacy; many members of the community may know about the rape and make judgments about the survivors and why the rape occurred. Escape to other communities will not solve this problem because it is likely that Deaf people elsewhere have heard about the rape and/or know the rapist. (pp. 326–327)

As with other linguistic minorities, the Deaf community experiences significant barriers in communicating with the hearing population (Anderson

& Kobek Pezzarossi, 2014; Parasnis, 1998), which may have an impact on access to resources. Deaf and hard-of-hearing victims' access to services is severely limited because most services in hearing agencies are unavailable to them (Sadusky & Obinna, 2002). Even if services are available, Deaf victims are likely to encounter many barriers from providers who are not prepared to address a Deaf person's communication and sociocultural needs (Mastrocinque et al., 2015). Mistrust of service providers and the use of interpreters make Deaf individuals reluctant to seek assistance for abuse (Anderson, 2014). Deaf individuals are sometimes reluctant to trust interpreters when discussing their experiences because of confidentiality issues in the small Deaf community (Obinna et al., 2006; Sadusky & Obinna, 2002), concerns about the interpreters' ability to accurately convey their sexual violence experience (Sadusky & Obinna, 2002), and afraid about interpreters who belong to the same social circles as the victim or perpetrator (Barber et al., 2010).

Additionally, many Deaf victims of sexual violence perceive a lack of support within the Deaf community, particularly if the perpetrator is also Deaf. Noting the difficulties faced by Deaf victims of sexual violence, Sheridan (1999) said, "When Deaf women are physically or sexually assaulted by Deaf men, the cohesiveness of the Deaf community contributes to a fear of ostracism that often prevents Deaf women from reporting the assault and obtaining needed support" (p. 384). Accordingly, Deaf victims will often try to protect the cultural identity, including denying instances of sexual violence, especially if the abuser is Deaf (Obinna et al., 2006). Mastrocinque and colleagues (2015) conducted interviews with Deaf women about their experiences with sexual violence and partner violence. Results showed that many Deaf survivors of sexual violence and abuse never reported their experiences because they were concerned about rumors being spread about them in the community or afraid that the Deaf community would not believe them because of the Deaf perpetrator's popularity.

Although few studies have examined sexual violence among college (or college-age) students with disabilities, the majority of studies in this area have focused on Deaf and hard-of-hearing college students' experiences with sexual violence. In an earlier study, about one fourth of Deaf or hard-of-hearing college students reported having been forced to have sex against their wishes on at least one occasion (Joseph, Sawyer, & Desmond, 1995). This study, however, did not place age limits on these occurrences, so it is unknown whether these experiences took place during years in college. Later studies support these earlier findings and suggest that Deaf and hard-of-hearing college students experience sexual violence at a significantly higher rate than their hearing peers (Anderson, 2010; Anderson & Leigh, 2011; Barrow, 2008; Porter & McQuiller Williams 2011a, 2011b).

Even more limited in number than studies examining sexual violence among Deaf and hard-of-hearing college students is the examination of sexual violence among Deaf and hard-of-hearing college students who are gay, lesbian, or bisexual (GLB). Only one study to date has examined the relationship between auditory status and sexual orientation and experiences of interpersonal violence (i.e., sexual, physical, and emotional abuse; Porter & McQuiller Williams, 2013). Through the lens of social structural theory, the authors hypothesized that students who occupy the dual status of GLB and Deaf or hard of hearing would have a greater risk of IPV while at college than students who are heterosexual and hearing.

According to social structural theory, individuals and groups that differ from the majority in attributes and characteristics are more likely to suffer. Individuals with sexual orientations that are different from the mainstream and who are Deaf or hard of hearing will be less likely to have access to resources. These populations experience unique issues that may limit or prevent access to seeking help, including discrimination and fear of being outed for those who are GLB (Freedberg, 2006), and discrimination, language, lack of communication to access service providers, communication, and lack of confidentiality in the Deaf community for those who are Deaf or hard of hearing (Barber et al., 2010). This theory looks at various interactions between groups that have unequal resources. Those groups underrepresented in the population, such as Deaf and hard of hearing and GLB, typically have barriers to resources such as education, services, and employment, among others. Socially stigmatized groups may "lack culturally-relevant services and resources which may contribute to isolation and silence about abuse" (Johnston-McCabe et al., 2011, p. 63).

Johnston-McCabe and colleagues (2011) found that students who were Deaf or hard of hearing had close to twice the risk of sexual abuse and a little more than two and a half times the risk of physical abuse and psychological abuse than students who were hearing. Students whose sexual orientation was GLB had a much higher risk for all three categories of IPV, more than six times as likely for sexual abuse, about four times the risk for physical abuse, and about three times as likely for psychological abuse when compared with heterosexual students. It is important to note that the combination of sexual orientation and auditory status was statistically significant for all three measures of IPV, which supports social structural theory. Students who were GLB and Deaf or hard of hearing were more likely to experience sexual abuse, psychological abuse, and physical abuse than the mainstream majority groups (Porter & McQuiller Williams, 2013).

These findings illustrate the need for administrators and health professionals working with college populations to understand how the nature of abuse and barriers for seeking help are unique among different populations. Students who are Deaf or hard of hearing, for example, may be exposed to "disability-specific forms of violence" by partners, such as destruction of communication devices (Powers et al., 2009, p. 1041), isolation manifested by checking or reviewing the information on the victim's communication devices, "insulting the victim by calling [her or him] 'hearing' or making fun of [her or his] ASL [American Sign Language] skills" (Anderson et al., 2011, p. 204), or tying the victim's hands to prevent the victim from signing (Packota, 2000). These coercive tactics are used to further isolate and control Deaf victims and may make them less likely to seek help psychologically and physically through the use of communication devices. Similarly, GLB students may be exposed to unique forms of abuse such as the threat of out-ing a partner (i.e., revealing sexual orientation) to others (Carvalho, Lewis, Derlega, Winstead, & Viggiano, 2011). Victims or survivors of IPV who are Deaf or hard of hearing and occupy minority sexual status experience unique stresses and therefore may be more reluctant to seek assistance from health care professionals or the legal system, fearing limited access to resources or audism (i.e., discrimination toward Deaf people) and homophobia.

Recommendations

Given that Deaf or hard-of-hearing college students are at a heightened risk of experiencing sexual violence than students without disabilities (Anderson, 2010; Anderson & Leigh, 2011; Barrow, 2008; Porter & McQuiller Wil-liams, 2013), educators and health care providers need to place greater attention on ways to prevent and reduce the incidence of abuse among this population. Moreover, these studies illustrate the importance for college health professionals and others dealing with college populations to avoid a one-size-fits-all approach to addressing sexual abuse. When developing pro-grams and services, practitioners and college health professionals must strive for inclusivity as well as develop targeted approaches for outreach to popula-tions on their campuses that may be at greater risk for sexual violence.

An important first step to prevention is raising awareness of sexual violence among Deaf and hard-of-hearing college students through col-laboration efforts between departments that provide victims with services and programs that serve those with disabilities. These collective efforts may encourage the development of specific and targeted education, awareness, prevention, and intervention strategies. For example, White, McQuiller Wil-liams, and Cho (2003) described research measuring the effectiveness of a social norms intervention to reduce coercive sexual behaviors among Deaf and hard-of-hearing college students. Specifically, the college social norms campaign, developed in collaboration with the victims' center and disability center, was designed for Deaf and hard-of-hearing students and corrected misperceptions of consent behaviors with a subsequent reduction in sexual violence (White et al., 2003). The campaign was developed after an unsuccessful social norms marketing campaign to prevent sexual violence targeting all students (including those who were Deaf and hard of hearing). The redesigned campaign addressed the needs, culture, and communication styles of Deaf and hard-of-hearing students, including marketing and delivery of all messages in ASL. This study illustrates that strategies to reduce or prevent sexual violence must take into account specific audiences, particularly when an audience is an underrepresented group, in the development and implementation of interventions.

The provision of sensitive and population-appropriate information is very important in gaining maximum participation when implementing programs (Heppner, Neville, Smith, Kivlighan, & Gershuny, 1999). Thus, providing information in a manner that is understandable and accessible to Deaf or hard-of-hearing students is vital. Although this may seem simple, it is not enough to merely provide interpreters. Deaf or hard-of-hearing survivors may have different communication styles, whereby some may use sign language while others may lip read. Moreover, given the significance of communication abuse in the Deaf community, providers and college health professionals should be educated on this unique form of abuse.

In addition to targeted prevention and intervention strategies for Deaf and hard-of-hearing college students, it could be helpful to provide general sexual and health education to this population. For example, individuals with disabilities do not always receive and have access to the same sexual education information as individuals without disabilities (Andrews & Veronen, 1993). Deaf and hard-of-hearing students in particular have "historically lacked access to comprehensive health and sex information" (Anderson & Kobek Pezzarossi, 2014, p. 4). Along these lines, many Deaf individuals have low health literacy because of a number of factors including the lack of access to auditory incidental learning and the lack of health education programs provided in ASL (McKee, 2009). Consequently, Deaf individuals may be less likely to recognize abuse and seek appropriate services. Research has found that Deaf female college students do not label their experiences of partner violence as abuse, even when these experiences included severe physical and sexual violence (Anderson & Kobek Pezzarossi, 2014). Thus, programs that address sexual and health education can be useful in reducing and preventing sexual violence among Deaf and hard-of-hearing college students.

Moreover, because victims or survivors of IPV who are male, Deaf or hard of hearing, and sexual minorities are more likely to experience abuse than those in the majority, it is vital to use inclusive terms (i.e., *sexual assault* rather than rape) when educating people about sexual violence to help demonstrate that this issue does not solely occur among women and in heterosexual relationships. When developing programs and services, practitioners and college health professionals must strive for inclusivity as well as develop targeted approaches for outreach to populations on their campuses that may be at greater risk. Including survivors who are disabled and GLB can contribute to an increased understanding of the intersections of sexual orientation, disability, and sexual violence. Lesbians with disabilities are not recorded in studies of either abuse or disability but they frequently experience discrimination in other health and mental health care settings because of their sexual identity, their identity as disabled, and the interaction between the two (O'Toole & Brown, 2003). Research is needed to help understand these types of sexual and disability identity complexities, which can greatly influence the acceptability and accessibility of safety-related information (Powers, Hughes, & Lund, 2009).

At the college level, hotlines could be a useful tool to address sexual violence to provide information about agencies that offer certain services such as sexual violence or abuse services, domestic abuse or violence information, and counseling, among others. Often, efforts to educate the general population on campus about sexual orientation are implemented through speakers, forums, films, posters, and other types of outreach to students. Education should also address auditory status. Certainly, such efforts, courses, groups, safe zones, and hotlines should be encouraged on any campus. In addition, school policies ought to support an inclusive climate for individuals of all sexual orientations and abilities. Mandatory training about sexual orientation, gender identity, and auditory status included as part of freshman orientation programs might be helpful in establishing a greater understanding among students and tolerance for others.

Conclusion

The homogenizing of sexual violence among college students severely limits our understanding of the experiences of sexual violence and help-seeking behaviors of Deaf and hard-of-hearing students. As this chapter shows, Deaf and hard-of-hearing college students encounter unique barriers regarding sexual violence that have implications for education and intervention. As Deaf and hard-of-hearing students constitute a linguistic minority, understanding the cultural context of sexual violence in the Deaf community is a vital first step. Moreover, it is also important to recognize that Deaf and hard-of-hearing college students, similar to other groups, have multiple identities and in turn may face compounded barriers as a result of their auditory status *and* gender, race, and sexual orientation. Therefore, education, outreach, and intervention programs must be tailored to meet the needs of the Deaf and hard-of-hearing heterogeneous college population.

References

Anderson, M. L. (2010). *Prevalence and predictors of intimate partner violence victimization in the deaf community* (Unpublished doctoral dissertation). Gallaudet University, Washington, DC.

Anderson, M. L. (2014). Intimate partner violence in the Deaf community: 5 things you need to know & 5 things you can do. *Psychiatry Information in Brief, 11*(1), Article 1. Retrieved from http://escholarship.umassmed.edu/pib/vol11/iss1/1

Anderson, M. L., & Kobek Pezzarossi, C. M. (2014). Violence against Deaf women: Effect of partner hearing status. *Journal of Deaf Studies and Deaf Education, 19*, 411–421.

Anderson, M. L., & Leigh, I. W. (2011). Intimate partner violence against Deaf female college students. *Violence Against Women, 17*, 822–834.

Anderson, M. L., Leigh, I. W., & Samar, V. J. (2011). Intimate partner violence against Deaf women: A review. *Aggression and Violent Behavior, 16*, 200–206.

Andrews, A. B., & Veronen, L. J. (1993). Sexual assault and people with disabilities. Special issue: Sexuality and disabilities: A guide for human service practitioners. *Journal of Social Work and Human Sexuality, 8*, 137–159.

Ballan, M. S., & Freyer, M. B. (2012). Self-defense among women with disabilities: An unexplored domain in domestic violence cases. *Violence Against Women, 18*, 1083–1107.

Banyard, V. L., Ward, S. S., Cohn, E. S., Plante, E. G., Moorhead, C. C., & Walsh, W. W. (2007). Unwanted sexual contact on campus: A comparison of women's and men's experiences. *Violence and Victims, 22*, 57–70.

Barber, S., Wills, D., & Smith, M. (2010). Deaf survivors of sexual assault. In I. W. Leigh (Ed.), *Psychotherapy with Deaf clients from diverse groups* (pp. 320–340). Washington, DC: Gallaudet University Press.

Barrow, L. B. (2008). *Criminal victimization of the Deaf.* New York, NY: LFB Scholarly.

Benedet, J., & Grant, I. (2014). Sexual assault and the meaning of power and authority for women with mental disabilities. *Feminist Legal Studies, 22*, 131–154.

Brownlie, E., Jabbar, A., Beitchman, J., Vida, R., & Atkinson, L. (2007). Language impairment and sexual assault of girls and women: Findings from a community sample. *Journal of Abnormal Child Psychology, 35*, 618–662.

Burnash, D. L., Rothman-Marshall, G., & Schenkel, L. S. (2010, November). *Child maltreatment in Deaf college students: An analysis of the prevalence, characteristics, and clinical outcomes.* Poster session presented at the 44th Annual Convention of the Association for Behavioral and Cognitive Therapies, San Francisco, CA.

Carvalho, A. F., Lewis, R. L., Derlega, V. J., Winstead, B. A., & Viggiano, C. (2011). Internalized sexual minority stressors and same-sex intimate partner violence. *Journal of Family Violence, 26*, 501–509.

Casteel, C., Martin, S. L., Smith, J. B., Gurka, K. K., & Kupper, L. L. (2008). National study of physical and sexual assault among women with disabilities. *Injury Prevention, 14*, 87–90.

Chin, N. P., Cuculick, J., Starr, M., Panko, T., Widanka, H., & Dozier, A. (2013). Deaf mothers and breastfeeding: Do unique features of Deaf culture and language support breastfeeding success? *Journal of Human Lactation, 29*, 564–571. Retrieved from http://jhl.sagepub.com/content/early/2013/03/08/0890334413476921.full

Curry, M. A., Renker, P., Hughes, R. B., Robinson-Whelen, S., Oschwald, M. M., Swank, P., & Powers, L. E. (2009). Development of measures of abuse among women with disabilities and the characteristics of their perpetrators. *Violence Against Women, 15*, 1001–1025.

DuMont, J., Chertkow, L., Macdonald, S., Asllani, E., Bainbridge, D., Rotbard, N., & Cohen, M. M. (2012). Factors associated with the sexual assault of students: An exploratory study of victims treated at hospital-based sexual assault treatment centers. *Journal of Interpersonal Violence, 27*, 3723–3738.

Findley, P. A., Plummer, S., & McMahon, S. (2015). Exploring the experiences of abuse of college students with disabilities. *Journal of Interpersonal Violence*. Advance online publication. Retrieved from http://jiv.sagepub.com/content/early/2015-/05/06/0886260515581906.long

Fisher, B. S., Cullen, F. T., & Turner, M. G. (2000). *The sexual victimization of college women*. Washington, DC: National Institute of Justice.

Freedberg, P. (2006). Health care barriers and same-sex intimate partner violence: A review of the literature. *Journal of Forensic Nursing, 2*(1), 15–24.

Hamblet, E. C. (2009). Helping your students with disabilities during their college search. *Journal of College Admission, 205*, 6–15.

Haydon, A. A., McRee, A. L., & Halpern, C. T. (2011). Unwanted sex among young adults in the United States: The role of physical disability and cognitive performance. *Journal of Interpersonal Violence, 26*, 3476–3493.

Heppner, M. J., Neville, H. A., Smith, K., Kivlighan, D. M., Jr., & Gershuny, B. S. (1999). Examining immediate and long-term efficacy of rape prevention programming with racially diverse college men. *Journal of Counseling Psychology, 46*, 16–26.

Hines, D. A. (2007). Predictors of sexual coercion against women and men: A multilevel multinational study of university students. *Archives of Sexual Behavior, 36*, 403–422.

Hines, D. A., & Saudino, K. J. (2003). Gender differences in psychological, physical, and sexual aggression among college students using the Revised Conflict Tactics Scales. *Violence and Victims, 18*, 197–217.

Holcomb, T. (2012). *Introduction to American Deaf culture*. New York, NY: Oxford University Press.

Job, J. (2004). Factors involved in the ineffective dissemination of sexuality information to individuals who are deaf or hard of hearing. *American Annals of the Deaf, 149*, 264–273.

Joharchi, H. A., & Clark, M. D. (2014). A glimpse at American Deaf women's sexuality. *Psychology, 5,* 1536–1549.

Johnston-McCabe, P., Levi-Minzi, M., Van Hassely, V. B., & Vanderbeek, A. (2011). Domestic violence and social support in a clinical sample of Deaf and hard of hearing women. *Journal of Family Violence, 26,* 63–69.

Joseph, J. M., Sawyer, R., & Desmond, S. (1995). Sexual knowledge, behavior and sources of information among Deaf and hard of hearing college students. *American Annals of the Deaf, 140,* 338–345.

Lightfoot, E., & Williams, O. (2009). The intersection of disability, diversity, and domestic violence: Results of national focus groups. *Journal of Aggression, Maltreatment and Trauma, 18,* 133–152.

Martin, S. L., Ray, N., Sotres-Alvarez, D., Kupper, L. L., Moracco, K. E., Dickens, P. A., . . . Gizlice, Z. (2006). Physical and sexual assault of women with disabilities. *Violence Against Women, 12,* 823–837.

Mastrocinque, J. M., Thew, D., Cerulli, C., Raimondi, C., Pollard, R. Q., & Chin, N. P. (2015). Deaf victim's experiences with intimate partner violence: The need for integration and innovation. *Journal of Interpersonal Violence.* Advance online publication. Retrieved from http://jiv.sagepub.com/content/early/2015/09/11/0 886260515602896.long

McKee M. (2009). *Better health through accessible communication* [PowerPoint slides]. Retrieved from www.urmc.rochester.edu/MediaLibraries/URMCMedia/ncdhr/publications-presentations/documents/BetterCommunicationBetterHealth.pdf

Mitra, M., Lu, E., & Manning, S. L. (2012). Physical abuse around the time of pregnancy among women with disabilities. *Maternal and Child Health Journal, 16,* 802–806.

Mitra, M., & Mouradian, V. E. (2014). Intimate partner violence in the relationships of men with disabilities in the United States: Relative prevalence and health correlates. *Journal of Interpersonal Violence, 29,* 3150–3166.

Mitra, M., Mouradian, V. E., & Diamond, M. (2011). Sexual violence victimization against men with disabilities. *American Journal of Preventive Medicine, 41,* 494–497.

National Center for Education Statistics. (2015). *Fast facts: Students with disabilities.* Retrieved from https://nces.ed.gov/fastfacts/display.asp?id=60

National Institute on Deafness and Other Communication Disorders. (2014). *Quick statistics.* Retrieved from www.nidcd.nih.gov/health/statistics/pages/-quick.aspx

Nomeland, M. M., & Nomeland, R. E. (2012). *The Deaf community in America: History in the making.* Jefferson, NC: McFarland.

Nosek, M. A., Howland, C. A., & Young, M. E. (1997). Abuse of women with disabilities: Policy implications. *Journal of Disability Policy Studies, 8,* 157–176.

Obinna, J., Krueger, S., Osterbaan, C., Sadusky, J. M., & DeVore, W. (2006). Understanding the needs of the victims of sexual assault in the Deaf community: A needs assessment and audit. Retrieved from www.ncjrs.gov/pdffiles1/nij/grants/212867.pdf

O'Toole, C., & Brown, A. (2003). No reflection in the mirror: Challenges for disabled lesbians accessing mental health services. *Journal of Lesbian Studies, 7*(1), 35–49.

Packota, V. J. (2000). *Emotional abuse of women by their intimate partners: A literature review*. Retrieved from www.springtideresources.org/resource/emotional-abuse-women-their-intimate-partners-literature-review

Parasnis, I. (1998). *Cultural and language diversity and the Deaf experience: On interpreting the Deaf experience within the context of cultural and language diversity*. New York, NY: Cambridge University Press.

Plummer, S. B., & Findley, P. A. (2012). Women with disabilities' experience with physical and sexual abuse: A review of the literature and implications for the field. *Trauma, Violence, & Abuse, 13*, 15–29.

Pollard, R. Q., Sutter, E., & Cerulli, C. (2014). Intimate partner violence reported by two samples of Deaf adults via a computerized American sign language survey. *Journal of Interpersonal Violence, 29*, 948–965.

Porter, J. L., & McQuiller Williams, L. (2011a). Auditory status and experiences of abuse among college students. *Violence and Victims, 26*, 788–798.

Porter, J. L., & McQuiller Williams, L. (2011b). Intimate violence among underrepresented groups on a college campus. *Journal of Interpersonal Violence, 26*, 3210–3224.

Porter, J. L., & McQuiller Williams, (2013). Dual marginality: The impact of auditory status and sexual orientation on abuse in a college sample of women and men. *Journal of Aggression, Maltreatment & Trauma, 22*, 577–589.

Powers, L. E., Curry, M. A., Oschwald, M., Maley, S., Saxton, M., & Eckels, K. (2002). Barriers and strategies in addressing abuse: A survey of disabled women's experiences. *Journal of Rehabilitation, 68*, 4–13.

Powers, L. E., Hughes, R. B., & Lund, E. M. (2009). *Interpersonal violence and women with disabilities: A research update*. Retrieved from www.vawnet.org .applied-research-papers/print-document.php?doc_id=2077

Powers, L. E., Renker, P., Robinson-Whelen, S., Oschwald, M., Hughes, R., Swank, P., & Curry, M. A. (2009). Interpersonal violence and women with disabilities: Analysis of safety promoting behaviors. *Violence Against Women, 9*, 1040–1069.

Sadusky, J., & Obinna, J. (2002). *Violence against women: Focus groups with culturally distinct and underserved communities*. Minneapolis, MN: Rainbow Research.

Scherer, H. L., Snyder, J. A., & Fisher, B. S. (2013). A gendered approach to understanding intimate partner victimization and mental health outcomes among college students with and without disability. *Women & Criminal Justice, 23*, 209–231.

Sheridan, M. (1999). Deaf women now: Establishing our niche. In L. Bragg (Ed.), *Deaf world: A historical reader and primary coursebook* (pp. 380–389). New York: New York University Press.

Sullivan, P., Vernon, M., & Scanlan, J. (1987). Sexual abuse of Deaf youth. *American Annals of the Deaf, 132*, 256–262.

Westcott, H. L., & Jones, D. P. H. (1999). Annotation: The abuse of disabled children. *Journal of Child Psychology and Psychiatry, 40*, 497–506.

White, J., McQuiller Williams, L., & Cho, D. (2003). A social norms intervention to reduce coercive behaviors among Deaf and hard of hearing college students. *Report on Social Norms, 2*(4).

8

QUEER-SPECTRUM STUDENT SEXUAL VIOLENCE

Implications for Research, Policy, and Practice

Jason C. Garvey, Jessi Hitchins, and Elizabeth McDonald

Women's National Basketball Association (WNBA) players Brittney Griner and Glory Johnson are known throughout queer communities, not only for their athletic achievements on the court but also for championing their queer relationship off the court in an athletic culture that is not typically supportive of queer relationships. According to their Instagram feeds, they were a couple very much in love and were engaged to be married; however, in April of 2015, Griner and Johnson were arrested at a Phoenix-area home for suspicion of assault and disorderly conduct. This event gained some national traction on the news; however, when compared to Ray Rice of the Baltimore Ravens football team and his domestic violence trial, the Griner-Johnson incident (a queer relationship) did not receive nearly as much attention. The entirety of this event, ranging from the minimal national coverage of the WNBA players' arrests to the quick succession of media outlets to newer stories, reveals a reluctance to speak about queer-spectrum sexual violence because of fear of the unknown and lack of knowledge.

When discussing sexual violence, national leaders often use heteronormative language to focus on the narratives of straight cisgender women, diminishing national discourse on the topic to "what she was wearing [and] her prior sexual history" (White House, 2014b, p. 13). Similarly, higher education scholars often center conversations about sexual violence on heteronormative contexts, largely ignoring experiences of queer-spectrum students (Potter, Fountain, & Stapleton, 2012). A report published by the Association of American Universities (Cantor et al., 2015) states that queer-spectrum students are more likely to experience sexual assault, but the authors neither specifically highlight the experiences of queer-spectrum students nor give indications why these students experience violence at such higher rates than heterosexual students. Thus, practitioners and policymakers are left without proper resources to facilitate queer-conscious practice, policy, and research on sexual violence in higher education.

Contextual Overview

In this chapter we provide insights concerning sexual violence prevention and response for queer-spectrum students. We begin our chapter with a contextual overview, providing deeper understanding of our use of the term *queer spectrum* and our inclusion of sexual violence and intimate partner violence. We also review the prior literature on the prevalence and dynamics of sexual violence in queer-spectrum communities and provide a brief introduction to queer theory as a theoretical framework for our chapter, outlining the ways we use queer theory to explore and complicate narratives of sexual violence in higher education. In the remaining sections of our chapter, we focus on sexual violence research, policy, and practice for higher education and student affairs administrators. We use queer theory in each section to illuminate the current status and inefficiencies of research, policy, and practice for queer-spectrum sexual violence and provide recommendations to improve scholarship, policy, and services for queer-spectrum communities.

As a coalition of queer-spectrum and ally scholars, we implore our readers to note that the work for equity and inclusion of marginalized groups is constantly evolving. This chapter should be used only as a starting point to delve into the complications of serving queer-spectrum people within the realm of sexual violence.

Language Clarification

Throughout this chapter, we use the term *queer spectrum* to include those who identify as gay, lesbian, bisexual, queer, or another sexual orientation other than straight. Given the fluid and evolving nature of sexual identities, we use the term *queer spectrum* to value myriad ways in which individuals identify themselves. Using a spectrum of identities, as opposed to placing individuals into fixed and socially constructed categories of sexuality, embraces discursive fluidity of queer theory and encompasses a broader range of the lived experiences of people (Rankin, Weber, Blumenfeld, & Frazer, 2010). However, in a majority of the literature about queer-spectrum students, researchers use other terminology to refer to sexual minorities such as *lesbian, gay, bisexual,* and *queer* (LGBQ). In our summaries of prior literature, we use terminology the authors used in their work and use queer-spectrum language when synthesizing or discussing our own recommendations.

Although we focus on sexual violence among queer-spectrum students, we recognize that gender identity and gender expression are entangled with sexuality. For example, the 2010 Dear Colleague letter issued by the U.S. Department of Education Office of Civil Rights (OCR) states that Title IX indirectly serves queer-spectrum people via gender discrimination (Ali, 2010). This letter collapses gender identity and sexual orientation into the same identity in an effort to extend protections by Title IX of the 1972 Education Amendments to queer-spectrum individuals. Although we problematize the conflation of gender identity and sexual orientation, OCR's interpretation of Title IX reveals the ways these identities are socially and culturally amalgamated. By viewing sexual orientation and gender identity in tandem, we are able to imagine the complexities and the silencing that individuals and communities create and perpetuate because "heterosexuality both depends upon and produces gendered identities, meanings, and practices" (Pascoe, 2011, p. 28). Therefore, higher education practitioners must acknowledge and negotiate radical changes in working with and serving queer-spectrum survivors of sexual violence in complicated and interwoven understandings of sexual orientation and gender identity.

In this chapter we focus on sexual violence and intimate partner violence. Sexual violence encompasses "rape (forced penetration, attempted forced penetration, and alcohol or drug facilitated penetration), being made to penetrate someone else, sexual coercion, unwanted sexual contact, and non-contact unwanted sexual experiences" (Black et al., 2011, p. 17). Intimate partner violence includes "physical violence, sexual violence, threats of physical or sexual violence, stalking and psychological aggression (including coercive tactics) by a current or former intimate partner" (Black et al., p. 37). To date, campus resource providers have focused on addressing sexual violence perpetrated by strangers, largely ignoring intimate partner violence or sexual violence perpetrated by an acquaintance (Burrows, 2014). With the exception of gay men, queer-spectrum women and bisexual men experience intimate partner violence incidences higher than the national averages, with bisexual women affected at twice the national average (Walters, Chen, & Breiding, 2013). To effectively support queer-spectrum survivors of sexual violence, practitioners must acknowledge sexual violence by any perpetrator and consider the entanglements and complexities of sexual and intimate partner violence for queer-spectrum survivors.

Prevalence and Dynamics of Sexual Violence in Queer-Spectrum Communities

Queer-spectrum people are at increased risk for sexual violence victimization, from sexual harassment to rape (Black et al., 2011; Rothman, Exner, & Baughman, 2010). Gay and bisexual men are up to 27 times more likely to be victims or survivors of sexual violence compared to straight men, with reported prevalence of lifetime sexual violence between 12% and 54% among gay and bisexual men (Black et al., 2011; Rothman et al., 2010). Lesbian and bisexual women are up to 7.5 times more likely to experience sexual violence in relation to straight women, with reported incidents of lifetime sexual violence between 16% and 85% among lesbian and bisexual women (Rothman et al., 2010). This range is significantly large because of the vast differences between people who identify as bisexual and lesbian or gay.

In particular, people of all genders who identify as bisexual, pansexual, polysexual, fluid, or another all-gender-loving identity are at a significantly higher risk than any other population to be survivors of sexual violence (Black et al., 2011; San Francisco Human Rights Commission [SFHRC], 2011). For example, nearly 75% of bisexual women are survivors of sexual violence other than rape, which is notably higher than national averages for heterosexual or lesbian women (SFHRC, 2011). The large discrepancy in data that report incidents of sexual violence for queer-spectrum people is troubling and points to the inefficiency of current reporting structures for tracking sexual violence among queer-spectrum individuals, including sampling techniques that do not wholly capture varied experiences in queer-spectrum communities and data consolidation techniques that essentialize queer-spectrum narratives.

When discussing sexual violence prevention and response, we aspire to bring forth the complexities of sexual identities and experiences. As such, we use queer theory throughout this chapter to capture nonnormative narratives and disrupt assumptions on sexual violence. The following section outlines our approach to incorporating queer theory into our discussions of sexual violence research, policy, and practice.

Queer Theory

We use queer theory to explore and complicate the narratives on sexual violence on college campuses. As a theoretical framework, queer theory has neither a fundamental logic nor a shared set of characteristics (Jagose, 1996). Queer theory consists of vague and indefinable practices and positions to challenge normative knowledge and identities (Sullivan, 2003). Scholars who use queer theory attempt to deconstruct normalized and static assumptions of sexuality and gender that have historically privileged some and silenced others (Tierney & Dilley, 1998). Queer theory provides knowledge for scholars to disrupt binaries, including gay/straight, male/female, and man/woman, and allows a more social, fluid, and multiple understanding of sexuality and gender (Britzman, 1995; Lugg, 2003). Scholars employ this theoretical tool to dismantle structural forces of oppression and unveil the strategic silencing of marginalized individuals (Tierney & Dilley, 1998). As the lived experiences of queer-spectrum people include heterosexism, homophobia, biphobia, queerphobia, and other forms of oppression, a queer theoretical perspective is an appropriate frame to unveil these forces. For example, queer theory enables individuals to conceptualize gender expression as fluid, contextual, and situational. Rather than placing masculinity as a static performance centered on men and males, queer theory enables scholars to disrupt notions of masculinity across genders and sexualities to complicate assumptions of alignment across social identities and experiences (Sullivan, 2003).

Scholars have called for the increased use of queer theory as a lens to examine various contexts and experiences in higher education (Renn, 2010). Throughout our chapter, we use queer theory to bring forth the narratives of queer-spectrum students and deconstruct normalcy in sexuality and gender. In other words, we do not assume a normative narrative of sexual violence based solely on heterosexuality (Potter et al., 2012). In the following sections, we use queer theory to interrogate the representation of sexual violence in queer-spectrum communities in colleges and universities. We situate our conversations on three facets of higher education scholarship: research, policy, and practice. Although we discuss these three facets separately, each of them is tightly intertwined with the other. Therefore, themes and concepts overlap within the sections.

Research on Sexual Violence

Although sexual violence in higher education has received greater attention from researchers and scholars in recent years, most data collection instruments assume survivors and perpetrators are straight and cisgender (Balsam, Rothblum, & Beauchaine, 2005). Most scholarship and campus initiatives are aimed at straight, cisgender women, but this population is not the only one in which sexual and relationship violence is an issue (Potter et al., 2012). Rates of sexual violence among queer-spectrum survivors and in same-gender relationships have received little research attention (Todahl, Linville, Bustin, Wheeler, & Gau, 2009). Empirical and data-driven research about queer-spectrum student sexual violence is essential for several reasons.

For instance, researchers can use data to educate service providers, law enforcement, allied medical professionals, staff at rape crisis centers, and campus administrators on the narratives of queer-spectrum sexual violence survivors. The experiences of queer-spectrum sexual violence survivors may likely involve unique factors related to homo/queerphobia and other forms of oppression as well as heterosexist assumptions in service availability and reporting structures such as the omission of same-gender relationship statuses on intake forms (Bieschke, Perez, & DeBord, 2007). These unique factors translate into poor access to services for sexual violence survivors and poor responses to disclosure across various sectors, including health professions, law enforcement, and social work (Girshick, 2002). In fact, more than two thirds of queer- and trans-spectrum people do not think law enforcement is well equipped to handle incidents of sexual violence in queer- and trans-spectrum communities (Todahl et al., 2009). Policy and practice grounded in empirically valid scholarship can assist practitioners in developing culturally relevant outreach and services that accommodate survivors across all sexual identities. This approach to research may begin to dispel negative stereotypes and myths about gender violence among queer-spectrum individuals.

Queer- and trans-spectrum community members frequently ignore or minimize experiences with sexual violence to avoid further discrimination or oppression, which leads to feelings of guilt for sharing experiences of sexual violence, greater protection with secrecy, feelings of being trapped, increased isolation, victim blaming, lack of support, and self-degradation (Todahl et al., 2009). Rigorous research can decrease misunderstandings and increase awareness about the unique narratives of queer-spectrum student sexual violence survivors by illuminating the voices of queer-spectrum sexual violence survivors and encouraging more survivors to share their experiences. Multiple approaches may make sexual violence research more inclusive of queer-spectrum students, including collecting more information on surveys, using qualitative inquiry, constructing research designs using intersectionality as a theoretical lens, and creating outcome-based research.

Recommendations for Research on Sexual Violence

In this section we provide recommendations for researchers and other data collection personnel to create more queer-friendly reporting structures and services for sexual violence prevention and survivors. First, to foster inclusion, scholars must revisit data collection via large-scale surveys. For example, the Bureau of Justice Statistics' (BJS') National Crime Victimization Survey (NCVS) collects information on nonfatal crimes reported and not reported to police against people age 12 or older (Sinozich & Langton, 2014). BJS produces reports to compare rape and sexual violence victimization of college students and nonstudents from 1995 to 2013. The NCVS does not note respondents' sexual identity, nor does the survey ask about the gender of the perpetrator in questions about forced or unwanted sexual acts. The National Intimate Partner and Sexual Violence Survey (NISVS), administered by the Centers for Disease Control and Prevention (Black et al., 2011), presents data about intimate partner violence, sexual violence, and stalking. Different from the NCVS, the NISVS asks respondents to provide perpetrator information including the sex of the perpetrator (male/female) and relationship of the perpetrator to the survivor, but it does not ask about respondents' sexual identity.

The Campus Sexual Assault (CSA) Study (Krebs, Lindquist, Warner, Fisher, & Martin, 2007) was funded by the National Institute of Justice and assessed various types of sexual violence experienced by university students. The CSA assessed students' demographics and dating (including sexual orientation) and the gender of the perpetrator (man/woman). Although the NISVS and CSA provide opportunities to understand queer-spectrum student sexual violence survivors, there are greater opportunities to collect better empirical data to more adequately represent the narratives and experiences of queer-spectrum students through more inclusive and expansive question formatting and an increased number of questions or items focused on identities, expressions, and relationships.

In addition to assessing demographic questions of the sexual violence survivor and perpetrator and their relationship (e.g., intimate partner, acquaintance, stranger), survey designers must ask respondents to provide information about their sexual behavior, which is especially important for researchers to understand students who are exploring their sexual identities through same-gender sexual experiences. In other words, a person may identify as a straight man but engage in sexual behavior with people across multiple genders. To fully understand sexual violence in the queer community, scholars must examine identity and experiences. Asking respondents to identify their sexual orientation and sexual behavior encourages a queer theoretical understanding of sexual violence because it further complicates assumptions about the relationship between identity and experiences among survivors and perpetrators.

Survey methodologists must also use sampling techniques that attract a larger sample of queer-spectrum sexual violence survivors to participate in research. Such community-responsive data collection and sampling techniques include nonprobabilistic chain-referral sampling (Semaan, Lauby, & Liebman, 2002), point people (Miles & Huberman, 1994), snowball sampling (Faugier & Sargeant, 1997), and social media survey distribution (Johnson, Drezner, Garvey, & Bumbry, in press). By administering a national survey that focuses on the unique experiences of queer-spectrum students, researchers can ask community-specific questions related to discrimination, oppression, and social identities (e.g., identity, behavior, attraction, performance) to capture the nuanced narratives of queer-spectrum student survivors of sexual violence.

Second, scholars must also use qualitative inquiry to further understand queer-spectrum sexual violence. Despite preliminary work to understand queer-spectrum student sexual violence, few scholars have provided opportunities for queer-spectrum students to discuss their personal narratives regarding sexual violence. Qualitative inquiries provide opportunities for queer-spectrum survivors of sexual violence to share their stories about the structural and oppressive forces in higher education that interact with their sexualities as they relate to sexual violence to broaden services and policies to be more inclusive of all sexualities and experiences. Researchers may employ qualitative methods with queer theoretical frameworks to disrupt normative assumptions of sexuality, gender, and sexual violence in higher education (Britzman, 1995). A queer theoretical approach may enable qualitative scholars to critically examine various contexts and experiences in higher education, including gender-normative reporting structures for sexual violence in higher education, heterocentric student services for sexual violence, or assumptions of heterosexuality when reporting campus sexual violence in college or university media (Renn, 2010).

Third, scholars must adopt an intersectional approach to understand the complexity of social identities. Developed through Black feminist thought and originally coined by Crenshaw (1991), intersectionality refers to the interaction between gender, race, and other categories of difference and the outcomes of these interactions as they relate to power. Intersectionality encourages scholars to examine how various systems of oppression interact to create political and cultural structures that shape the experiences of oppressed individuals. Intersectional scholars are interested in the relationship among all groups in each social category (McCall, 2005). Scholars can use this approach to understand the role of sexuality, gender, and other social identity classifications in sexual violence, within and across communities. For example, when conducting quantitative analyses about sexual violence, researchers can create demographic interaction effects among gender, sexuality, race, or any number of social identity combinations to empirically test within- and between-community experiences. Combining intersectionality and queer theory within one theoretical construction may encourage researchers to disrupt notions of sexual orientation and behavior in relation to other social identities like race, gender, or ability.

Fourth, scholars who examine sexual violence within queer-spectrum communities must use outcome-based research. Until recently, most research about queer-spectrum students focused on visibility, campus climate, and identity and experiences (Renn, 2010). Rankin and Garvey (2015) advocated that outcome-based assessments should be the future of queer-spectrum student research and assessments. Outcome-based assessment focuses on knowledge, skills, attitudes, and habits that directly relate to student learning and development (Schuh & Associates, 2009). Continuing their recommendation, scholars must explore other outcomes for queer-spectrum student survivors of sexual violence, including resiliency, health and well-being, academic success, identity development, and self-authorship, among others. By examining student learning and development in relation to sexual violence, researchers may uncover unique environmental contexts to better serve queer-spectrum sexual violence survivors. Focusing on queer-spectrum student outcomes also encourages scholars to dismantle deficit-based research and recognize achievements and resiliency among queer-spectrum students (Tierney & Dilley, 1998).

Sexual Violence Policy

Policies are formal (e.g., nondiscrimination policies) and informal (e.g., dress codes, personal office decor) in that they are manifested in procedural manners and through structural, department, or office practices (Ballard, 2006). Policies in any form are often framed as neutral, value free, apolitical, and ahistorical; however, these policies often have specific aims and unintended consequences (Allan, 2008; Shaw, 2004). The presence or lack of policies signifies structural values of an institution and often affect particular groups of students, faculty, staff, or other constituents. For example, when an institution lacks specific and visible support for queer-spectrum people via policies, administrators and policymakers demonstrate their devaluing of queer-spectrum people. In this particular realm, sexual violence policies are no different.

Historically, administrators constructed sexual violence policies to protect white, middle-class, able-bodied, straight cisgender women through the second-wave feminist surge for advocacy and justice (Allan, 2008; Crenshaw, 1991). For example, marginalized people are not targeted by these policies so they might not be aware that resources even exist or trust the system of resources to begin with (Crenshaw, 1991). Although policymakers enacted such policies with good intentions in an effort to curb sexual violence and to assist survivors, they did not consider the ways policy formation silenced other marginalized populations and deflected responsibility from potential bystanders or perpetrators (Crenshaw, 1991). To illustrate this point, policymakers who focus on risk reduction reinforce rape culture by targeting potential victims on campus (e.g., in printed materials and services specifically directed at women-identified organizations) rather than explicitly demanding that the campus not tolerate perpetrators of this crime (Burrows, 2014). Although it is crucial that survivors know their resources, the culture of sex negativity and silence on campus is unchecked for potential bystanders or perpetrators, thus continuing the cycle of violence. Furthermore, by focusing on straight cisgender women, administrators deflect prevention and response policies to serve other populations, including queer-spectrum individuals and communities.

Even when policymakers develop, establish, and implement official policies, their policy processes ignore queer-spectrum communities. For example, campus policymakers seldom consult experts who serve marginalized groups, including queer-spectrum students, in developing sexual violence policies (Iverson, 2012). Additionally, senior administrators and policymakers are overwhelmingly straight cisgender men who construct policies and reports as a paternalistic mechanism to save and protect vulnerable and fearful women and girls (Allan, 2008; Iverson, 2012). In doing so, policymakers reinforce heteronormative assumptions about sexual violence, which has unintended gaps and consequences for queer-spectrum people.

Policymakers often use language that reflects assumptions about sexual violence as centered on straight cisgender women. In *Not Alone: The First Report of the White House Task Force to Protect Students From Sexual Assault* (White House, 2014b), the authors employed a framework of women as survivors of sexual violence and men as perpetrators. The report indicated that men are survivors of sexual violence but gave no indication on who perpetrates violence against men as it did with women victims and survivors. Specific gender language in the report for survivor (i.e., she/her/woman/ female) and perpetrator (i.e., he/him/man/male) reinforces heteronormative and cisnormative assumptions, effectively erasing queer-spectrum narratives in sexual violence (Calton, Cattaneo, & Gebhard, 2015). Furthermore, the authors of the report state men have a responsibility to interrupt sexual violence if they observe other men attempting or completing violence against women, only giving cursory acknowledgment that women may also intervene. Such language situates women as passive observers whereas only men are capable of actively participating in bystander intervention (Calton et al., 2015). Given the importance of the White House report, there are nationwide implications for campus knowledge and outreach for preventing and responding to sexual violence, and using normative language silences sexual violence knowledge and outreach to various communities, including queer-spectrum individuals.

As noted earlier, policymakers often envision sexual violence survivor prevention and response through dominant heteronormative narratives and contexts, thus actively excluding queer- and trans-spectrum individuals as well as straight cisgender men from accessing tangible resources for sexual violence prevention and response, including shelters and advocacy centers (Gilbert, 2014). For example, by enacting formal and informal policies, administrators create barriers such as *only* serving straight cisgender women at sexual violence shelters or labeling a sexual violence advocacy program as being for women (e.g., Women's Center). Such structural policy inequalities reinforce heteronormativity and cisnormativity and diminish the effectiveness of policy formation, structure, and implementation.

Recommendations for Sexual Violence Policy

In this section we provide recommendations to policymakers to more effectively serve queer-spectrum people in college and university campus communities. First, policies should have flexibility to change and grow. Language choice matters in policies, and administrators should use language that reflects current trends that describe marginalized people and communities (Calton et al., 2015). Gender-nonspecific language is useful (e.g., survivor, perpetrator, partner) and using such language aligns with queer theory in that it more adequately captures the complexities of gender and sexuality among individuals (Britzman, 1995; Lugg, 2003). When giving information and naming services on a college or university campus, administrators must specify that personnel serve victims and survivors of all identities, paying particular attention to the spectra of sexual and gender identities. For example, university and college administrators can employ purposeful language in their policies and survivor services that include statements such as, "We serve any person regardless of gender identity and sexual orientation, and regardless of the gender identity and sexual orientation of the perpetrator." Queer theory also opens possibilities for policymakers to reduce the effects of heteronormativity and cisnormativity in policy development and implementation (Sullivan, 2003). By queering sexual violence prevention and response policies, administrators can include information related to all expressions of sexuality (e.g., lesbian, gay, bisexual, queer, asexual, polyamorous, and bondage, dominance, submission, masochism, and other interpersonal dynamics [BDSM]).

Second, policymakers and administrators, as well as faculty, staff, student, and community representatives, should regularly review policies related to sexual violence. When soliciting feedback from representative constituencies, policymakers and administrators must seek varied perspectives across social identities (e.g., race/ethnicity, faith/religion, gender, sexuality, age) and professional responsibilities (e.g., exempt staff, tenured faculty, part-time students). A positive and affirming policy for one group or person may be exclusionary or alienating for another. For example, campus administrators who provide facilities open to all genders may marginalize people whose religious practices require separation of genders. Administrators must be cognizant of experiences across all social identities and serve students with intersectional cultural competencies. To encourage campus participation and representation, administrators could convene an annual open task force and host a well-publicized town meeting for all constituencies (e.g., faculty, staff, students, community members) to proactively review policies.

Third, policies need to reach and reflect all people in the campus community. Campus leaders must develop creative and inclusive ways to engage a variety of populations and provide safe and confidential reporting that is free from repercussion or judgment. Simply building Web pages that address particular affinity groups within the context of sexual violence has the potential to alleviate fears and encourage individuals to seek assistance (Calton et al., 2015). Administrators should include links on their university's advocacy or Title IX Web page that provide resources and responses to frequently asked questions for queer-spectrum individuals. Rather than reactively serving queer-spectrum sexual assault survivors on a case-by-case basis, policymakers must be proactive in creating sexual violence policies that include people across all sexualities and sexual behaviors. Policymakers must be conscious of how restrictive or omitted language manifests itself in exclusionary practices. Administrators and policymakers must therefore continually review and update written and unwritten policies as new insights and information become available.

Practice Related to Sexual Violence Prevention and Response

With renewed focus on Title IX legislation and sexual violence, college and university administrators have heightened awareness, prevention, and response for sexual violence. However, as most student services focus on the experiences of heterosexual cisgender women, there are few resources for queer-spectrum student survivors of sexual violence, and student affairs administrators are therefore poorly prepared to support student survivors across sexual identities and experiences.

The 2014 presidential memorandum (White House, 2014a) and the Task Force to Protect Students From Sexual Assault (White House, 2014b) were created to assist college and university administrators in sexual assault prevention and response practices. Unfortunately, the memorandum includes only two small notations on how to best serve queer-spectrum students. The general omission of queer-spectrum individuals from national reports on sexual violence in higher education creates a dominant heteronormative lens nationally, thereby influencing the ways individual campuses respond to and create practices for students. Queer-spectrum students notice the heterocentric campus sexual violence policies, as illustrated by the fact that 59% of queer students have little to no faith that their institution would take queer-spectrum students' reports of sexual assault seriously (Cantor et al., 2015). Without guidance from national leaders on sexual violence, student affairs practitioners and service providers cannot learn about or train people in specific contexts for queer-spectrum student sexual violence.

Student affairs professionals and service providers frame sexual assault conversations around four tenets: response, awareness and risk reduction, bystander intervention, and primary prevention (Burrows, 2014). Within these four categories, one of the largest issues that college crisis centers must navigate is reframing risk reduction. Particularly when using consent-based models that educate students about resisting peer pressure, student affairs professionals seldom create prevention programming that is beneficial to queer-spectrum students (Rothman & Silverman, 2007). In the past, practitioners framed risk reduction as offering self-defense courses and safety tips, all of which perpetuate the myth of heterocentric stranger-based sexual violence and the culture of victim blaming (Burrows, 2014).

The flaws that Rothman and Silverman (2007) point to in prevention programming can be seen in online sexual misconduct training programs (SMTPs). These programmatic training sessions cover definitions and overviews for key terms such as *consent, sexual* and *relationship violence, sexual intercourse and contact, stalking,* and *sexual coercion* (Worthen & Baker, 2014). Although SMTP training typically has widespread campus support, queer-spectrum students often have mixed reactions to the training because topics on queer-spectrum sexuality are frequently superficial, impersonal, and biased, with little translation to actual campus actions or queer-specific services. To incorporate more queer-spectrum student experiences into SMTP training, practitioners must use gender-neutral pronouns and queer-specific examples to validate all sexual identities and experiences.

Queer-spectrum survivors of interpersonal violence also experience a lack of information on partner abuse and face judgment and homophobic or queerphobic attitudes from service providers. Often, queer-spectrum students seek anonymity in the initial response to their mental and physical needs and concerns and therefore turn to online sources first to seek help (e.g., counseling center websites, college rape center websites; McKinley, Luo, Wright, & Kraus, 2015). Without welcoming communication, queer-spectrum students are less likely to report incidents of violence (Rothman & Silverman, 2007). If a queer student survivor of interpersonal violence does report the incident, there is an additional risk that service providers themselves will harbor homophobic or queerphobic attitudes or have a lack of knowledge about the queer community. Service providers may knowingly or unknowingly create hostile environments, online or in person, for queer-spectrum survivors if they have ineffective communication on their websites or improper screening procedures (The Network/La Red, n.d.).

Recommendations for Sexual Violence Prevention and Response

In this section, we provide recommendations to student affairs practitioners and service providers in regard to sexual violence prevention and response services for queer-spectrum students. To create more welcoming services for queer-spectrum students, practitioners must employ more inclusive communication techniques when discussing sexual violence. One of the most basic and crucial interventions all providers must adopt is asking clients about their sexual identity and behaviors. It is worth noting that sexual identities and behaviors may not always align, and service providers must understand that one does not necessarily predict the other. In other words, how students identify sexually or romantically does not have to directly link to their sexual or romantic interactions. Practitioners must recognize the complexities of identities and expressions and escape fixed, binary constructions of sexuality and gender (Britzman, 1995; Lugg, 2003). As noted earlier, students who identify as bisexual, pansexual, polysexual, or another all-gender-loving sexual identity are often invisible in conversations about sexual violence. Asking about students' sexual identities and behaviors removes the stigma that queer students often face when seeking services related to sexual violence. Intake forms for service providers and on-campus student services must also collect similar data for survivors of sexual violence. Intake forms with inclusive language across sexual and gender identities will not only increase awareness of queer-spectrum students but also decrease stigmatization and increase comfort between survivors of sexual violence and service providers.

Staff at college crisis centers can turn to their community-based counterparts to learn specific needs and wants from queer-spectrum sexual violence survivors. One such community-based crisis organization is The Network/ La Red, a Massachusetts-based social justice organization that is survivor-led and focused on ending partner abuse in LGBTQ, polyamorous, and BDSM communities. Administrators of The Network/La Red (n.d.) strongly suggest including information about LGBTQ partner abuse in a center's outreach material, educating service providers on LGBTQ issues/sensitivity training, and conducting screening practices that are contextualized in the queer-spectrum experience. A center's outreach material must emphasize that abuse is not exclusive to straight relationships. Outreach materials need to publicize a more specific definition of *partner abuse* that is "a systematic pattern of behaviors where one person tries to control the thoughts, beliefs, and/or actions of their partner, *someone they are dating or had an intimate relationship with* [emphasis added]," regardless of sexual orientation (The Network/La Red, n.d., p. 1). Additionally, these outreach materials need to be available on the center's website to allow ease of access for queer students who seek anonymity.

Queer-specific training for practitioners and service providers is also a crucial step in providing a safe space for queer-spectrum survivors of sexual and interpersonal violence (Brown & Groscup, 2008; Ford, Slavin, Hilton, & Holt, 2012). Without specialized training and understanding, service providers are unable to recognize their biases and judgments about relationships and sexuality when working with queer-spectrum survivors. With proper training on queer-spectrum sexual violence, service providers are able to recommend appropriate resources, services, and referrals in a culturally relevant and affirming approach. Through training, service providers should better understand how to effectively and thoughtfully screen survivors and abusers, and also offer to refer them to queer-friendly services. Training sessions may also educate service providers on the pervasiveness and systemic nature of heterosexism, homophobia, biphobia, queerphobia, and other forms of oppression against queer-spectrum people, and about ways to dismantle such oppressive forces (Sullivan, 2003).

Practitioners must be skilled in recognizing the nuances and complications of queer-spectrum interpersonal relationships and understand that queer-spectrum survivors may have the same support systems as their abuser or may be closeted and cannot reach out for the appropriate services. On many college campuses, queer communities are close knit and are vital support systems for the students within them. If an abusive queer relationship exists in this community, and the queer-spectrum survivor chooses to report the abuse, the survivor may experience feelings of isolation from the close-knit community. Resources from the National Coalition Against Domestic Violence (www .ncadv.org) and the Northwest Network (www.nwnetwork.org) can assist practitioners in crafting screening questions that determine which partner in a queer relationship has more power and control over the other partner.

Conclusion

Researchers, policymakers, and campus practitioners must recognize the detrimental effects of pervasive heteronormativity when examining sexual violence prevention and response. Throughout this chapter, we described common assumptions about sexual violence largely dominated by discourse about straight cisgender women in heterosexual relationships. Being a social justice–oriented and identity-conscious researcher, policymaker, and administrator requires constant reflection on normative assumptions that permeate conversations about sexual violence. Although we focus specifically on queer-spectrum student survivors of sexual violence, we encourage readers to consider the intersections and complexities of social identities (Crenshaw, 1991), recognizing there is no singular or grand narrative for sexual violence in higher education. Similarly, contexts and language consistently shift and are shaped by emerging identities and experiences. In the same way that we do not assume a normative narrative of sexual violence based solely on heterosexuality (Potter et al., 2012), we must also not generate a normative narrative for queer-spectrum individuals.

References

Ali, R. (2010, October 26). *Dear colleague letter*. Retrieved from http://www2 .ed.gov/about/offices/list/ocr/letters/colleague-201010.pdf

Allan, E. J. (Ed.). (2008). *Policy discourses, gender, and education: Constructing women's status*. New York, NY: Routledge.

Ballard, R. M. (2006). *Queer women in higher education: Tales from out of the closet* (Unpublished doctoral dissertation). University of Alabama, Tuscaloosa.

Balsam, K. F., Rothblum, E. D., & Beauchaine, T. P. (2005). Victimization over the life span: A comparison of lesbian, gay, bisexual, and heterosexual siblings. *Journal of Consulting and Clinical Psychology, 3*, 477–487.

Bieschke, K. J., Perez, R. M., & DeBord, K. A. (2007). *Handbook of counseling and psychotherapy with lesbian, gay, bisexual and transgender clients* (2nd ed.). Washington, DC: American Psychological Association.

Black, M. C., Basile, K. C., Breiding, M. J., Smith, S. G., Walters, M. L., Merrick, M. T., . . . Stevens, M. R. (2011). *The National Intimate Partner and Sexual Violence Survey: 2010 summary report*. Atlanta, GA: National Center for Injury Prevention and Control and Centers for Disease Control and Prevention.

Britzman, D. (1995). Is there a queer pedagogy? Or stop thinking straight. *Educational Theory, 45*, 151–165.

Brown, M., & Groscup, J. (2008). Perceptions of same-sex domestic violence among crisis center staff. *Journal of Family Violence, 24*(2), 87–93.

Burrows, E. (2014). Spotlight on campus sexual violence. *Sexual Assault Report, 17*(5), 65–67.

Calton, J. M., Cattaneo, L. B., & Gebhard, K. T. (2015). Barriers to help seeking for lesbian, gay, bisexual, transgender, and queer survivors of intimate partner violence. *Trauma, Violence, & Abuse*, 1–16.

Cantor, D., Fisher, B., Chibnall, S., Townsend, R., Lee, H., Bruce, C., & Thomas, G. (2015). *Report on the AAU Campus Climate Survey on Sexual Assault and Sexual Misconduct*. Washington, DC: Association of American Universities.

Crenshaw, K. (1991). Mapping the margins: Intersectionality, identity politics, and violence against women of color. *Stanford Law Review, 43*, 1241–1299.

Faugier, J., & Sargeant, M. (1997). Sampling hard to reach populations. *Journal of Advanced Nursing, 26,* 790–797.

Ford, C. L., Slavin, T., Hilton, K. L., & Holt, S. L. (2012). Intimate partner violence prevention services and resources in Los Angeles: Issues, needs, and challenges for assisting lesbian, gay, bisexual, and transgender clients. *Health Promotion Practice, 14,* 841–849.

Gilbert, J. (2014). *Sexuality in schools: The limits of education.* Minneapolis: University of Minnesota Press.

Girshick, L. B. (2002). No sugar, no spice: Reflections on research on woman-to-woman sexual assault. *Violence Against Women, 8,* 1500–1520.

Iverson, S. V. (2012). Constructing outsiders: The discursive framing of access in university diversity policies. *The Review of Higher Education, 35,* 149–177.

Jagose, A. (1996). *Queer theory: An introduction.* New York: New York University Press.

Johnson, S., Drezner, N. D., Garvey, J. C., & Bumbry, M. (in press). Social media use for survey distribution. In M. Gasman (Ed.), *Academic going public: How to write and speak beyond academe.* New York, NY: Taylor & Francis/Routledge.

Krebs, C. P., Lindquist, C. H., Warner, T. D., Fisher, B. S., & Martin, S. L. (2007). *The Campus Sexual Assault (CSA) Study.* Retrieved from www.ncjrs.gov/pdffiles1/nij/grants/221153.pdf

Lugg, C. (2003). Sissies, faggots, lezzies, and dykes: Gender, sexual orientation, and a new politics of education? *Educational Administration Quarterly, 39,* 95–134.

McCall, L. (2005). The complexity of intersectionality. *Signs, 30,* 1771–1800.

McKinley, C. J., Luo, Y., Wright, P. J., & Kraus, A. (2015). Reexamining LGBT resources on college counseling center websites: An over-time and cross-country analysis. *Journal of Applied Communication Research, 43,* 112–129.

Miles, M. B., & Huberman, M. (1994). *Qualitative data analysis: An expanded sourcebook.* San Francisco, CA: SAGE.

The Network/La Red. (n.d.). *Information for domestic violence providers about: LGBTQ partner abuse.* Retrieved from www.avp.org/storage/documents/Training%20 and%20TA%20Center/2010_TNLR_Partner_Abuse_Handout_for_Providers .pdf

Pascoe, C. J. (2011). *Dude, you're a fag.* Berkeley: University of California Press.

Potter, S. J., Fountain, K., & Stapleton, J. G. (2012). Addressing sexual and relationship violence in the LGBT community using a bystander framework. *Harvard Review of Psychiatry, 20,* 201–208.

Rankin, S., & Garvey, J. C. (2015). Identifying, quantifying, and operationalizing queer spectrum and trans-spectrum students: Assessment and research in student affairs. *New Directions for Student Services, 152,* 73–84.

Rankin, S., Weber, G., Blumenfeld, W., & Frazer, M. S. (2010). *State of higher education for LGBT people.* Charlotte, NC: Campus Pride.

Renn, K. A. (2010). LGBT and queer research in higher education: The state and status of the field. *Educational Researcher, 39,* 132–141. doi:10.3102/0013189X10362579

Rothman, E., Exner, D., & Baughman, A. L. (2010). The prevalence of sexual assault against people who identify as gay, lesbian, or bisexual in the United States: A systematic review. *Trauma, Violence, & Abuse, 12*(2), 55–66.

Rothman, E., & Silverman, J. (2007). The effect of a college sexual assault prevention program on first-year students' victimization rates. *Journal of American College Health, 55*, 283–290.

San Francisco Human Rights Commission. (2011). *Bisexual invisibility: Impacts and recommendations*. Retrieved from http://sf-hrc.org/sites/sf-hrc.org/files/migrated/ FileCenter/Documents/HRC_Publications/Articles/Bisexual_Invisiblity_ Impacts_and_Recommendations_March_2011.pdf

Schuh, J. H., & Associates. (2009). *Assessment methods for student affairs*. San Francisco, CA: Jossey-Bass.

Semaan, S., Lauby, J., & Liebman, J. (2002). Street and network sampling in evaluation studies of HIV risk-reduction interventions. *AIDS Review, 4*, 213–223.

Shaw, K. M. (2004). Using feminist critical policy analysis in the realm of higher education: A case of welfare reform as gendered educational policy. *Journal of Higher Education, 75*, 56–79.

Sinozich, S., & Langton, L. (2014). *Rape and sexual violence victimization among college-age females, 1995–2013*. Washington, DC: Bureau of Justice Statistics.

Sullivan, N. (2003). *A critical introduction to queer theory*. New York: New York University Press.

Tierney, W. G., & Dilley, P. (1998). Constructing knowledge: Educational research and gay and lesbian studies. In W. F. Pinar (Ed.), *Queer theory in education* (pp. 49–72). New York, NY: Routledge.

Title IX of the Education Amendments, 20 U.S.C. §1681 et seq. (1972).

Todahl, J. L., Linville, D., Bustin, A., Wheeler, J., & Gau, J. (2009). Sexual assault support services and community systems: Understanding critical issues and needs in the LGBTQ community. *Violence Against Women, 15*, 952–976.

Walters, M. L., Chen, J., & Breiding, M. J. (2013). *The National Intimate Partner and Sexual Violence Survey (NISVS): 2010 findings on victimization by sexual orientation*. Atlanta, GA: National Center for Injury Prevention and Control and Centers for Disease Control and Prevention.

White House, Office of the Press Secretary. (2014a, January 22). *Memorandum— Establishing a White House Task Force to Protect Students From Sexual Assault* [Press release]. Retrieved from https://obamawhitehouse.archives.gov/the-press-office/2014/01/22/memorandum-establishing-white-house-task-force-protect-students-sexual-a

White House. (2014b). *Not alone: The first report of the White House Task Force to Protect Students From Sexual Assault*. Retrieved from www.notalone.gov/assets/ report.pdf

Worthen, M., & Baker, S. (2014). Consent is sexy: Analyzing student reactions to a campus mandatory online sexual misconduct training program. *Sexual Assault Report, 17*(5), 65–75.

PART THREE

COALITION BUILDING FOR
THE FUTURE

9

INTERSECTIONALITY, POWER, PRIVILEGE, AND CAMPUS-BASED SEXUAL VIOLENCE ACTIVISM

Chris Linder and Jess S. Myers

Although mainstream media and higher education scholars frequently herald the 1960s as the beginning of campus-based activism (Astin, Astin, Bayer, & Bisconti, 1975; Broadhurst, 2014; Rhoads, 1998), student activists have challenged campus administrators on a variety of issues since colleges were founded in the United States (Broadhurst, 2014; Rhoads, 1998). Early student activists advocated for better living conditions and dining hall food and curricular changes on campus (Altbach, 1989; Broadhurst, 2014). Students have also worked to raise awareness about critical social issues throughout history, including protesting war, divesting from particular businesses and countries, and increasing access to higher education (Altbach, 1989; Broadhurst, 2014). Additionally, some student activists engaged in identity-based activism on and off campus related to race, gender, sexual orientation, and additional minoritized social identities (Rhoads, 1998). Today, two of the most visible activist movements on college campuses are identity related: sexual violence awareness and racial justice activism (Wong, 2015).

Using campus- and identity-based activism as a background, the purpose of this chapter is to explore the strategies of campus sexual violence activists (CSVAs), highlighting specific tensions related to power, privilege, and oppression. We provide a conceptual framework highlighting the literature about campus-based activism, then present findings from our study exploring the strategies of CSVAs. We conclude the chapter with implications and recommendations for educators to support CSVAs through a power-conscious lens.

Campus Sexual Violence Prevention and Response Activism

Activists, specifically women of color activists, have worked to raise intersectional awareness about sexual violence for hundreds of years (Chapter 3; Freedman, 2013; Giddings, 2007; McGuire, 2010). However, many historians and feminist authors credit (white) feminist consciousness-raising of the 1970s as the beginning of sexual violence activism (Corrigan, 2013). Centering white women as the initiators of sexual violence prevention and response activism ignores the significant contributions of women of color. Additionally, as white women initiated awareness prevention and response campaigns on campus, they frequently did so from a race- and power-neutral perspective, resulting in limited strategies for addressing sexual violence (Corrigan, 2013). For example, white feminists centered on police and legal responses in their activism, failing to account for the tumultuous and racist history of the relationship between legal systems and communities of color (INCITE!, 2006).

As (white) activist consciousness-raising groups gained attention on college campuses in the 1970s and 1980s, women of color and poor women frequently organized in communities outside college campuses, calling attention to the intersections of race, class, and gender in sexual violence responses (Bevacqua, 2000; INCITE!, 2006). Unfortunately, few college activists followed this intersectional approach and anchored their work in an identity-neutral or woman-only perspective (e.g., Bohmer & Parrot, 1993), resulting in less than inclusive efforts to address sexual violence on campus. For example, texts written in the 1990s about sexual violence on college campuses rarely examined race, class, or sexual orientation in relationship to sexual violence (see Bohmer & Parrot, 1993; Warshaw, 1994).

On college campuses, scholars, educators, and policymakers have historically approached sexual violence from a power-neutral perspective, failing to consider social identities other than woman when examining sexual violence (e.g., Bohmer & Parrot, 1993). Using a power- and identity-neutral lens results in the uncritical centering of cisgender, white, heterosexual women in sexual violence prevention and response on campuses. For example, prevention programs have historically focused on teaching women to fear a stereotypical perpetrator (often men of color) and to be aware of their surroundings rather than highlighting the reality that most sexual violence happens between two people who know each other and may happen in same-sex relationships as well as heterosexual ones. Additionally, scholars researching sexual violence rarely examine experiences of people other than cisgender, heterosexual, white women (see Chapter 1).

Social Identities and Campus Activism

Power, privilege, and identity significantly influence the experiences and strategies of campus-based activists (Rhoads, 1997). Students of color, women, queer and trans* students, and poor students frequently engage in activism related to one of their subordinated identities (Rhoads, 1997) but often do not identify with the term *activist*. Students who engage in social change related to a subordinated identity often consider their work a burden or a strategy for survival (Linder & Rodriguez, 2012) rather than activism, leadership, or cocurricular activities. For example, students involved in racial justice initiatives on campus rarely discuss their experiences as a form of leadership; rather, they minimize or even hide their experience with activism when applying for jobs to minimize their chances of being seen as a troublemaker in the workplace. Students organizing on issues directly affecting them (e.g., identity politics) are frequently considered rabble-rousers and administrators discuss ways to manage them rather than address the issues students raise (e.g., White, 2013).

Conversely, administrators and educators may herald students who engage in activism not directly tied to the university as good leaders. For example, students who participate in international service or mission work or volunteer at a local soup kitchen receive university resources, support, and recognition. Students may engage in this type of service as a result of socialization in their dominant identities such as white, middle or upper class, or Christian, but it is rarely named as such because these are dominant, often normalized and invisible, identities. This kind of service or activism does not directly affect the university's policies and practices, yet it benefits the university by demonstrating engagement on the part of its students (Linder, 2015).

Students from privileged backgrounds may have access to time and resources their less privileged peers do not have (Altbach, 1989; Broadhurst, 2014). For example, students from economically privileged families may not need to hold jobs while they are students, resulting in more time for them to organize and participate in activism. Students from privileged backgrounds frequently have access to networks of policymakers and knowledge about the ways things work, resulting in them spending less time figuring out bureaucracy and more time addressing issues of concern (Altbach, 1989; Linder, 2015).

Social identities and the power associated with them also results in some activists failing to consider an intersectional perspective related to their activism. For example, heterosexual cisgender white women may fail to consider homophobia, transphobia, and racism in sexual assault activism because they have not had to consciously consider those factors in their own experiences.

Similarly, consequences of traditional forms of activism, such as arrests for civil disobedience, are different for students from a variety of populations. The monetary costs of an arrest have differential impacts on students with fewer financial resources. Similarly, the consequences for an arrest may be significantly different for white students compared to students of color. Any sort of a criminal record has significant implications for the future employment of students of color as documented by studies indicating that people of color without a criminal record are less likely to be hired than a white person with a criminal record (Ross, 2014). Finally, queer and trans* students face significantly more dangerous conditions in jail cells than heterosexual and cisgender students. Power and privilege associated with identity has significant implications for the ways students engage in various forms of activism, and failing to acknowledge this privilege results in severing of movements because some activists do not feel welcome or included in certain activist spaces. For example, if sexual violence activists are not conscious of racism, some activists of color may not feel comfortable attending events, resulting in less than effective organizing because some people are not represented in the work.

Social Media and Activism

Given that consequences of traditional activism are different for different populations, social media has become an important counterspace for identity-based activism (Bonilla & Rosa, 2015; Yang, 2007), including sexual assault activists (Linder, Myers, Riggle, & Lacy, 2016). Online tools amplify voices of minoritized people historically ignored by mainstream media (Bonilla & Rosa, 2015) and provide a space for minoritized people to come together to share stories, connect, and begin to heal from their experiences with trauma (Conley, 2014).

Some cynics argue that online activism does not translate to *real* activism. They maintain that "slacktivism" (Glenn, 2015) allows people to demonstrate awareness of social and political issues online without actually engaging in action (Fatkin & Lansdown, 2015). Other scholars argue online and offline engagement intersect; they do not exist in isolation from one another (Bonilla & Rosa, 2015; Fatkin & Lansdown, 2015; Nielsen, 2013). In fact, most activists who use social media consider it a "mundane internet tool" (Nielsen, 2013, p. 173). Social media is a part of many people's everyday experiences, a tool activists use for a variety of reasons including activism. Those who argue online activism is slacktivism fail to consider ways online activism contributes to the increased visibility of minoritized communities and provides unique opportunities for connection and solidarity (Bonilla & Rosa, 2015).

Globally, feminists have used social media to address issues of oppression and violence. For example, women in South Africa raised money via social media for the Saartjie Baartman Centre for Women and Children as it faced significant financial difficulties (Mudavanhu & Radloff, 2013). Similarly, feminists in Spain raised awareness about interpersonal violence using social media to "organize direct actions, share information and resources, and coordinate activities" (Puente, 2011, p. 335). In Egypt, feminists developed HarassMap, a technological tool designed to "undermine the climate of social acceptability for sexual harassers" (Peuchaud, 2014, p. i115) by documenting stories of harassment and assault. Feminists in other North African countries also use HarassMap to "detail the brutality and frequency of sexual harassment" (Skalli, 2014, p. 245).

In the United States, feminists have harnessed the power of social media to raise awareness about issues of violence against women. Women of color, specifically, have used social media as a counterspace to share stories about violence and raise awareness about the ways white feminists frequently ignore their unique experiences with violence. Building on Collins's (2000) work highlighting the significance of "safe spaces" (p. 98) for Black feminists to come together to "contest the ideologies that perpetuate the objectification and oppression of Black women" (Rapp, Button, Fleury-Steiner, & Fleury-Steiner, 2010, p. 249), Black women have used online environments to grieve the loss of community members and to "authenticate their voices" (Rapp et al., 2010, p. 249). Similarly, hashtags created by Black feminists contribute to a sense of solidarity by attempting to "counteract the emotional and psychological trauma of marginalization, colonization, and essentially death" (Conley, 2014, p. 1112). For example, Black feminists created #RememberingRenisha, #IStandWithJada, and #WhyWeCantWait on Twitter, making those virtual spaces places for Black women to come together in solidarity to tell the stories of Black women ignored by media and some feminist and Black civil rights organizations (Conley, 2014; Rapp et al., 2010; Williams, 2015). Students on college campuses have used social media to establish community and connect with activists on other campuses attempting to address similar issues. For example, students across the country united using #carrythatweight as a place to raise awareness about university responses to sexual violence (Hess, 2014).

Building on the framework of social media as a counterspace for identity-based activism, we use Internet-related ethnography (Postill & Pink, 2012) to examine the strategies of CSVAs and the role of social media in sexual violence activism. Specifically, we explore the influence of power and privilege on the strategies of CSVAs and provide implications for educators striving to support CSVAs.

Methodology

We employed Internet-related ethnography (Postill & Pink, 2012) to examine sexual assault activism and the role of social media in activism. The research questions for this study were: What are the strategies of campus sexual assault activists? and What role did social media play in campus sexual assault activism?

Ethnography

Ethnographic researchers engage in data collection over a prolonged period of time, attempting to understand a culture of interest or a phenomenon (Wolcott, 2008). Internet-related ethnography allows researchers to use ethnography in online spaces to examine the role of technology in the development of communities and processes (Postill & Pink, 2012). Researchers using Internet-related ethnography integrate traditional forms of data collection, such as interviews, with new forms of data collection, such as participating in online communities.

Data Collection

Members of this research team include four cisgender women with current or previous experiences working in campus-based women's centers supporting sexual violence survivors and activists. Three researchers identify as white and one as Black; two identify as queer and two as straight. We possess educational privilege as all of us hold master's degrees in student affairs and higher education, one has a doctoral degree, and two are in doctoral programs in higher education and student affairs.

Guided by Postill and Pink's (2012) strategy of "living part of one's life on the Internet, keeping up-to-date and participating and collaborating in social media discussions" (p. 128), each of us followed a variety of conversations about sexual violence online. We followed the Know Your IX Facebook Group and several hashtags on Twitter, including #survivorprivilege, #RapeCultureIsWhen, and #KnowYourIX. We observed Tumblr and Instagram posts when Facebook and Twitter directed us there. Additionally, we collected clipped newspaper articles, screenshots of text message exchanges between members of the research team, reflections about trending topics on Twitter and Facebook, notes about sexual assault–related programs and events we attended on our campuses and in our communities, and researcher reflections immediately after interviews with activist survivors in a shared electronic notebook. The notebook included 304 notes collected over a period of eight months.

We identified participants by reviewing articles from national news sources (e.g., *The Chronicle of Higher Education, New York Times*, and *Huffington Post*) and compiling a list of student activists featured in those articles. We contacted potential participants through various forms of social media, posted a call for participants on Facebook and Twitter, and sent a call for participants to an electronic mailing list of staff at a women's center. In the e-mail sent to the electronic mailing list, we sought "current or recent students engaged in sexual assault activism" and "who use social media." After each interview, we asked participants to share the call for participants with their networks, resulting in a snowball sample. We interviewed 23 campus activists using Skype or Google Hangouts.

Participants

We interviewed 23 activists involved with campus sexual assault activism on national and local levels in the United States. Participants included current undergraduate students (11), current graduate students (2), and recent alumni (10) and ranged in age from 19 to 37, with 16 participants between the ages of 19 and 24. Five participants attended college in the southeastern region of the United States, five in the mid-Atlantic, four in the West, two in the Mountain states, three in the Midwest, three in the Northeast, and one in the Northwest. Fourteen participants attended public institutions, including one community college; nine attended private institutions. Of the 23 participants, 3 identified as men, 20 as women, and none as transgender. Ten activists identified as white, six as Asian, five as multiracial, two as Latina, and no one identified as African American or Native American. Fifteen participants identified as heterosexual, six as queer, one as bisexual, and one participant preferred not to answer.

Data Analysis

Data analysis included a three-cycle coding process (Saldaña, 2009) in which each transcript was read by at least two researchers. In the first cycle of coding, we reviewed the transcripts, making note of initial codes relevant to the research questions. In the second cycle of analysis, we discussed the initial codes generated and developed a list of common codes, collapsed by similarity and overlap from the first round, then reread and recoded the transcripts using the agreed-on codes. Finally, in the third cycle, we regrouped the codes into overarching themes (Saldaña, 2009).

Findings

CSVAs engage in a variety of strategies to address sexual violence on college campuses and frequently use social media as a tool for engaging in activism. Some CSVAs also grapple with the nuances of power, privilege, and oppression as related to activism. In this section, we explore the strategies of CSVAs, including the role of social media. We also describe ways some students intentionally think about power and privilege in their activism, resulting in more nuanced approaches to sexual violence prevention and response.

Strategies of Activists

CSVAs in this study employed a variety of strategies to raise awareness about sexual violence on college campuses. Specifically, activists used social media to engage in awareness-raising, to connect with other activists, to expand the movement beyond the scope of their invetigation, and to intentionally shape messages about sexual violence.

Awareness-raising. Activists highlighted the significance of raising awareness about issues of sexual violence and the role social media played in this awareness-raising. Specifically, activists described posting survivors' stories and articles about campus sexual violence on social media accounts including Facebook and Twitter. Activists used Facebook and Twitter to share information about campus events and encourage people to attend protests and rallies and sign petitions. Additionally, participants discussed using their Instagram accounts to post pictures of events as they were happening and to raise awareness by addressing issues of sexual violence in captions of their everyday photos. For example, Gina shared how she used a space that was designed for one purpose for another purpose. She used the popular hashtag #OOTD (outfit of the day) to post information about sexual violence against American Indian women. She explained how the activism project worked: "You post [a picture] but your caption is completely unrelated to the outfit. It has to do with social justice." She explained that "because it's eye-catching . . . hopefully they'll read the caption and be like, 'Oh, I learned something today.'"

Similarly, Louisa said she noticed the ways her friends began to follow and pay attention to specific sexual violence–related social media after a post she made on her personal page, demonstrating to her the effectiveness of sharing through her personal social media accounts:

> Since I started with [the group] on Twitter, I've seen my own circle on Twitter change, and I have professors now on my Twitter and they are actually willing to retweet stuff that I share. . . . I think my favorite part of doing the [organization's] page is seeing my own personal friends start following them, especially when they don't even know that I'm in charge of that page.

Participants described using social media as a tool for activism rather than as the actual activism (Nielsen, 2013). Several activists discussed the significance of reaching people who otherwise might not be reached through social media including Facebook, Twitter, and Instagram by regularly posting articles about sexual violence in places they already interacted with in social media. Further, activists described using social media to connect with other activists.

Connecting with other activists. Participants used social media to connect with activists on other campuses. Several activists in our study mentioned a private Facebook group called IX Network, which had more than 900 members, providing a space for campus activists to come together to share challenges and strategies. We did not observe this group because it was private and we did not have permission to observe private groups; however, activists described a sense of solidarity from connecting with other activists on other campuses through participation in this Facebook group. Several activists reflected on the reality that connecting with others via social media allowed them to keep moving forward and engaging in activism when they otherwise felt exhausted. Lynn explained,

> There's just a wonderful solidarity of knowing that you're not alone . . . and as painful as it is to find other people who have been through what you've been through, there is an incredible level of empowerment that comes from knowing that somebody else has that experience.

Sally discussed the idea that activists often felt as though they were working in isolation, but social media provided an avenue for them to connect with each other:

> So when a group at [the institution] was trying to put a lot of work into something, they would get kind of far and they would all graduate and then the administration would drop it. So now we have this massive network of people saying, "Me too, the same issues are existing, this is what's happening for us, this is what's working, this is what's not."

Consistent with previous research highlighting the significance of online spaces as sites of solidarity and healing (Bonilla & Rosa, 2015; Conley, 2014), participants in this study described the importance of connecting with other activists. Forming national networks allowed activists to share ideas with each other, find emotional support to keep working, and strategically formulate messages about sexual violence, which we discuss in the next section.

Intentionally shaping messages. Activists also described intentionally shaping messages to focus on agency rather than victimhood and to ensure that people understood sexual violence is a national issue, not something happening on individual campuses. For example, because of the connections that activists built with each other in online spaces, they worked to shift the framework about sexual violence on college campuses, as one participant said, from an individual issue to a "national epidemic." Activists sought to push policymakers to address sexual violence from a systemic perspective, rather than an individual perspective. Lynn explained,

> Rather than framing it about victimhood, which a lot of it has before, the conversation is now about empowerment . . . and taking actions. It's not about whose case is worse, whose case is more egregious, who has really been treated the worst. It's about the fact that no matter what has happened, the connection is it's a national epidemic.

Framing issues of sexual violence on college campuses as an epidemic pushed policymakers to address sexual violence through more closely monitoring violations of Title IX of the 1972 Education Amendments and introducing national and state legislation to hold colleges and universities accountable for addressing sexual violence.

Another strategy for intentionally framing messages about sexual violence included activists specifically focusing on themselves as activists, not victims, as Lynn previously stated. Although some activists explicitly identified as survivors of sexual violence, not all participants disclosed a personal experience with sexual violence. Participants described the media's obsession with knowing the intimate details of sexual violence, which, for them, led to the public's making judgments about what kind of assault was real assault. Many of the activists refused to share their specific stories about sexual violence, instead focusing on the ways they were working to raise awareness about sexual violence and framing themselves as activists, not victims. This strategy also led activists to consider sharing and disclosing their privileged and marginalized identities as a means to moving their activism forward.

Activists' Intersecting Identities

Although activists worked to shift the framework informing coverage of sexual violence in the national media from victim to activist, they also made critical decisions related to naming and claiming their own social identities within this framework. Activists discussed intersectionality and how navigating identities such as gender, race, class, and disability influenced their activism. For example, some participants shared their decisions of either intentionally coming out or not coming out as queer identified.

Peter, who was assaulted by a man, shared his realization that his coming forward as a survivor and activist meant he "was going to [have] to claim a queer identity and there was no way around it." Conversely, Lynn reflected that her experience as a queer woman did not correlate with her identity as a survivor. She shared, "I wasn't raped by a woman. I was raped by a white man. . . . This is not about sexuality. Being queer did not make me more susceptible." Unlike Peter, Lynn felt that she wasn't "the queer person to talk about" the experience of lesbian, gay, bisexual, transgender, or queer sexual assault as she crafted her activist messages related to sexual assault. She continued, "And I think a lot of us don't come out publicly because we don't want to be like, 'Oh, look at all these lesbians.'" While not disclosing her queer sexual identity was purposeful, Lynn reflected on the impact this had on the overall campus sexual assault movement as appearing very white and very heterosexual. "We cannot be what they want us to be, [but] I will say, most of us are not heterosexual."

Some participants were clear about the ways their identities provided them with access and privilege in particular settings, especially related to legal and political issues. For example, Peter discussed ways he "played" with his identities to access certain spaces, for example, "being able to wear a suit and be straight passing, take off my nail polish, hide my earings, things like that has [sic] allowed me access to spaces especially in terms of law making, in terms of spaces that are really dominated by the male establishment."

Similarly, Chad, who is mixed race but often perceived as white, acknowledged the privilege associated with being "one who appears to be white." He explained that his ability to maintain his activism as a male survivor and have enough support from others is connected to "the social capital that comes with being white, male, from an upper-middle-class background, and having gone to Ivy League universities." Lynn also understood the importance of crafting social capital for herself. Despite many of her fellow activists pushing her to be more vocal about some of her marginalized identities, she purposely stuck to a message absent of subordinated identities. She explained, "I didn't make it a point to talk about my sexuality. . . . And I definitely didn't make it a purpose to say I had PTSD [post-traumatic stress disorder] and I was disabled. You know, I was just like, I didn't use these words." Although participants did not discuss the long-term consequences of masking salient social identities, they did understand the short-term benefits of hiding or minimizing particular aspects of their identities, a strategy not available to all of their peers, especially those who could not hide identities.

Wrestling With Identity, Intersectionality, and Power

Through this research, we wanted to better understand how activists thought about and navigated power associated with identity. Some participants described complex understandings of intersectionality, including the influence of social identity power and privilege in sexual violence movements. Several participants noted the ways sexual violence has been framed in some mainstream media outlets as an issue affecting a very specific population of students—white heterosexual women. Additionally, some participants discussed tension in the movement related to identity politics and people not understanding the complexity of identity in sexual violence–related activism.

Power and privilege in institutions. Peter observed that educators, policymakers, and media outlets tend to center "pretty, white, skinny women who look like they come from the upper middle class who go to an elite school" in sexual assault prevention and response initiatives on college campuses. He described this as a "white saviorhood complex," in which media outlets frequently cater toward the "sellable" story centering white, pretty, "good girls" as more "savable" than others. Peter gave specific examples from his time as an activist that illustrated the challenges of mainstream media's representation of sexual violence. Representatives from more than one national media outlet refused to cover his story and the stories of women of color in their work because the stories were "too 'alternative.'" He continued, sharing that filmmakers creating a documentary about sexual violence "only interviewed our two youngest, whitest, prettiest [female] individuals" involved with an organization that had a high number of men and women of color survivors. From these experiences he concluded,

> There's definitely a racist and sexist element going on and it's very much that news outlets are looking for stories of people that they can save, that they feel that they can save and also that they have a desire to save. And so that means that someone who is appealing to a demographic, so that's straight-presenting white cisgender women who look like they come from upper middle class.

Similarly, Deb shared that "the struggle has been how to balance what we know with what [the public understands] because if you go on CNN and start talking about intersectionality people are going to turn [off] the TV." Likewise, Gina said that stories of women of color and trans* women "are told by people who don't have a right to tell them" in mainstream media and are frequently being misrepresented or appropriated.

In the context of activism taking place specifically on college campuses, participants wrestled with the complexities between those who were willing and unwilling to address sexual assault with an intersectional lens. For example, Lory shared that her campus's task force connected to sexual assault found it challenging to focus on queer women and women of color as survivors. She went on to say, "That's something people don't want to talk about. They don't want to address . . . race or sexuality." Tina and Ariel also shared similar experiences when working with upper-level administrators on their campuses. Tina reflected, "I think what really hit me" when talking and working with many of the people in administration was that "the real power behind all of it tends to be straight white men" who most likely "haven't had experience creating a safe environment." Similarly, Ariel spoke of a "generation gap between the stereotypical old white male that's a college administrator" and the college activists such as herself who grew up being more exposed to or at least aware of sexual assault. She went on to say that "he just didn't get it." In addition to recognizing intersectional oppression in institutions, participants described challenges with helping people understand the significance of intersectionality in interpersonal relationships.

Intersectionality and tension among activists. In addition to wrestling with identity and power with people and systems outside the movement, activists shared ways identity politics and a disparity of understanding or awareness about intersectionality created tension with each other from within the movement. Many student activists consider their work a form of survival (Linder & Rodriguez, 2012). Although many of the participants were working on behalf of their personal experience and identity connected to sexual violence, not all of them felt the same responsibility to do their activist work from an intersectional approach, and participants demonstrated varying levels of understanding intersectionality. Vee, a queer woman of color, said, "Intersectionality really informs what I do because it pushes me to do better and go outside my comfort zone. And, it also pushes me to expect that of others who are in the movement." She explained that when she sees white people always featured in media "it makes [her] feel like [she doesn't] belong," and that she really knows "what it feels like to be invisiblized or to feel like really marginalized. And I don't want that to happen to anyone."

Other activists noted the importance of incorporating intersectionality into their activism work, but without personal identities connected to marginalized experiences of race, sexual orientation, or gender, they felt incapable of moving forward on a path of understanding. Tina expressed concern about the lack of diversity in her activist student group:

> How do we make sure that it's not just the loudest voices or the most obvious voices that are having a say in what's happening and how do we make sure that, like, we're incorporating groups that are relatively marginalized here?

Another participant, Ariel, explained her concern about not understanding or centering marginalized experiences because of her own privileged identities. "I'm cisgender heterosexual white female, middle class. I am all of those things, and sometimes I'm like just give me something that's not normal. I'm the definition of average," she said.

The continuum on which participants found themselves related to their understanding and awareness of intersectionality was also evident on social media. Although social media has served as a critical space for activists in creating counterspaces (Bonilla & Rosa, 2015; Conley, 2014), it also became a location for conflict. Amanda reflected on being a part of one of the closed Facebook groups as she watched the "negotiations of power and in terms of who can speak and who can't speak." Amanda acknowledged the role of social identities in these power negotiations, recognizing that most people who spoke up in this group were white women at elite institutions who received significant media coverage. She said that "there were some people who felt like their voices weren't being heard" and that a "big blowup" happened when "some women of color were coming in and saying that their voices weren't heard and they wanted intersectionality to be considered." Demonstrating a less nuanced understanding of intersectionality, Deb minimized these negotiations when she discussed the blowup by saying that in "a group of 800 people who have survived something awful who haven't been listened to" by their institution, the media, police, friends, and family, "they're going to take it out on the people where they feel like they can because they're not being heard anywhere else."

The role of social identities, power, privilege, and intersectionality in activism cannot be overstated. Although most activists had at least some awareness of the significance of power in their work as activists, they reflected the mainstream feminist movement of essentializing and minimizing identities other than woman when it came to acting on and incorporating an intersectional framework in their sexual violence activism. Consistent with earlier sexual violence activism, participants in this study frequently failed to consider identity in their work, which results in centering on people with dominant identities: white cisgender heterosexual women from middle-class backgrounds. Even participants with multiple marginalized identities often minimized the significance of oppression in their work as activists. Although some activists consistently challenged their peers to consider multiple and intersecting identities in their work, most had a cursory understanding and failed to address the complexities of oppression in their work.

Implications and Strategies

Campus-based activists reflect the complexities of addressing power and privilege in larger social movements. Although well intentioned, many activists become narrowly focused on issues related to their personal identities when engaging in activism. Additionally, activists demonstrated a continuum of awareness related to power, privilege, and oppression in sexual violence activism. For example, some activists clearly understood and attempted to incorporate nuanced perspectives about gender, race, sexual orientation, class, and immigration status in their work; others preferred to minimize those differences, focusing instead on the issue of sexual violence. Failing to acknowledge and address intersections of oppression based on racism, classism, sexism, homophobia, and imperialism results in ineffective strategies for addressing sexual violence. Given that rates of sexual violence on college campuses have not changed in 60 years (Adams-Curtis & Forbes, 2004), educators, activists, and policymakers must do something differently to effectively address sexual violence. Educators supporting student activists on college campuses must better understand the role of power and privilege in social identity movements and challenge and support students as they also explore this complexity.

Encourage and Support Coalition Building

A resurgence of campus-based activism provides unique opportunities for organizing across identities and issues. Racial justice activists and campus sexual violence activists appear to be working toward a common goal: socially just campuses allowing all students access to an education. Although the movements have similar goals, it appears the activists in these movements are working parallel to each other rather than with each other. Racial justice movements have been critiqued for failing to address sexism and homophobia (Rapp et al., 2010) just as sexual violence movements have been critiqued for failing to address racism and cisgenderism (INCITE!, 2006). What might be different if sexual violence and racial justice activists came together and shared expertise, resources, and perspectives? By sharing experiences and strategies, sexual violence and racial justice activists may learn to adopt more inclusive strategies to advance both movements. Sexual violence activists may become more aware of ways racism influences sexual violence, including problems with the heavy legal focus on reform, and racial justice activists may become more aware of ways sexism influences how some people experience racism.

Current student activists would likely benefit from working in conjunction with community-based sexual violence activists with a strong intersectional focus. INCITE! Women of Color Against Violence, established in the late 1990s, provides significant resources for addressing sexual violence at the intersection of racism, classism, sexism, and imperialism (see www.incite-national.org). Student activists may also be well suited to engage in more intergenerational activism. Current activists may learn from the mistakes of previous activists and benefit from better understanding of histories of sexual violence activism. For example, if current students were to talk with activists in the 1970s who also advocated for tough-on-crime legislation similar to what some activists today are advocating, they might learn some of the limitations of this approach and consider some more nuanced approaches to legislation, crime, and sexual violence.

Provide Room and Support for Development

Current student activists have created significant change locally and nationally, especially related to awareness about sexual violence on college campuses. However, many of these activists are also still navigating complexities of their own identity. Although people negotiate identity for a lifetime, college students, specifically, are in a heightened time of identity development and negotiation (Patton, Renn, Guido, & Quaye, 2016). Educators must provide spaces for students to explore these identities, examining the ways they experience privilege and oppression in their identities. In addition to providing the space for students to explore this, especially in relation to their survivor or activist identities, educators must continue to do this work for themselves. Ongoing reflection and self-awareness contributes to educators being better positioned to support students negotiating complexities of identities. Further, many students have a more nuanced understanding of intersectionality from their lived experiences than some educators do; educators must be open to listening to and learning from students.

In addition to providing space for students to explore identity, educators must work to interrupt identity and power-neutral approaches to sexual violence. Student activists cannot be the only ones addressing sexual violence from a complex, critical, and nuanced perspective. When educators observe campus policy or practice that approaches sexual violence as an issue affecting only white cisgender heterosexual women, they must interrupt and address this with their colleagues.

Use Social Media as a Tool

As exemplified in the literature review and study findings shared in this chapter, activists who use social media can engage in consciousness-raising, create connections, and intentionally shape messages for media and additional audiences. Educators may also use social media to produce similar results related to sexual violence on college campuses. Some educators may feel cautious about using social media to interact with students, citing reasons such as privacy, boundaries, or being unfamiliar with certain social media platforms. Yet, calling to mind the common phrase used among student affairs professionals of "meeting students where they are," it is important for educators to meet CSVAs where they are on social media.

Following groups such as Know Your IX (knowyourix.org), End Rape on Campus (endrapeoncampus.org), or current activists in the movement can be an excellent way for educators to continue their own education and awareness about campus-based sexual violence issues as well as the activism connected to the issue. By reading similar articles or following the same popular hashtags as CSVAs, educators can engage in issues of sexual violence from a more student-based perspective. Using social media to increase personal awareness may also help educators shape conversations and build connections offline with CSVAs and other survivors of sexual violence. Just as important, educators may use their voice on social media to fill in gaps or help model ways students can practice more power-conscious and intersectional activism by sharing articles and resources that address these concerns.

Conclusion

Student activists approach sexual violence activism with passion, heart, and commitment. Some of these activists also have a strong understanding of intersectionality and power and their relationship to sexual violence; some do not. As shown by previous activism in sexual violence prevention and response, a failure to approach sexual violence at the intersections of racism, classism, homophobia, sexism, genderism, and nationalism will result in continued high rates of sexual violence. Supporting campus-based activists to better understand and address power in activism will contribute to more inclusive movements and, ultimately, a reduction in the prevalence of sexual violence.

References

Adams-Curtis, L. E., & Forbes, G. B. (2004). College women's experiences of sexual coercion: A review of cultural, perpetrator, victim, and situational violence. *Trauma, Violence, & Abuse, 5*, 91–122.

Altbach, P. G. (1989). Perspectives on political student activism. *Comparative Education, 25*(1), 97–110.

Astin, A. W., Astin, H. S., Bayer, A. E., and Bisconti, A. S. (1975). *The power of protest*. San Francisco, CA: Jossey-Bass.

Bevacqua, M. (2000). *Rape on the public agenda: Feminism and the politics of sexual assault*. Boston, MA: Northeastern University Press.

Bohmer, C., & Parrot, A. (1993). *Sexual assault on campus: The problem and the solution*. New York, NY: Lexington Books.

Bonilla, Y., & Rosa, J. (2015). #Ferguson: Digital protest, hashtag ethnography, and the racial politics of social media in the United States. *American Ethnologist, 42*(1), 4–17. doi:10.1111/amet.12112

Broadhurst, C. J. (2014). Campus activism in the 21st century: A historical framing. *New Directions for Higher Education, 167*, 3–15.

Collins, P. H. (2000). *Black feminist thought: Knowledge, consciousness, and the politics of empowerment.* New York, NY: Routledge.

Conley, T. L. (2014). From #RenishaMcBride to #RememberingRenisha: Locating our stories and finding justice. *Feminist Media Studies, 14*, 1111–1113. doi:10.1080/14680777.2014.975474

Corrigan, R. (2013). *Up against a wall.* New York: New York University Press.

Fatkin, J., & Lansdown, T. C. (2015). Prosocial media in action. *Computers in Human Behavior, 48*, 581–586.

Freedman, E. B. (2013). *Redefining rape: Sexual violence in the era of suffrage and segregation.* Cambridge, MA: Harvard University Press.

Giddings, P. (2007). *When and where I enter: The impact of Black women on race and sex in America.* New York, NY: HarperCollins.

Glenn, C. L. (2015). Activism or "slacktivism?": Digital media and organizing for social change. *Communication Teacher, 29*(2), 81–85.

Hess, A. (2014, October 30). *Emma Sulkowicz inspired students across the country to carry their mattresses. Now what?* Retrieved from www.slate.com/blogs/xx_factor/2014/10/30/carry_that_weight_emma_sulkowicz_s_mattress_becomes_a_national_movement.html

INCITE! Women of Color Against Violence. (Ed.). (2006). *The color of violence: The INCITE! anthology.* Boston, MA: South End Press.

Linder, C. (2015, November). *An intersectional approach to supporting student activists.* Paper presented at the annual meeting of the Association for the Study of Higher Education, Denver, CO.

Linder, C., Myers, J. S., Riggle, C., & Lacy, M. (in press). From margins to mainstream: Social media as a tool for campus sexual violence activism. *Journal of Diversity in Higher Education.*

Linder, C., & Rodriguez, K. (2012). Learning from the experiences of self-identified women of color activists. *Journal of College Student Development, 53*, 383–398.

McGuire, D. L. (2010). *At the dark end of the street: Black women, rape and resistance—a new history of the civil rights movement from Rosa Parks to the rise of Black power.* New York, NY: Random House.

Mudavanhu, S., & Radloff, J. (2013). Taking feminist activism online: Reflections on the "Keep Saartjie Baartman Centre Open" e-campaign. *Gender & Development, 21*, 327–341. doi:10.1080/13552074.2013.802881

Nielsen, R. K. (2013). Mundane Internet tools, the risk of exclusion, and reflexive movements—Occupy Wall Street and political uses of digital networked technologies. *Sociological Quarterly, 54*, 159–228.

Patton, L. D., Renn, K. A., Guido, F. M., & Quaye, S. J. (2016). *Student development in college: Theory, research, and practice* (3rd ed.). San Francisco, CA: Jossey-Bass.

Peuchaud, S. (2014). Social media activism and Egyptians' use of social media to combat sexual violence: An HiAPcase study. *Health Promotions International, 29*(Suppl. 1), i113–i120. doi:10.1093/heapro/dau046

Postill, J., & Pink, S. (2012). Social media ethnography: The digital researcher in a messy web. *Media International Australia, 145*, 123–134.

Puente, S. N. (2011). Feminist cyberactivism: Violence against women, Internet politics, and Spanish feminist praxis online. *Continuum: Journal of Media & Cultural Studies, 25*, 333–346.

Rapp, L., Button, D. M., Fleury-Steiner, B., & Fleury-Steiner, R. (2010). The Internet as a tool for Black feminist activism: Lessons from an online antirape protest. *Feminist Criminology, 5*, 244–262. doi:10.1177/1557085110371634

Rhoads, R. A. (1997). Interpreting identity politics: The educational challenge of contemporary student activism. *Journal of College Student Development, 38*, 508–519.

Rhoads, R. A. (1998). *Freedom's web: Student activism in an age of cultural diversity.* Baltimore, MD: Johns Hopkins University Press.

Ross, J. (2014, May 27). African-Americans with college degrees are twice as likely to be unemployed as other graduates. *National Journal.* Retrieved from www .nationaljournal.com/next-america/education/african-americans-with-college-degrees-are-twice-as-likely-to-be-unemployed-as-other-graduates-20140527

Saldaña, J. (2009). *The coding manual for qualitative research.* Thousand Oaks, CA: SAGE.

Skalli, L. H. (2014). Young women and social media against sexual harassment in North Africa. *Journal of North African Studies, 19*, 244–258.

Title IX of the Education Amendments, 20 U.S.C. §1681 et seq. (1972).

Warshaw, R. (1994). *I never called it rape: The Ms. Report on recognizing, fighting, and surviving date and acquaintance rape.* New York, NY: HarperCollins.

White, L. (2013). *Protests, activism, and student riots.* Paper presented at the annual Conference on Legal Issues in Higher Education, University of Vermont, Burlington. Retrieved from www.forstudentpower.org/sites/default/files/protestsactivistsriots.pdf

Williams, S. (2015). Digital defense: Black feminists resist violence with hashtag activism. *Feminist Media Studies, 15*, 341–344. doi:10.1080/14680777.2015.1 008744

Wolcott, H. F. (2008). *Ethnography: A way of seeing.* Lanham, MD: AltaMira Press.

Wong, A. (2015, May 21). The renaissance of student activism. *Atlantic.* Retrieved from www.theatlantic.com/education/archive/2015/05/the-renaissance-of-student-activism/393749

Yang, K. W. (2007). Organizing MySpace: Youth walkouts, pleasure, politics, and new media. *Educational Foundations, 21*(1/2), 9–28.

AN EMPOWERMENT-BASED MODEL OF SEXUAL VIOLENCE INTERVENTION AND PREVENTION ON CAMPUS

Naddia Cherre Palacios and Karla L. Aguilar

This chapter explores the nuances of sexual violence intervention and prevention on college campuses. We offer strategies and provide insight into how educators on college campuses may respond to the needs of those who have experienced sexual violence prior to or during their college years. We do not claim to have all the solutions or complete answers to every component of campus sexual violence, but we attempt to provide insight into improving support for survivors and empowering community members to become change agents in their campus environment. In this chapter, we define *sexual violence* as any unwanted sexual experience or unwanted sexual contact. For the purposes of responding comprehensively to gender-based violence, sexual violence here also encompasses responses and prevention related to intimate partner violence (dating violence), stalking, and other forms of sexual harassment. Gaining an understanding of the differing types of sexual violence and how they manifest themselves on specific campuses is essential to educating and programming on this issue.

We also explore the differences, similarities, and interactions among sexual violence intervention, advocacy, prevention, and education. We argue that educators and policymakers must understand the differences between an advocacy and prevention model and the need to implement both separately, simultaneously, and in association with one another. Sexual violence intervention and advocacy focus on exploring practices and frameworks that respond to survivors' immediate needs and facilitate the healing, recovery, and empowerment process. This may include responses to immediate medical care, navigation through on- and off-campus systems, and elaboration on trauma-informed and holistic advocacy frameworks that expand beyond students' college experience. Primary prevention and education efforts highlight practices that mediate and prevent the victimization and perpetration of sexual violence before it happens.

Prior to delving deeper into this chapter, we find it necessary to position ourselves in this work. Naddia Palacios oversees advocacy and intervention services at a large public state institution in Southern California. Naddia also works closely with other large institutions, developing their system-wide advocacy approaches. Karla Aguilar oversees advocacy and prevention education programs at a small, private liberal arts college and volunteers as a community advocate at a local rape crisis center. We are both certified sexual violence and domestic violence counselor advocates and have worked extensively in developing and implementing prevention education programs, training, and curricula. When used intentionally, we believe certification can serve as a tool to allow community members to become certified sexual violence counselors without having to become psychologists. We both worked to implement the Office of Violence Against Women Grant to Reduce Sexual Violence, Domestic Violence, Dating Violence, and Stalking on Campus Program aimed at providing technical assistance in coordinated community responses, prevention education material, and judicial and policy and campus security coordination to institutions of higher education. We find solidarity with other sexual violence grassroots movements, antioppression collectives, advocates and organizers, pioneers, experts, and leaders in the campus sexual violence movement. Alongside our community, we are gradually working toward regulating and responding to sharing college institutionalized practices in which many people facilitate and create the avenues necessary for coordination and collaboration among involved stakeholders (Klein & Seshadri, 2016).

Empowerment-Based Advocacy on College Campuses

Some institutions have employed long-standing, designated staff members to provide sexual violence advocacy services to the campus community. For instance, University of California, San Diego founded its Sexual Assault Resource Center in 1987; University of Michigan founded its Sexual Assault Prevention and Awareness Center in 1986; and Indiana University's Sexual

Assault Crisis Services was founded more than 20 years ago. Although these resources are not new to the college campus, campus staff and offices dedicated to sexual violence advocacy have become an increasingly standard practice within the past two years. In April 2014 the federal government began to encourage higher education institutions to hire or designate someone who can provide confidential advocacy services on campus (White House, 2014). As practitioners and advocates, we have seen a drastic increase in the number and variety of professionals charged with addressing sexual violence across institutions, which has resulted in heightened media and governmental attention to sexual violence on the college campus.

Often, these professionals do not have direct or previous experience understanding and working with the complexities of sexual violence on the college campus. They may have previously worked in off-campus settings as counselors, psychologists, social workers, and psychiatrists but have little to no previous experience working with sexual violence in a college setting. Although hiring knowledgeable advocates from any realm of society to fill these positions has many pros (e.g., they hold specific skills; they are able to come in with a fresh understanding) there are many aspects to consider when searching for campus advocates. In our work, we have observed the need for administrators to consider several aspects when selecting people to oversee sexual violence advocacy on campuses, including administrative background, trauma-informed status, ability to navigate campus culture, inclusive approach to practice, creativity to produce engaging and contemporary material, capacity to oversee an autonomous office, and the ability to effectively integrate oneself into an already established campus culture. College and university administrators must also look at their long-standing structures to find the best way to incorporate sexual violence prevention and intervention programs and services into their institution. With these considerations in mind, the following section explores comprehensive strategies and action-oriented steps campus leaders can take to build an effective sexual violence prevention and intervention program on their campus.

Trauma-Informed Foundation

Many rape crisis agencies offer state-certified training accessible to college practitioners. States such as California have set training standards (California Coalition Against Sexual Assault [CALCASA], 2001) developed by coalitions to meet certification standards for sexual assault counselors. Per state code, a sexual assault counselor in California must receive a minimum of 40 hours of training before being issued a certificate of completion and before being able to counsel victims of sexual violence. The delivery of this curriculum varies with each organization and differs even more if the organization acts as a dual agency that provides services for survivors of domestic violence *and* sexual assault. Many agencies cover similar and critical topics that are important for practitioners to understand when creating a campus advocacy program. Some of the topics included in the CALCASA training standards include types and definitions of *sexual assault*, the differing impact of sexual assault for different populations, cultural considerations in providing services, effects of sexual abuse in children, and crisis intervention (CALCASA, 2001).

The aforementioned topics pertain to off-campus and on-campus systems that student survivors may encounter and that campus advocates must be knowledgeable of to adequately support survivors of sexual violence on campus. It is critical for campus advocates to make participation in state-certified training a priority, especially certified training that protects them with confidentiality. However, we also acknowledge and recognize that not all certification programs are the same, and some may perpetuate the trauma of sexual violence. Many certification programs have been co-opted by federal institutions, which are embedded in and controlled by dominant individuals, groups, and systems, thus resulting in a depoliticized and identity-neutral stance. Often, when the government or large corporations take over certification, it becomes increasingly less common to find nuanced training that addresses the unique needs of specific communities and identities. Therefore, we look to local community agencies to provide training and certification. Rape crisis agencies and certifications in our Los Angeles community remain grassroots driven, inclusive of multiple identities, and community oriented, but this is not often the case. Therefore, it is imperative that the certification campus advocates on which embark is critical, community oriented, and inclusive of multiple identities and complexities of sexual violence. Stated bluntly, institutional leaders must do their research on sexual violence certifications to determine if they are truly invested in supporting all student survivors. Increasing their knowledge in this area and understanding the role of off-campus advocates and community agencies will assist campus advocates in creating a trauma-informed campus program that has reconsidered and evaluated all components of how the campus responds to a survivor in light of a basic understanding of the role violence plays in the lives of survivors (Harris & Fallot, 2001).

It is also important for staff at higher education institutions to assist rape crisis agencies in their community with outreach and collaboration. A minimal amount of students receive assistance from victim-survivor service agencies (Bureau of Justice Statistics, 2014). Institutions must foster partnerships with rape crisis agencies to assist in the continuation of care of campus survivors throughout college, as well as postgraduation. In a webinar hosted by the Office of Victims of Crime in collaboration with the Victim Rights Law Center, both organizations encouraged community rape crisis coalitions to form partnerships with campus advocates. Speakers highlighted the importance of campus advocates' ability to connect student survivors with services (Aldrich & Walsh, 2015), particularly when student survivors are not ready to make an official report via the campus Title IX office but need assistance in creating a safety and wellness plan on and off campus.

Creation of Empowerment-Based Intervention Services on Campus

In our experience, institutional leaders often expect professionals overseeing an advocacy office to create a campuswide sexual violence advocacy program that is sustainable and integrated into campus culture. Given the current spotlight on sexual violence, administrators and activists expect many newly created offices to develop protocols and systems that address sexual violence almost instantaneously. They are also expected to create new student-friendly media and access points that lead students to the right information in times of need. With the understanding that college students are in need of several tools to access services, including websites, hotlines, text chats, apps, and printed materials, it is best to customize advocacy materials to specific individual campuses. It is also imperative for administrators to not outsource this material or turn to national organizations to provide general tools for sexual violence prevention and advocacy. Instead, practitioners must use institutional resources and local information to design campus-specific tools that will allow students to learn at their own pace. Creating the tools at a local level will convey to students that the issue of sexual violence is important to their institution.

Because sexual violence advocacy is not a one-size-fits-all approach, processes, systems, and tools need to take account of different stages of students' development. A campus advocate cannot expect every student to consume and react to tools, posters, sessions, programs, and such in the same way. Educators must consider the different periods of cognitive development our students are in, as many might just want to acknowledge and read the posters, while others may want to actively engage and think about what the marketing conveys (Long, 2012). College educators must come up with several types of easily accessible media for students with varying backgrounds.

Educators should ensure that campus sexual violence marketing is gender neutral. Advocacy services must account for every student on campus.

Practitioners must be inclusive of members of their entire community, look objectively at the illustrations used, and make sure they incorporate a diverse group of students. Sexual violence does not discriminate and neither should outreach efforts. To have further reach, educators must think about alternative marketing strategies such as audio format, braille, and closed-captioned video. All members of the campus community should feel empowered by and knowledgeable from marketing messages on campus.

There are also factors to consider for the range of experiences that sexual violence survivors encounter. For example, consider how the provision of resources may differ for a survivor who has recently experienced trauma and the survivor who experienced it several weeks or months ago and is now seeking resources. The advocate must gather as much information as possible from on-campus and off-campus partners alike to address a range of experiences. A necessary start is to identify all partners, including law enforcement, sexual assault nurse examiners, and district attorney victim services offices, and schedule meetings with each to gather information concerning what a campus survivor may need at different points and times.

Meetings and information could inform a comprehensive, campus-specific guide that compiles access points and connects services for survivors. Because the guide will most likely be read without the presence of the advocate, the document must have a tone of empowerment that allows the reader to feel that the guide as well as the advocate is ever present as a support mechanism. A tone of empowerment aligns with the empowerment model of advocacy and informs the campus survivor that he or she is believed and supported while also validating the survivor's journey. A tone of empowerment is reflected in the following excerpt from a campus guide we designed:

> We believe survivors are the experts of their own experience. You might be feeling overwhelmed during this time. It's okay to feel this way. Whoever your support network is currently might be advising you to move forward, to not say anything or they simply may not know how to address what you are going through; and this might be overwhelming as well.
>
> However, we want you to remember that this is your process, your healing journey, and you have every right to feel what you are feeling and decide what your next steps are. In this booklet, we have provided you with a series of resources that can allow you to explore and identify what you might be feeling and where you can find emotional support and resources.
>
> Take a deep breath. Let's begin.

The guide should also address common feelings after the violence, legal rights and protections, on-campus intervention services, off-campus intervention services, medical care, reporting on campus, Title IX reporting flow chart, responsible employees, information about Title IX of the Education Amendments of 1972, reporting off campus, making a police report, order of events in a criminal proceeding, what to expect in court, and definitions of *sexual violence* on and off campus. A section may also be included for survivors to write about their experiences, reflections, and feelings. This writing space offers a way for campus survivors to process their experiences in a manner that may be more comfortable to them, at that moment, than talking with others. Once the campus-specific guide is complete, it should be made available in several places around campus where students congregate such as residence halls, multicultural offices, student unions, the advocacy office, the counseling office, medical services, and campus Title IX offices.

The Importance of Being Inclusive in Advocacy

Campus advocacy offices are available to serve all members of the institution who have experienced sexual violence. However, an array of communities are often forgotten about or excluded from the national and campus discourses on sexual violence, such as communities of color; students with disabilities; lesbian, gay, or bisexual students; and men. Campus advocates should make it a part of their job assignment to learn more about how trauma affects diverse populations and place this at the forefront of campus advocacy so that advocates may be better equipped to understand and serve all students, identities, and their intersections. For example, about one in four girls and one in six boys are sexually abused before the age of 18 (Felitti et al., 1998). This statistic is crucial in helping us assess and include the victimization of college students prior to and during college and expanding our outreach to this student population. Additionally, student victims who identify as transgender, genderqueer, nonconforming, and questioning (TGNQ) report the highest rates of sexual violence and intimate partner violence (Cantor et al., 2015), especially those belonging to racial minorities (Grant et al., 2011), yet many educators and policymakers still view sexual violence through a heteronormative lens. Remaining conscious of these often forgotten findings and populations is imperative when striving to create an inclusive campus advocacy office. Practitioners must pause and assess if they are truly addressing and supporting the entire student population, including those who have been victimized prior to college. Campus advocates must acquire knowledge from conferences, books, newsletters, electronic mailing lists, research, journal articles, rape crisis centers in the surrounding communities, and other resources.

Educators and policymakers on campus must realize that not all students will be ready to talk about sexual violence openly and candidly. Research suggests that male survivor disclosure rates are lower than female disclosure rates, because male survivors of sexual violence feel isolated because of the common misconception that men are not victims (Sorsoli, Kia-Keating, & Grossman, 2008). Given that sexual violence education and outreach has become a common topic on college campuses, incoming students are expected to immediately and fully embrace sexual violence prevention, policies, and education as soon as they set foot on campus. Campus administrators must consider creating an all-encompassing and inclusive advocacy office that fosters an environment in which all survivors feel they can disclose their experiences and all students can learn and speak openly about campus violence. Advocacy services must be crafted with the understanding of men's hesitancy to disclose as well as prior-to-college victimization rates and be inclusive of diverse communities. Administrators should also consider the physical location of advocacy offices, as the location of the space might send students messages that convey the space is for only one gender, race, or specific campus population.

It is important for practitioners to acknowledge the direct links between advocacy and prevention education and vice versa. Essentially, advocacy efforts and services are publicized through prevention education training, programming, and campuswide events. Peer-to-peer outreach can become an effective vehicle. As mentioned earlier, advocacy messaging and branding also affects the way students perceive prevention and education efforts regarding their participation in active bystander and other prevention strategies. Consistent communication between the office of intervention and prevention is critical. In cultivating this relationship, practitioners can gain a better understanding of trends and cultures and assess the climate of the college, whereas prevention education can simultaneously implement and address those relevant changes in campus climate.

Empowerment-Based Prevention Education on College Campuses

Responding to incidents of sexual violence requires a multipronged approach. To effectively prevent and respond to the intricacies of campus sexual violence requires higher education administrators, students, and community partners to proactively address the issue. Educators must implement primary prevention strategies to prevent perpetration and victimization from occurring in the first place. Primary prevention efforts focused on reducing sexual violence examine risk and protective factors found in individual, relationship, community, and systemic-level dynamics that facilitate changes in areas on sexual health, gender, sexual orientation, and gender identity (Lee,

Guy, & Perry, 2008). Research on campus-based gender violence prevention has progressed rapidly in the past several years compared to previous decades; however, this body of research continues to lack a critical understanding of the experiences of minoritized communities in regard to race, gender, ability, and the intersections of identities. Studies that focus on the effectiveness of prevention programming on college campuses and explore various models of campus-based prevention programs showcase various findings that support active bystander intervention training and empathy development (DeGue, 2014). However, to our knowledge, no research demonstrates a link between campus-based sexual violence prevention programs and a subsequent campuswide reduction in the incidences of sexual violence (see Chapter 1). For this reason, governmental and nonprofit agencies, such as the Centers for Disease Control and Prevention, are eagerly working toward finding solutions, model programs, and insights into prevention programs that actually reduce sexual violence on campus.

Although there is no concrete evidence of the cause-and-effect nature of prevention programs, we maintain that trauma-informed prevention programming may be helpful in preventing sexual violence on college campuses. Trauma-informed prevention programs have the capacity to create safe climates where survivors feel supported and empowered in disclosing to departments such as the campus Title IX office, advocacy offices, counseling centers, and off-campus rape crisis centers. They also increase students' knowledge about rape, changing attitudes related to rape so that they do not blame but empathize with survivors of sexual violence (Gibbons & Evans, 2013). By promoting a culture of survivor support and reporting, comprehensive prevention allows the cultivation of empathy, fosters a culture of caring for one another, and strengthens community accountability in practicing prevention principles.

Prevention efforts that have been found to show positive behavioral change and perceptions include various modes of educational platforms, theoretical frameworks, and comprehensive skill-based programs. Many programs include facilitated dialogues that explore the notions of how power-based violence is culturally constructed and perpetuated. Some programs include activities aimed to increase the likelihood that participants will intervene in potentially risky situations through increasing resistance strategies and skills (Nation et al., 2003).

Most important, prevention efforts that acknowledge and are implemented through an intersectional framework take into account that violence is created and perpetuated through the interconnections among systems of oppression that not only influence individual identity and experience but also are entangled, coconstructed, and mutually dependent (Shlasko, 2015).

Sexual violence doesn't emerge or occur in siloed and narrow experiences; to be truly effective, sexual violence prevention must work with other antidomination initiatives on and off campus.

Program Staff and Training

Before conceptualizing or developing sexual violence prevention programs, events, or training, educators must understand the training and skills necessary to provide quality, effective, and dynamic steps for prevention. Through our work, we have come to understand that employing passionate, well-trained, full-time staff is the most important aspect of providing effective prevention education. *Passionate* and *well trained* implies that sexual violence educators must be vested not only in issues of sexual violence but also in other facets of antidomination work such as racial and gender justice. This includes recruiting, cultivating, and sustaining staff who are competent on issues of diversity and can effectively facilitate dialogues and advocate for inclusive policy and structural change efforts that address the intersectionality of sexual violence experiences and frameworks (Adams, Bell, & Griffen, 2007). Most often, students' first interactions with violence prevention will involve the aforementioned staff members. Similar to how a survivor's experience of healing is determined by how others react to his or her initial disclosure (Ahrens, 2006), prevention educators must acknowledge that their first interactions with training and programming determine how students will perceive, connect, and find relevant sexual violence issues with antidomination efforts on campus (Klein & Seshadri, 2016).

Institutionally based support programs must be committed to continuously developing staff and providing support in several ways. Professional program managers and program coordinators should have extensive training in sexual violence, intimate partner violence, and stalking intervention and prevention. Practitioners should be certified and seek continuing education with sexual violence counselor advocates from local rape crisis agencies and domestic violence training. Ongoing training may include in-service education provided by local community partners (e.g., American College Personnel Association [ACPA]; the Rape, Abuse, and Incest National Network [RAINN]), organizational webinars and training sessions, and subscribing to prevention education electronic mailing lists and networks.

Students who serve as peer educators or programming assistants should also be extensively trained and supervised closely for several reasons. For example, one training model requires violence prevention student program assistants to first complete extensive professional and leadership development training in the summer as well as participate in a personal development retreat. This professional and leadership development training focuses on participants' becoming familiar with the intricacies of sexual violence, intimate partner violence, child sexual abuse, stalking prevention education, related crisis intervention, and facilitation and community engagement skills. Ongoing training for students also allows these peer educators to develop their own leadership styles, cultural competency, conflict-mediation tools, and skills to work with diverse groups. Most important, the personal development training focuses on participants' becoming familiar with stress management; self-care; preventing and dealing with vicarious trauma; sensitivity training; team-building processes; and empowering students to lead with passion and compassion through their own abilities, stories, and strengths.

Principles of Effective Prevention Programming for Sexual Violence

Researchers have concluded that sexual violence prevention on college campuses can be more effective when considering specific values of prevention. Effective programs mitigate risk and protective factors of perpetration and victimization, increase skill building, and offer strategies that foster strong, positive relationships and programs that are relevant to cultural beliefs and practices to specific groups. These include implementing strategies that include multiple components and affect multiple settings to address a wide range of risks and protective factors (DeGue, 2014). Some practitioners, activists, and advocates tend to criticize colleges that engage in risk-reduction strategies in prevention frameworks, which many would call victim blaming and unconducive to the antipolicing efforts of individuals' bodies. However, like empowerment-based advocacy, prevention should also provide an array of options that may provide individuals with several options for processing and reflecting. Appropriately timed prevention strategies include reaching first-year students in the red zone, a time frame many consider to be the first six weeks of college, when many students experience sexual violence (DeGue, 2014). The program should foster strong, stable, and positive relationships. Socioculturally relevant programs must be tailored to meet cultural beliefs and practices of specific groups and community norms. Essentially, the ultimate goal of prevention education is to cultivate healthy relationships; thus, prevention staff and peer educators will serve as role models. Evaluation and assessment components of a program should also be prioritized. Without ongoing assessment, programs run the risk of disconnecting from community needs as well as lacking transparency in their efforts.

Branding and Marketing

Branding and brand associations in the context of violence requires an examination of how violence prevention offices create and develop inclusive, nonbiased, and gender-nonconforming concepts in prevention efforts. Recommendations from the Office of Violence Against Women on college-based sexual violence prevention programming suggest that acknowledging programs, images, brands, language, and examples that "blame survivors" creates unrealistic expectations of students to step up in risky situations (Edwards, 2009). Educators should consider color schemes that are nontraditional such as orange, green, and teal and avoid colors such as red or pink that traditionally imply danger and perpetuate a gendered undertone. Normalizing positive messaging that promotes a culture of care and branding that connects students to relevant cultural themes is key. Creating inclusive brands that target multiple populations and the intersections of identities has the potential to change the greatest amount of behaviors and perceptions.

Social Media Marketing and Engagement

Social marketing campaigns have been widely used in primary prevention efforts in order to target whole communities on particular issues such as high-risk behaviors, HIV/AIDS prevention, emergency contraception, and smoking (Gibson et al., 2010). The overall goal of social marketing campaigns has two components: to increase the amount of public knowledge on a given topic and to use the knowledge to provide members of the public with specific directions for changing their current behavior (Gibson et al., 2010). Social marketing campaigns can be effective with widespread audiences and consume fewer resources. These campaigns are able to raise awareness of an issue, help individuals see consequences of behavior, and increase support for the benefits of taking action. Several of the advantages of using social marketing campaigns is that focused media can target specific community social norms or rape myths and address common relationship violence behaviors (Edwards, 2009). Prevention support programs at colleges across the United State often use social media and social marketing campaigns (e.g., Facebook, Instagram, Twitter, Vine, videos) managed by student program assistants and staff to demonstrate prosocial behaviors during and after incidences of sexual violence. Media platforms that can be shared with students and in online community groups are also used to disseminate resources, articles, surveys, videos, and other media to gain a better understanding of advocacy and role-model bystander behavior.

Bystander Intervention

Historical or traditional awareness and education prevention programs have not always been successful in reducing the statistics of sexual violence (Katz & Moore, 2013). Onetime wide-scale events, traditional programming, and training that only focus on disseminating statistics may be successful at increasing knowledge on sexual violence but have not been effective in improving violence-behavior attitudes and/or the use of direct services (Gibbons & Evans, 2013). For this reason, other approaches that focus on bystander intervention must be considered.

One such innovative program at Occidental College, Oxy Upstander, is based on an adaptation of Green Dot's community mobilization strategy (Coker et al., 2011). Characterized as a bystander intervention model, the Green Dot model is based on decades of research grounded in four different yet interrelated areas: acknowledgment that violence prevention education solely based on statistics and definitions of *power-based violence* alone has not been successful in reducing power-based violence; bystander behavior literature; perpetrator data; and, as a prevention tool, the research on diffusion of innovation and social diffusion theory (Coker et al., 2011).

The developers of Green Dot have taken a different approach. The program incorporates data that suggest perpetrators consist of about 5% of the population, repeatedly perpetrate violence, and exhibit certain behaviors (Coker et al., 2011). Considering that perpetrators may be about 5% of a population, mobilizing the bystander population is an integral component to addressing violence on campus (Lisak & Miller, 2002).

The bystander intervention component of Occidental College's empowerment-based violence prevention training is based on tenets of bystander behavior in that when individuals are faced with potentially risky, dangerous, or emergency situations, the following can occur: (a) a diffusion of responsibility, meaning individuals will not react because they assume someone else will handle it; (b) evaluation apprehension, which means when faced with a high-risk situation individuals will not act for fear of looking foolish; (c) pluralistic ignorance, which is when faced with a high-risk or an ambiguous situation, individuals will defer to the cues of those around them before they decide to respond; (d) confidence in skills, when individuals are more likely to intervene when they feel confident that their intervention will be effective; and (e) modeling, which means individuals are most likely to intervene in high-risk situations when they have seen someone else model it first (Coker et al., 2011). Based on this research, Occidental College adapted Green Dot's (2011) Direct, Distract, and Delegate skill-building model to "Be Upfront, Distract and Entrust" (Oxy Upstander, n.d.). Through this exercise, students are able to either confront a person engaging in risky behavior, create a distraction to prevent the incident from happening, or entrust someone else to intervene for them by being up front or distracting (Coker et al., 2011). The college's workshop creates a space for role modeling and developing the skills necessary for such intervention.

According to research on bystander intervention as well as Green Dot's approach on the dissemination of information, it is important to think about the premise for how behavior change can occur on a greater cultural scale (Cook-Craig et al., 2014). Using theoretical research that pertains to the diffusion of innovation and social diffusion theory in Green Dot's prevention model, research suggests that systematically identifying, recruiting, and training influential popular opinion leaders can serve as behavioral change endorsers in various communities and spheres of influence (Cook-Craig et al., 2014). Influential leaders, in this case students on campus, who hold high amounts of social and network capital, will diffuse new behaviors naturally and gradually as well as visibly adopt, endorse, and support bystander behavior (Cook-Craig et al., 2014). For this reason, having peer educators or programming assistants who vary in social and professional areas from athletics, Greek culture, cultural organizations, and peer health groups can create, present, and disseminate new bystander behaviors.

Training Content

Empowerment-based violence prevention begins before students arrive on campus. Educators must introduce community norms and normalize a culture of care prior to these students stepping foot on campus. Institutions may use an online education program to introduce students to the basics of sexual violence, dating and domestic violence, stalking, and active bystander techniques. Many online programs provide students with an exciting, dynamic, and technologically friendly interface that actively works with first-year and transfer students. These students may benefit from a more personal, intimate discussion and exploration of the topic from the safety of their computer desk and personal space. Developmentally, students may come with different levels and emotional capacities to process topics that are sensitive, allowing students to initially explore the issue privately and feel more comfortable in familiarizing themselves with language, intersecting experiences, or particular triggers before they engage in a wider system (e.g., campuswide training, orientation). Participating at orientation, students may then grasp and understand information more in depth with peers and peer leaders as opposed to entering an unfamiliar climate and dialogue.

Continuing students and upper-division students, who may be in a different developmental space than first-year and transfer students, may thrive and be better served in interventions and programs that foster ownership and professional development on violence prevention. For example, conducting training sessions and workshops that entail discussing sexual harassment or active bystanders in professional settings may challenge and prepare students to deal with real-life situations postgraduation. This programming may also benefit students who are venturing off campus for work and internships, which may require a deeper understanding of power, privilege, sexism, and harassment in the workplace.

After introducing students to a basic understanding of violence, placing them in relational settings and training will scaffold this new knowledge. An initial presentation at orientation could serve as a catalyst for follow-up trainings where students who want more information or want to be more involved may participate. Each presentation is based on the audience's need and should take into consideration age, setting, developmental stage, environment, and educational needs. Preassessment intake forms and consultation meetings must be held with groups prior to the training to better assess which type of intervention would be best. As part of the presentation adaptation, training sessions should include topics that pertain to various communities on campus, including Greek life, athletics, residential life, and other communities where certain language, themes, and situations might be more common, relatable, and realistic.

Prevention Programming

Prevention programming must be ongoing and inclusive. As mentioned in the previous sections, sexual violence prevention should be a commitment to coordinating, cooperating, and collaborating with antidomination efforts on and off campus. In critically thinking about approaches to sexual violence, exclusive programming on sexual violence that focuses on one particular topic may limit the ability of students, faculty, practitioners, and advocates to make connections across experiences of oppression and may conjure feelings in individuals of having to choose one identity-specific issue to fight for or address (Klein & Seshadri, 2016). For example, if a department on campus were to host a program regarding violence against TGNQ, and the violence prevention office were to organize a sexual violence program regarding the experience of marginalized communities at the same time, students would have to choose which program to attend. Instead, choosing to work with other departments collaboratively and working toward building programs that dismantle systems of oppression through intersectional spaces would allow students to begin to see connections among various identities. With the absence of collaboration, campus departments then begin to cross program and compete with department programs instead of building productive dialogues and strategic plans toward integrating and streamlining inclusive and intentional programming.

Conversations that focus on the intersectional experiences of those who experience violence elevate the voices of those who have often been silenced and/or not previously provided with space to share their stories. Transmitting these stories and programs can take place through various platforms including social media by developing virtual community spaces where participants and communities post, share, and process information regarding sexual violence. Traditional prevention programming, such as Take Back the Night, where survivors have the opportunity to share their stories in solidarity with other survivors; RAINN Day, in which college campuses take a day to bring awareness to sexual violence and connect students to on-campus resources; or Empowerment Week, a program dedicated toward creating awareness on dating and domestic violence and stalking are other opportunities to involve multiple and diverse communities. These programs also highlight how historical issues of power, violence, and sexism have had an impact on campuses and specific communities on campus. These national programs also allow students, administrators, faculty, and survivors to connect with other individuals across campuses.

Local or institution-specific programming can also take on issues of sexual violence and intersectionality of identities and communities. Educators must connect with campus offices and departments that develop programs and focus on issues of gender, inequality, race, critical theory, and social justice. Administrators should also collaborate with faculty, possibly inviting them to participate in monthly seminars and brown-bag lunches, and encourage faculty to integrate issues of sexual violence into their academic curriculum. Finally, campus educators must integrate and align first-year core academic opportunities and programs with violence prevention programs to engage students in sexual violence awareness in and out of the classroom.

Evaluation and Feedback

Evaluation is a necessity in ensuring program efficiency and outcomes. Developing several methods of evaluation is helpful not only in evaluating knowledge and behavior but also in addressing community needs and climate. Quantitative and qualitative assessments are important in examining programs. One form of evaluation can be conducted pre- or postengagement in sexual violence interventions on campus. Time should also be set aside during workshops so that participants can provide in-situ feedback. A three-month, six-month, and one-year follow-up using logic models, directed outcomes, and collecting an array of feedback is also necessary to measure program outcomes. Additionally, evaluation and assessment may be different for different campus environments, given variations in demographics, organizational structure, and institutional type.

Noting that sexual violence climate surveys are now in progress and/or have been completed at several institutions (i.e., from the Higher Education Data Sharing Consortium and the Association of American Universities), prevention programs and offices may run the risk of overpolling students or creating survey fatigue. This consideration is especially important when specific groups (e.g., athletics, Greek members, and students of color) are targeted for ongoing feedback or focus group participation. This may be particularly true for smaller colleges, where students are bombarded with surveys because of the small sampling size (which may increase trauma in students by constantly revisiting the issue), as opposed to larger institutions that have access to a larger student body. Remaining transparent about evaluation with groups, allowing several modes of access such as online surveys, e-mail feedback, focus groups, and conversations with students allows variety of intake while also building rapport. Practicing inclusivity in evaluation strategies is critically important for accessing groups that have historically been marginalized from mainstream research methods. Coordinating with offices that work with students with disabilities can result in staff lending their expertise to working with students who may need accommodations such as interpreters or other forms of survey instruments and providing insight on the experiences and barriers that may exist. Other aspects may include administering questions that are gender inclusive and informed, surveys that allow individuals to choose how they identify, and instruments that do not assume cisgender and heteronormativity. Finally, instruments and survey language that evaluate particular incidents or experiences of violence may or may not coincide with or feel relevant to marginalized students. Allowing students to be part of the development of instruments for evaluation can allow greater accessibility and outreach.

It is vital for evaluation efforts to be carried out in collaboration with other offices and departments that may already have data available or are in the process of developing similar assessments. Office staff should also consider the possibility of joint assessment strategies to minimize assessment fatigue for students. It is helpful to connect with any institutional research departments that may guide or provide evaluation platforms already structured in academic areas.

Our Purpose as Practitioners in the Movement

Institutions must explore and undertake ways to go about developing, implementing, and evaluating sexual violence advocacy and prevention strategies. Prevention and advocacy efforts at institutions live through core values and beliefs developed with students and the community at large. Institutions and educators must empower survivors, meet individual and community members where they are, build critical consciousness and awareness on sexual violence, be inclusive of multiple populations, collaborate with community partners, and remain aware of students' development and identities. Finally, efforts must not only prevent sexual violence but also strive to build a culture of care; cultivate relationships of respect; and recognize the value, privilege, power, and worth and dignity of every person in the campus community. Through passionate, committed individuals and research-informed and innovative programs, institutions may transform and elevate human relationships in their communities, which is one of the main goals of critically informed and empowerment-based violence intervention and prevention.

References

Adams, M., Bell, L. A., & Griffen, P. (Eds.). (2007). *Teaching for diversity and social justice* (2nd ed.). New York, NY: Routledge.

Ahrens, C. E. (2006). Being silenced: The impact of negative social reactions on the disclosure of rape. *American Journal of Community Psychology, 38*, 263–274. doi:10.1007/s10464-006-9069-9

Aldrich, L., & Walsh, A. (2015). *Safety planning with campus sexual assault victims* [Webinar]. Washington, DC: U.S. Department of Justice, Office of Justice Programs, Office for Victims of Crime. Retrieved from www.ovcttac.gov/eblast/ TitleIX_Eblast_3-1.HTML

Bureau of Justice Statistics. (2014). *Special report on rape and sexual violence victimization among college-age females*. Retrieved from www.bjs.gov/content/pub/pdf/ rsavcaf9513.pdf

California Coalition Against Sexual Assault. (2001). *Sexual assault training standards: A trainer's guide*. Retrieved from www.calcasa.org/wp-content/uploads/2011/05/ Training-Standards.pdf

Cantor, D., Fisher, B., Chibnall, S., Townsend, R., Lee, H., Bruce, C., & Thomas, G. (2015). *Report on the AAU Campus Climate Survey on Sexual Assault and Sexual Misconduct*. Retrieved from www.aau.edu/Climate-Survey.aspx?id=16525

Coker, A., Cook-Craig, P., Williams, C. M., Fisher, B. S., Clear, E. R., Garcia, L. S., & Hegge, L. M. (2011). Evaluation of Green Dot: An active bystander intervention to reduce sexual violence on college campuses. *Violence Against Women, 17*, 777–796. doi:10.1177/1077801211410264

Cook-Craig, P., Coker, A., Clear, E., Garcia, L., Bush, H., Brancato, C., . . . Fisher, B., (2014). Challenge and opportunity in evaluating a diffusion-based active bystanding prevention program: Green Dot in high schools. *Violence Against Women, 20*, 1–4. doi:10.1177/1077801214551288

DeGue, S. (2014). *Preventing sexual violence on college campuses: Lessons learned from research and practice.* Retrieved from https://notalone.gov/assets/evidence-based-strategies-for-the-prevention-of-sv-perpetration.pdf

Edwards, D. (2009). *Branding & marketing: Comprehensive prevention and education technical assistance.* Washington, DC: Office of Violence Against Women.

Felitti, V., Anda, R., Nordenberg, D., Williamson, D., Spitz., A., Edwards, V., . . . Marks, J. (1998). Relationship of childhood abuse and household dysfunction to many of the leading causes of death in adults: Adverse childhood experiences study. *American Journal of Preventative Medicine, 14,* 245–258.

Gibbons, R., & Evans, J. (2013). *The evaluation of campus-based gender violence prevention programming: What we know about program effectiveness and implications for practitioners.* Retrieved from www.vawnet.org/assoc_files_vawnet/ar_evaluationcampusprogramming.pdf

Gibson, D., Zhang, G., Cassady, D., Pappas, L., Mitchell, J., & Kegeles, J. (2010). Effectiveness of HIV prevention social marketing with injecting drug users. *American Journal of Public Health, 100,* 1828–1830 doi:10.2105/AJPH.2009.181982

Grant, J., Mottet, L., Tanis, J., Harrison, J., Herman, J., & Keisling, M. (2011). *Injustice at every turn: A report of the National Transgender Discrimination Survey.* Retrieved from www.thetaskforce.org/static_html/downloads/reports/reports/ntds_full.pdf

Green Dot. (2011). *An overview of the Green Dot strategy.* Retrieved from www.calcasa.org/wp-content/uploads/2011/04/Curriculum-Summary.pdf

Harris, M., & Fallot, R. D. (Eds.). (2001). Using trauma theory to design service systems. *New Directions for Mental Health Services,* 89.

Katz, J., & Moore, J. (2013). Bystander education for campus sexual assault prevention: An initial meta-analysis. *Violence and Victims, 28,* 1054–1067.

Klein, L. B., & Seshadri, M. (2016, February 17). You say potato, I hear tomato: Cognitive dissonance & navigating institutional bureaucracy [Webinar]. Campus Advocates and Prevention Professionals Association. Retrieved from www.nationalcappa.org/cappalive-4/

Lee, D., Guy, L., & Perry, B. (2008). *Shifting the paradigm: Primary prevention of sexual violence.* Linthicum, MD: American College Health Association.

Lisak, D., & Miller, P. (2002). Repeat rape and multiple offending among undetected rapists. *Violence and Victims, 17*(1), 80–82.

Long, D. (2012). Theories and models of student development. In L. J. Hinchliffe & M. A. Wong (Eds.), *Environments for student growth and development: Librarians and student affairs in collaboration* (pp. 41–55). Chicago, IL: Association of College & Research Libraries.

Nation, M., Crusto, C., Wandersman, A., Krumper, K. L., Seybolt, D., Morrissey-Kane, E., & Davino, K. (2003). What works in prevention: Principles of effective prevention programs. *American Psychologist, 58,* 449–456.

Oxy Upstander. (n.d.). Project safe. Retrieved from http://www.oxy.edu/project-safe/prevention-education/oxy-upstander

Shlasko, D. (2015). Using the five faces of oppression to teach about interlocking systems of oppression. *Equity & Excellence in Education, 48,* 349–360.

Sorsoli, L., Kia-Keating, M., & Grossman, F. K. (2008). "I keep that hush-hush": Male survivors of sexual abuse and the challenges of disclosure. *Journal of Counseling Psychology, 55*, 333–345. Retrieved from www.traumacenter.org/products/pdf_files/i_keep_that_hush_hush.pdf

Title IX of the Education Amendments, 20 U.S.C. §1681 et seq. (1972).

White House. (2014). *Not alone: Sample language for reporting and confidentially disclosing sexual violence.* Retrieved from www.notalone.gov/assets/reporting-confidentiality-policy.pdf

II

MAPPING IDENTITIES

An Intersectional Analysis of Policies on Sexual Violence

Susan V. Iverson

Many college and university administrators, faculty members, and students are "no longer surprised" by the "reprehensible" realities of sexual violence on campus; instead it has "become part of our normal" (Wooten & Mitchell, 2015, p. 186). This normal adheres to a dominant script: Sexual violence is a form of gendered violence committed by (cisgender) men against (cisgender) women. It fails to identify other dimensions of identity as important to consider (Belknap, 2015; Phipps, 2010; Wooten, 2015). In the 1970s, feminist activists removed the "cloak of invisibility" from women's victimization, empowering women to speak out about victimization (Belknap, 2015, p. xiv). Prior to this time, sexual violence was narrowly conceptualized as a "sex crime carried out by pathological men" (Fried, 1994, p. 562), conjuring images of a stranger in a back alley. Now, women were breaking the silence and making the scope of sexual violence visible and revealing that rape could occur "in bedrooms . . . at parties, in offices, and within families" (Kim, 2012, p. 264). The antirape movement, born in the 1960s, redefined *sexual violence* to include victim and survivor perspectives and to illuminate how male power is used as a form of social control over women (Donat & D'Emilio, 1998; Rose, 1977). However, perspectives of white cisgender, economically privileged women seemed to dominate the movement, and this may have had the unintended consequence of shaping conceptualizations of sexual violence as heteronormative and heterosexist (Wooten, 2015). This is seen in the absence of an analysis of sexism combined with racism and heterosexism as well as other forms of oppression (Belknap, 2015) in U.S. higher education policy on sexual violence.

214

In this chapter, I draw on intersectionality theory to uncover embedded assumptions and predominant meanings constructed through sexual assault policies. Employing an intersectional analysis, I seek to reveal how an over-reliance on one-dimensional analyses (meaning assumptions that all women experience sexual violence the same as white cisgender, economically privileged women) contributes to misunderstandings of sexual violence. I argue that an intersectional approach can illuminate how dimensions of identity (i.e., race, gender, sexuality) are socially constructed and too often seen as separate spheres of experience. These overlapping and interlocking spheres create complex intersections at which two or more dimensions of identity converge and determine social, economic, and political dynamics of oppression. In what follows, I provide a theoretical overview of intersectionality; I then discuss my findings from an intersectional analysis of sexual violence policies from 22 U.S. institutions of higher education, and I conclude with considerations for policymakers and future research.

Intersectionality Theory

Researchers are increasingly aware of the limitations of particular identity dimensions as singular analytic categories (Davis, Brunn-Bevel, & Olive, 2015; Mitchell, Simmons, & Greyerbiehl, 2014). For instance, feminist researchers (BacaZinn, Hondagneu-Sotolo, & Messner, 2000; Brah, & Phoenix, 2004; Collins, 1998) critique the use of gender as the sole analytic category. Black feminist thought in particular introduced the concept of intersectionality as a lens to see "distinctive systems of oppression as being part of one overarching structure of domination" (Collins, 1990, p. 122). Increasingly, scholars argue for intersectionality as a schema for understanding the interaction of different forms of oppression, including racism, homophobia, and sexism (Cole, 2009; Ken, 2008; McCall, 2005). Crenshaw (1991), typically cited as the scholar to first use the term *intersectionality*, critiqued the failure of "contemporary feminist and antiracist discourses" (p. 1242) to consider intersectional identities of immigrant women of color. Using men's violence against women of color as her focus, she asserted how the "experiences of women of color are frequently the product of intersecting patterns of racism and sexism" (p. 1243).

Crenshaw (1991) indicated that she was not offering a new explanatory theory of identity; rather she offered this as a "provisional concept" (p. 1244, note 9) for researchers to account for multiple categories of identity. Yet, this concept is far more than an accounting of differences regarding race, class, and sexuality, among other identity dimensions. The theory of intersectionality destabilizes identity categories (Jennrich & Kowalski-Braun, 2014) and emphasizes "the process by which social structures and power relations are written into identities and bodily repertoires and thus *shape* experience" (Phipps, 2010, p. 360, italics in original).

In the context of sexual violence, an intersectional analysis challenges the primacy of gender as the organizing and explanatory factor for sexual violence. It can illuminate multiple identity perspectives (e.g., race, class, sexuality), thus giving voice to a vast array of marginalized peoples (Tevis & Griffen, 2014). However, amplifying voices and including marginalized perspectives must also recognize and analyze "the hierarchies and systems of domination that permeate society and that systematically exploit and control people" (Andersen & Collins, 2001, p. 6). Just as a person never stands separate from race, gender, sexuality, national origin, and so forth, so too those dimensions of identity are never outside the social systems that construct and sustain them. Thus, as Rhedding-Jones (2002) observes, we "need to 'undo' texts" to "bring to life the complexities, intersections and dangers" of institutional practices that may actually reinscribe the very problem a policy seeks to alleviate (p. 92).

Questioning the Universality of Violence Against Women

The traditional (feminist) approach to sexual violence emphasized women's experiences and has been successful in forging a strong movement to combat violence against women. Yet, this approach has garnered criticism in that it has failed to "give voice to women marginalized by the largely white, middle-class feminist movement" (Sokoloff & Dupont, 2005, p. 41). Dominant ideologies of sexual violence typically frame the problem as something that a woman experiences, and this violence against women is represented in essentialist and heteronormative ways. For instance, in incidents of sexual violence, men are perpetrators and women are victims, and sexual assault occurs in opposite-sex relationships (Iverson, 2006; Wooten, 2015). Further, many have critiqued the dichotomous ways people are socially categorized, meaning that individuals are either male or female, white or Black, disabled or able-bodied (Andersen & Collins, 2001; Colker, 1996; Collins, 1990; Fine, 1994), and the ways such social constructions of difference are used "to include or exclude, reward or punish, credit or discredit, elevate or oppress, value or devalue, leave alone or harass" (Johnson, 2006, p. 16).

Calls have emerged for theoretical analytic tools, such as intersectionality, to describe the complexity of identity and interrelated forces acting on dimensions of identity. For instance, Crenshaw's (1991) use of men's violence against women of color illuminated how the "experiences of women of color are frequently the product of intersecting patterns of racism and sexism" (p. 1243). Such an analysis dismantles binaries (i.e., men/women) and reveals that power is not unidirectional (i.e., top down, or power over), but that "power operates in multiple directions simultaneously" (Harris & Hanchey, 2014, p. 3). Thus, collisions occur not only at the intersection of individual identities but also in the ways socially constructed contexts inscribe meaning, yielding differences in navigating the road map for "other" bodies. For instance, policy may advance universal definitions of *sexual violence*; however, in the United States, "white men have committed sexually violent acts with impunity because of their proximity to a discourse that hypersexualizes Black people and conscribes Black men as always violent" (Harris & Hanchey, 2014, p. 2). Katz (2006) adds that the "sinister influences of 'race' and 'culture' are only invoked when the perps are men of color" (p. 133). Thus, violence associated with whiteness becomes invisible (Harris & Hanchey, 2014).

Campus policy, the site for this investigation, has developed over the past two decades as a solution to sexual violence, largely in response to federal legislation; yet, little scholarship exists investigating the solution of policy to the problem of sexual violence (Wooten & Mitchell, 2015). This intersectional analysis is an extension of my previous study (Iverson, 2015) designed to investigate university diversity policies to understand how these documents frame diversity and what reality these diversity action plans produce. In this study, I observed that little institutional-specific considerations were evident in sexual violence policies and that the bodies regulated by policy were represented as monolithic rather than multidimensional (Phipps, 2010). An intersectional analysis, thus, is warranted to critically interrogate sexual violence as framed in university policies. Following a brief overview of the methods, I discuss the findings from this analysis.

Methods

The data include 22 sexual violence policies from 22 recipients of U.S. Department of Justice's (2015) Office of Violence Against Women (OVW) campus grants in 2012 (see Appendix 11.A for all data cited in this chapter). My rationale for this sampling strategy was that these 22 campuses, as recipients of federal funds to address sexual violence on their campuses, have (or are conducting revisions of) sexual violence policies. I did not assume these were model policies or reflected best practices; rather, these campuses are dedicating focused (and funded) efforts to the problem of sexual violence. Further, this sample reflected various institutional types, ranging from Christian four-year colleges (i.e., Samford University) to historically Black colleges and universities (i.e., Virginia State University), from public research universities (i.e.,

University of North Carolina at Chapel Hill) to a community college (i.e., Joliet Junior College). With the list of 22 grant recipients, I conducted a search on the website for each campus, using the search function and keywords *sexual violence* (or *misconduct* or *assault*) *policy*. All 22 institutions revealed they had something, ranging from lean policies (i.e., 1–3 pages) to comprehensive policies (i.e., 23–48 pages). The average policy length was 8 to 9 pages.

Building on my previous analysis (Iverson, 2015), I employed discourse analysis, a focused examination of language, text, and meaning that emerges from the text (Denzin & Lincoln, 2011), to code broad themes and predominant representations of women and men in the sexual violence policies. Using an intersectional lens to illuminate difference, I found what was missing; for example, the images of women and men did not identify race, sexuality, dis/ability, or other dimensions of identity. Then, using a critical, feminist analysis, I focused on those silences and exclusions (Reinharz, 1992) to make visible the missing data (Danner & Carmody, 2001).

Limitations

Some limitations exist with this study. The data for this investigation are exclusively written texts. A future study could involve an in-depth case analysis of one or more universities to understand the administrative and organizational factors that contribute to the generation and implementation of sexual violence policies. Similarly, analyses of prevention programming through an intersectional lens would be beneficial. Additionally, these policies were collected in the 2012–2013 school year, and some campuses have since updated their policies. For instance, since receiving the 2012 OVW grant, Virginia State University made a revised policy document accessible on its website. Additionally, the revised document provided a list of resources that include an off-campus lesbian, gay, bisexual, and transgender (LGBT) partner abuse help line, poverty law center, and on-campus ministries. Thus, a follow-up sampling of policies from these institutions would be warranted to examine (any) changes over time.

Findings and Discussion

Before discussing my findings, I offer an observation about the policies. Each policy was unique, but they had some shared elements. According to Thapar-Bjorkert and Morgan (2010), this reflects "an institutionalization of . . . vocabularies" (p. 50) rather than a standardization of policies. Specifically, certain content (e.g., consent-based language, protections against retaliation) and some phrases (e.g., defining *sexual harassment* as "unwelcome" and *sexual exploitation* as "intentional") were shared across most policies. However, in light of institutional differences, the policies were strikingly similar. Collecting policies from 22 OVW campus grant recipients enabled a cross-section of various institutional types. Yet, this knowledge of variance in institutional type, and thus in demographics of student population, illuminated even more starkly what and who had been left out of these policies and the unintended consequence of institutionalized vocabularies (Thapar-Bjorkert & Morgan, 2010). In my description of findings, I discuss what was missing, policy silences, and identity absences.

Heterosexism and Genderism in Sexual Violence Policies

Presumably in an effort to reject heteronormative descriptions of sexuality and possibly to be inclusive of gender-nonconforming students, the subjects in sexual violence policies are ungendered or neutrally gendered (meaning she and he are used). Several policies state that sexual violence occurs "regardless of sexual orientation" (i.e., Bucknell University, p. 3; University of Mississippi, p. 37). Clark University's policy defines *sexual misconduct* as offenses committed "by a man or woman upon a man or woman without effective consent," (p. 2) and the Joliet Junior College policy adds that the "harasser may be a woman or a man" and the "victim does not have to be of the opposite sex" (p. 2). On occasion, a policy will include educational missives about sexual behavior that consequently undermine the gender ambiguity. For instance, Fairmont State's policy has ungendered definitions of *sexual harassment* and *date rape* (referring to "a person"), but then, in its explanation of the role of alcohol in incidents of sexual violence, the policy asserts that

> *in men* [emphasis added], alcohol releases their inhibitions and they tend to say and do things that they normally wouldn't say or do. They tend to be more open and forward with women which can lead to a serious situation. *With women* [emphasis added], when they are under the influence they may tend to make decisions that they wouldn't make if sober. If the two mingle throughout the night, a situation could evolve that they both will wish never happened. (pp. 1–2)

The policy continues with behavioral guidance for men and women, for example, that men should understand "when you use force against your date to have sex, you are committing a crime," and that women should "avoid secluded places" (p. 2). The ungendered innocence of the policy is lost.

Several consequences are evident in the ungendering of sexual violence. First, in the absence of pronouns, subjectivities are invisible. The person who commits sexual violence is described as a "student who violates policy," the "accused" (University of North Carolina at Chapel Hill, p. 16), the "alleged offender" (Bucknell University, p. 7), the "respondent," and rarely the "attacker" (University of Mississippi, p. 34). The individual "upon" whom sexual violence has been committed is typically described as the "victim" (or "alleged victims"; Bucknell University, p. 6) or complainants, as individuals who "allege" or "believe" sexual misconduct has been committed, and rarely is the term *survivor* used (see Bucknell University, p. 17; College of St. Scholastica, p. 3). Situating this ambiguity within the dominant discourse of sexual violence as committed by men against women, most readers of policies will likely draw from existing cognitive gender schemas that inform gender stereotyping (Bem, 1985) and will associate victim/survivor with femininity and offender/perpetrator with masculinity (Wooten, 2015).

Second, this ambiguity further fails to acknowledge sexual and gender-nonconforming identities. Not all women who are raped by men "self-identify as 'straight' or heterosexual" (Wooten, 2015, p. 47) or as women or as men. This ungendering of policies and implicit heteronormativity has material realities and consequences for individuals experiencing, and reporting, sexual violence. For instance, individuals who are not out or "voluntarily open" about their sexual identity may remain silent about incidents of sexual violence (Sokoloff & Dupont, 2005, p. 43). Additionally, the trans* population has particularly high risk for sexual violence coupled with very low rates of reporting but is absent from policy (Stotzer, 2009).

Third, it is notable that in lists of resources (e.g., student health services, counseling services) delineated in the policies, none refer to LGBT centers as a resource, and very few (e.g., Old Dominion University) identify women's centers as a resource. A few policies (i.e., Clark University, Gallaudet University) give descriptions of off-campus resources, (i.e., hospitals) and denote that these facilities have specially trained personnel (e.g., sexual assault nurse examiner), but policies would benefit by adding an acknowledgment of personnel readiness to serve LGBT victims and survivors. All campus services are called on to complicate their responses to the question, Who are the victims (and perpetrators) of sexual violence? Service providers should be cognizant that not only is sexual identity important to consider in reports of sexual violence, but also are gender identity (e.g., Is this a trans* student?), racial identity (e.g., Is this lesbian student also Native American?), veteran status (e.g., Is post-traumatic stress disorder attributable to combat as much as to campus or military sexual violence?), among other intersecting identities.

Failing to Hear the Voices: Ableism in Sexual Violence Policies

Students with disabilities are often referred to as having minority status since they share certain conditions of marginalization (Jones, 1996; Tevis &

Griffen, 2014). However, students with disabilities are often ignored in the sexual violence literature, even though women with disabilities experience almost twice the rate of all forms of abuse compared to other populations, and thus college students with disabilities are likely at increased risk for sexual violence (Alriksson-Schmidt, Armour, & Thibadeau, 2010; Hollomotz, 2009; McFarlane et al., 2001; D. L. Smith, 2008).

I viewed the sexual violence policy at Gallaudet University, an institution whose mission is to serve Deaf and hard-of-hearing students, as a potential example of best practices for the accommodation of deaf/Deaf students. Gallaudet remains the only higher education institution in the United States in which all programs and services are specifically designed to accommodate deaf/Deaf and hard-of-hearing students. It is thus striking to see the limited attention to the identities of the student body. For instance, *consent* is defined using language found in most other policies: "Effective consent can be given by word or action, but *non-verbal consent is not as clear as talking* [emphasis added] about what a person wants sexually" (p. 1). No mention of sign language is included in the consent definitions. Only when defining *stalking* does the policy describe "VP calls" (videophones used for deaf/Deaf telephone communication) as a form of undesired or nonconsensual communication (Gallaudet University, p. 6).

Under the section headings Rights of the Complainant and Rights of the Respondent, no explicit rights are mentioned regarding accommodations (i.e., interpreters). One might argue this is because such mechanisms are standard practice at Gallaudet and thus do not warrant being named explicitly. Indicated only when referring to off-campus services (hospital, police), "sign language interpretation to aid deaf and hard of hearing citizens" (p. 26) is available. Finally, on the last pages of the policy under the heading of on- and off-campus resources, whether office phones have voice (V) or videophone/teletypewriter (VP/TTY) capabilities is indicated, and even then only half (9) of the (18) offices denote this. Throughout the policy, these indications are not made, even when the phone number of the Title IX coordinator is listed.

The little that is evident in Gallaudet's policy profoundly illuminates absences in all other policies in the sample. For instance, policies fail to include accessibility services as a resource, fail to say if phone numbers are V only or VP/TTY, and fail to indicate whether accommodations (i.e., interpreters) are available at on- and off-campus services (hospitals, police, conduct offices). Only University of Montana notes, "Consistent with state and federal law, reasonable accommodation will be provided to persons with disabilities" (p. 1).

Shining a light on what is missing in these policies makes it evident how ableism is operating, meaning able-bodied people are situated as the norm, and people with disabilities are "viewed as being abnormal" or as individuals who "cannot function as full members of society" (L. Smith, Foley, & Chaney, 2008, p. 304). To illustrate, consider the way nearly every policy refers to disability. In the definitions of *sexual violence (sexual misconduct)*, and in particular elaborations on *consent*, policies indicate that having sex with a person who is incapacitated is considered sexual assault. Policies state that incapacitation can occur when alcohol and drugs are involved. They further add that having a disability can constitute incapacitation, as the following excerpts illustrate:

- Samford University policy states, "An individual also may be unable to give consent due to an intellectual or other disability" (p. 1).
- Clark University states that the policy "covers someone whose incapacity results from mental disability" (p. 3).
- University of Mississippi policy states that "a person cannot give consent if he/she is unable to appreciate the nature of the sexual act, as with a person who has a disability that would impair understanding of the act" (p. 1).
- The definition of *consent* in the North Carolina Central University policy states that consent cannot be given when "the individual . . . has a mental or physical disability which inhibits his/her ability to give consent" (p. 4).
- In Minot State University policy, *sexual assault* is defined as having "non-consensual sexual contact" with a "person [who] suffers from a mental disease or defect which renders him or her incapable of understanding the nature of his or her conduct" (p. 1).

This ableist framing marks students with disabilities as functionally limited, incapable of giving consent, as the preceding policy excerpts attest. Further, as King (1993) has observed, the "acceptable appearance for a disabled woman" is to be "asexual" (p. 74). The conflation of disability with incapacitation reflects an "ostracization, marginalization, and distorted response to disability" (King, p. 73).

Although the specific data on students with disabilities are not known for the campuses in this sample, one could extrapolate from U.S. postsecondary data that students with disabilities represent 11% of the student population today (National Center for Education Statistics, 2015). Students with disabilities reported they had one or more of the following conditions: a specific learning disability, a visual handicap, hard of hearing, deafness, a speech disability, an orthopedic handicap, or a health impairment (National Center for Education Statistics, 2015). Therefore, when policies refer to intellectual disability, mental disorder, or a disability that would impair understanding of the act, it is not clear if all such characteristics fall within that 11% or may reflect a broader definition.

Finally, these limited and underdeveloped references to disability fail to consider possible intersections with other dimensions of identity. For instance, Black students constitute a larger percentage of undergraduates reporting disabilities than undergraduates without disabilities (18% versus 16%; National Center for Education Statistics, 2015). Thus, ignoring disability in policy (e.g., disabled people of color who are victims of sexual violence) renders their experiences invisible by the very institutions that are designed to protect and empower them. Policies developed through an intersectional lens may ask "if some differences coalesce to create a more abject form of oppression (e.g., being poor, Black, and disabled) or if some differences support both privilege/invisibility within the same oppressed community (e.g., being Black, wealthy, and gay)" (Erevelles & Minear, 2010, p. 129). (For more information on Deaf students, students with disabilities, and sexual assault on the college campus see Chapter 7.)

Religion and Sexual Violence

Religion is another dimension of identity that was largely invisible in the policies, even though a few campuses in the sample have a religious mission. Policies for Christian campuses (e.g., Samford University, Wheaton College) described how sexual violence is inconsistent with "Christian and moral values" (p. 1). However, professions of "moral, legal, physical, and psychological seriousness" of sexual assault (Wheaton College, p. 8) were similarly evident in secular institutional policies that have statements of commitment to creating safe environments of mutual respect, and assert that "sexual harassment and sexual assault subverts the mission of the university" (Humboldt State University, p. 1). Two other policies at Catholic institutions (College of St. Scholastica and Loyola University) also had little rhetoric that was unique. Neither had any references to the intersection of their religious mission and the offense of sexual violence. Loyola had no special accommodations or resources, whereas St. Scholastica mentioned campus ministry.

Policies also had limited references to religious accommodations. The Bucknell policy identified the chaplain as a resource, and Wheaton's policy indicated it would make changes in "chapel seating" to "prevent unwanted contact" (p. 1). However, when the policy "encourages victims involved in such incidents to seek counseling and/or identify a support person," the policy (only) identifies the counseling center, health services, and the Dean of Students office (Wheaton University, p. 1). The absence of campus ministries generally, or a chaplain specifically, is striking. Further, no mention of other religious identities is considered, such as Muslim, Jewish, or Buddhist students. This policy silence is even more notable when considering the number of international students on some campuses (e.g., 15% of Stony Brook University's student body is international; see "Student Profile," 2013), and that some institutions have campuses in other countries. Individuals who report incidents of sexual violence are never just women or men but are always also colocated in a particular class, race or ethnicity, religion, and/ or sexuality, among other identities (e.g., What does it mean to respond to a Muslim woman from Turkey or a Catholic woman from Italy?). Viewing these colocations through an uninterrogated lens of white Christian privilege enables policies and practices to focus on "poor choices of individuals, rather than a systemic issue" (Ferber, 2012, p. 74).

Research attests to positive associations between spirituality and mental and physical health (Larson & Larson, 2003), and that "spiritually minded individuals will be more likely to treat others with dignity and respect and to value helping others" (Berkel, Vandiver, & Bahner, 2004, p. 129). Thus, policies generally, and at nonsecular campuses in particular, would benefit from greater attention to the role that religion and spirituality can serve in antiviolence strategies (Ayyub, 2000; Horsburgh, 1995; Sokoloff & Dupont, 2005; West, 1999). Further, consideration of the intersection of religion and spirituality with other dimensions of identity reveals additional gaps in policy. For instance, the historically Black institutions (North Carolina Central University, Virginia State University) had no mention of religion or spirituality; yet, in a study of the role of religious involvement among African American survivors of domestic violence, Watlington and Murphy (2006) found a strong correlation between high levels of spirituality, greater religious involvement, and high levels of social support and fewer depression symptoms.

E-race-ing (Erasing) Sexual Violence

No policies specifically or explicitly described race or ethnicity as a characterization of sexual violence, revealing an assumption that sexual violence is a color-blind phenomenon. For instance, the Virginia State University policy provided an overview of the rates of victimization, stating that "9 of 10 rape or sexual assault offenders were known to the victim" and adding that these assaults occurred "on a date" or "involved alcohol." Yet, the Virginia State University policy, a historically Black university, does not describe other characteristics, such as racial demographics, as points to consider regarding perpetration or victimization. Although Virginia State University considers race as central to its institutional identity, all institutions in the sample have racial characteristics in their current demographics and in their history. For instance, Virginia State University describes its founding as an educational institution for Blacks, ultimately becoming "fully integrated" in 1982 ("History of VSU," n.d., para. 3). Samford University, in Alabama, was founded in 1841 as an educational institution for whites, admitting its first Black student in 1967 ("History of Samford University," n.d.). University of California, Merced, a public college founded in 2005, reports that 48% of its students are Hispanic, whereas only 12.7% are white (UC Merced, 2015). Yet, none of these campuses, or any in the sample, indicated race or ethnicity as meaningful to the experience of sexual violence. This color-blindness in policy serves as "camouflage for the self-interest, power, and privilege of dominant groups" (Villalpando, 2003, p. 623).

This failure to acknowledge race or ethnicity in policy not only erases an institution's history, mission, or current demographics but also ignores the reality that sexual violence is experienced differently across racial or ethnic lines (see Chapter 1). Some studies have quantified rates of victimization and perpetration and disaggregated those numbers by race and ethnicity (Tjaden & Thoennes, 2006). Beyond numbers, individuals do not experience sexual violence in the same way. Bograd (2006) notes that violence is "constituted, experienced, and addressed by intersectionalities that shape psyche, interpersonal experiences, family relationships, community location, and social value" (p. 34). For instance, women of color in relationships with Black men "may fear that calling the police will subject their partners to racist stereotypes of Blacks as violent" (Sokoloff & Dupont, 2005, p. 43). Crenshaw (1992) observes that "even when the facts of our stories are believed, myths and stereotypes about Black women influence whether the insult and injury we have experienced is relevant or important" (p. 1470). These contemporary realities are rooted in a history (e.g., a hierarchy of race over gender in America during slavery) that results in different outcomes today for Black and white American men and women (Nagel, 2003). The "privilege of masculinity" does not afford Black men "immunity from racist stereotypes" that cast them as more violent (Jaggers & Iverson, 2012, p. 195) and they are not "privileged and protected" by the "same 'benefit of the doubt' enjoyed by their white counterparts" (Harper et al., 2011, p. 192). Thus, the failure of policies to acknowledge that race matters is whitewashing the enduring relationship between race and ethnicity and sexual violence.

My discussion of race and ethnicity is complicit with a problem in the literature. Bograd (2006) observes that most of the scholarship on race and violence focuses on Black or Latino populations, and that "ethnic groups are often collapsed into a single category, such as Asians" (p. 27). I too have cited examples related to Black and Latino populations. Further, in my efforts to illuminate race and ethnicity, intersecting dimensions of identity are concealed. For instance, working-class women from minority ethnic groups are more likely to experience a "second rape" in the criminal justice system (Phipps, 2010, p. 370). Sokoloff and Dupont (2005) assert that "of the three interlocking systems of oppression," class analysis of interpersonal violence is "the least developed" in comparison to race and gender (p. 40), and some scholars have observed that racial differences disappear when other factors, such as social class, are controlled (Bograd, 2006; Cunradi, Caetano, Clark, & Schafer, 2000). Many other dimensions of identity were also absent from the policies and warrant further interrogation, such as citizenship status, veteran status, national origin, age, and whether one's first language is English. Further research is needed, but campus administrators (from policy authors to victim advocates) must also interrogate their policies and practices to reveal how individuals experience sexual violence differently.

Implications and Conclusions

My intersectional analysis of these identity categories risks reproducing some of the problems I seek to illuminate. By foregrounding particular dimensions of identity (e.g., race, religion, dis/ability), one might see only individual identity characteristics and not interlocking social structures that perpetuate inequality or might be "misconstrued or deliberately used against vulnerable populations" (Sokoloff & Dupont, 2005, p. 48). As policy authors become aware and begin to map identity onto policy, they might produce lists of resources based on difference (e.g., VP numbers in policy, inclusion of campus ministries, accessibility services, referrals to LGBT resources), but awareness of only individual difference would fail to destabilize how structures privilege some and systematically disadvantage others.

Instead, policy authors must interrogate structural oppression to reveal how privilege and advantage operate systemically (i.e., white victims and perpetrators receive benefits from their white skin privilege). Or, as Koestner (2000) observed, how "white skin, virginity, Christianity, . . . an upper-middle-class socioeconomic status, [and] heterosexuality" constituted "a 'perfect victim' image" (p. 33). The dominant image of a sexual violence victim is rooted in white, middle-class femininity (Iverson, 2006; Richie, 1996) and policy authors must disrupt the dominant construction of the perfect victim. Further, they must problematize dichotomous language that situates individuals as victims or survivors, as passive or resistant, or as victimized or empowered. Characterizations (victim and survivor) must be complicated to reflect the ways identity is socially constituted and thus sexual violence is experienced differently by, for example, a Vietnamese woman, a Black Muslim, or a Jewish lesbian, among others. So, while some studies report differences among victims and survivors of sexual violence (namely differences among women), policymakers may start to codify these differences. A focus on only individual difference will likely do little to interrogate "just what such differences mean beyond an apparently increased vulnerability to violence" (Razack, 1994, p. 892).

Failing to employ an intersectional analysis perpetuates the notion of universal risk, for it does not acknowledge how, for instance, poor women of color are "most likely to be in both dangerous intimate relationships *and* [emphasis added] dangerous social positions" (Richie, 2000, p. 1136). One campus in this study illustrates this: The student population at University of California, Merced is 48% Hispanic, 61% low income, and 63% of students speak a language other than English at home ("First Year Experience for Faculty," n.d.; "UC Is Best Top-Ranked University," 2004; UC Merced, 2015). An intersectional analysis calls for policymakers to move beyond institutionalized vocabularies and consider what individual and structural effects exist when sexual violence occurs at the intersections of ethnicity, language, and social class. Then, policy may describe differentiated resources, support services, prevention programming, and articulation of rights for respondent and complainant. And educators, administrators, and policymakers can begin to see how intersectionalities shape the ways that sexual violence "is experienced by self and responded to by others, how personal and social consequences are represented, and how and whether . . . safety can be obtained" (Bograd, 1999, p. 276).

This intersectional analysis revealed that policy is never neutral, and policy authors must "uncover power dynamics" embedded in policy (Phipps, 2010, p. 362). As policymakers codify the diversity of individual lived experiences with sexual violence, they must also employ a "structural analysis of particular differences" (Phelan, 1994, p. 8) to reveal how some dimensions of identity secure normative status (white, Christian, straight, able-bodied), whereas others are marginalized if not invisible. Further, an intersectional analysis is needed not only for the problem of sexual violence but also for the solutions whose usefulness is potentially limited for those who are "multiply disadvantaged by numerous systems of inequality" (Ferber, 2012, p. 64).

Finally, as Hunter (2008) argues, the focus must be not only on the "minoritized, queered, and/or feminized subjects" (p. 521) of the policy but also on the identities and social locations of the policymakers, including how systems of privilege provide a framework of "assumptions and rules that inform the decisions, behaviors, and interactions of individuals" (Ferber, 2012, p. 64). I believe policy as a solution to sexual violence can achieve emancipatory and not just compliance goals. An intersectional analysis, with its emphasis on individual and structural dimensions of sexual violence might make it more possible for policymakers to be cartographers of marginalization. Using an intersectional lens, they can map difference and make transparent "the interlocking or simultaneous grids of oppression and hierarchies" experienced by individuals as members of multiple groups (Phelan, 1994, p. 12).

References

Alriksson-Schmidt, A. I., Armour, B. S., & Thibadeau, J. K. (2010). Are adolescent girls with a physical disability at increased risk for sexual violence? *Journal of School Health, 80,* 361–367.

Andersen, M., & Collins, P. H. (2001). Introduction. In M. Andersen & P. H. Collins (Eds.), *Race, class, gender: An anthology* (4th ed., pp. 1–9). Belmont, CA: Wadsworth.

Ayyub, R. (2000). Domestic violence in the South Asian Muslim immigrant population in the United States. *Journal of Social Distress and the Homeless, 9,* 237–248.

BacaZinn, M., Hondagneu-Sotolo, P., & Messner, M. (Eds.). (2000). *Gender through the prism of difference* (2nd ed.). Boston, MA: Allyn & Bacon.

Belknap, J. (2015). *The invisible woman: Gender, crime, and justice* (4th ed.). Stamford, CT: Cengage Learning.

Bem, S. L. (1985, January). Androgyny and gender schema theory: A conceptual and empirical integration. In *Nebraska symposium on motivation* (Vol. 32, pp. 179–226). Lincoln, NE: University of Nebraska Press.

Berkel, L. A., Vandiver, B. J., & Bahner, A. D. (2004). Gender role attitudes, religion, and spirituality as predictors of domestic violence attitudes in White college students. *Journal of College Student Development, 45,* 119–133.

Bograd, M. (1999). Strengthening domestic violence theories: Intersections of race, class, sexual orientation, and gender. *Journal of Marital and Family Therapy, 25,* 275–289.

Bograd, M. (2006). Strengthening domestic violence theories: Intersections of race, class, sexual orientation, and gender. In N. J. Sokoloff (with C. Pratt), *Domestic violence at the margins: Readings on race, class, gender, and culture* (pp. 25–38). New Brunswick, NJ: Rutgers University Press.

Brah, A., & Phoenix, A. (2004). Ain't I a woman? Revisiting intersectionality. *Journal of International Women's Studies, 5*(3), 75–86.

Cole, E. R. (2009). Gender, narratives and intersectionality: Can personal experience approaches to research contribute to "undoing gender"? *International Review of Education, 55,* 561–578.

Colker, R. (1996). *Hybrid: Bisexuals, multiracials, and other misfits under American law.* New York: New York University Press.

Collins, P. H. (1990). *Black feminist thought: Knowledge, consciousness and the politics of empowerment.* Boston, MA: Unwin Hyman.

Collins, P. H. (1998). It's all in the family: Intersections of gender, race, and nation. *Hypatia, 13*(3), 62–82.

Crenshaw, K. (1991). Mapping the margins: Intersectionality, identity politics, and violence against women of color. *Stanford Law Review, 43,* 1241–1299.

Crenshaw, K. (1992). Race, gender, and sexual harassment. *Southern California Law Review, 65,* 1467–1476.

Cunradi, C. B., Caetano, R. Clark, C., & Schafer, J. (2000). Neighborhood poverty as a predictor of intimate partner violence among White, Black, and Hispanic couples in the United States. *Annals of Epidemiology, 10,* 297–308.

Danner, M. J., & Carmody, D. C. (2001). Missing gender in cases of infamous school violence: Investigating research and media explanations. *Justice Quarterly, 18,* 87–114.

Davis, D. J., Brunn-Bevel, R. J., & Olive, J. L. (Eds.). (2015). *Intersectionality in educational research.* Sterling, VA: Stylus.

Denzin, N., & Lincoln, Y. (Eds.). (2011). *The SAGE handbook of qualitative research* (4th ed.). Thousand Oaks, CA: SAGE.

Donat, P. L. N., & D'Emilio, J. (1998). A feminist redefinition of rape and sexual assault: Historical foundations and change. In M. E. Odem & J. Clay-Warner (Eds.), *Confronting rape and sexual assault* (pp. 35–49). Lanham, MD: Rowman & Littlefield.

Erevelles, N., & Minear, A. (2010). Unspeakable offenses: Untangling race and disability in discourses of intersectionality. *Journal of Literary & Cultural Disability Studies, 4,* 127–145.

Ferber, A. L. (2012). The culture of privilege: Color-blindness, postfeminism, and Christonormativity. *Journal of Social Issues, 68*(1), 63–77.

Fine, M. (1994). Working the hyphens: Reinventing self and other in qualitative research. In N. Denzin & Y. Lincoln (Eds.), *Handbook of qualitative research* (pp. 130–155). Thousand Oaks, CA: Sage.

First year experience for faculty. (n.d.). Retrieved from http://fye.ucmerced.edu/

Fried, A. (1994). "It's hard to change what we want to change": Rape crisis centers as organizations. *Gender & Society, 8,* 562–583.

Harper, S. R., Davis, R. J., Jones, D. E., McGowan, B. L., Ingam, T. N., & Platt, C. S. (2011). Race and racism in the experiences of Black male resident assistants at predominantly White universities. *Journal of College Student Development, 52,* 180–200.

Harris, K. L., & Hanchey, J. N. (2014). (De)stabilizing sexual violence discourse: Masculinization of victimhood, organizational blame, and labile imperialism. *Communication and Critical/Cultural Studies, 11*(4), 1–20.

History of Samford University. (n.d.). Retrieved from http://www.samford.edu/about/history

History of VSU. (n.d.). Retrieved from http://www.vsu.edu/about/history/history-vsu.php

Hollomotz, A. (2009). Beyond 'vulnerability:' An ecological model approach to conceptualizing risk of sexual violence against people with learning difficulties. *British Journal of Social Work, 39,* 99–112.

Horsburgh, B. (1995). Lifting the veil of secrecy: Domestic violence in the Jewish community. *Harvard Women's Law Journal, 18,* 171–217.

Hunter, S. (2008). Living documents: A feminist psychosocial approach to the relational politics of policy documentation. *Critical Social Policy, 28*, 506–528.

Iverson, S. V. (2006). Performing gender: A discourse analysis of theatre-based sexual violence prevention programs. *NASPA Journal, 43*, 547–577.

Iverson, S. V. (2015). The risky subject: A policy discourse analysis of sexual assault policies in higher education. In S. C. Wooten & R. W. Mitchell (Eds.), *The crisis of campus sexual violence: Critical perspectives on prevention and response* (pp. 15–32). New York, NY: Routledge.

Jaggers, D., & Iverson, S. V. (2012). "Are you as hard as 50 Cent?" Negotiating race and masculinity in the residence halls. *Journal of College and University Student Housing, 39*(1), 186–199.

Jennrich, J., & Kowalski-Braun, M. (2014). "My head is spinning": Doing authentic intersectional work in identity centers. *Journal of Progressive Policy & Practice, 2*, 199–211.

Johnson, A. (2006). *Privilege, power and difference* (2nd ed.). New York, NY: McGraw-Hill.

Jones, S. R. (1996). Toward inclusive theory: Disability as social construction. *NASPA Journal, 33*, 347–354.

Katz, J. (2006). *The macho paradox: Why some men hurt women and how all men can help*. Naperville, IL: Sourcebooks.

Ken, I. (2008). Beyond the intersection: A new culinary metaphor for race-class-gender studies. *Sociological Theory, 26*, 152–172.

Kim, J. (2012). Taking rape seriously: Rape as slavery. *Harvard Journal of Law & Gender, 35*, 263–310.

King, Y. (1993). The other body. *Ms, 3*(5), 72–75.

Koestner, K. (2000). The perfect rape victim. In J. Gold & S. Villari (Eds.), *Just sex: Students rewrite the rules on sex, violence, activism, and equality* (pp. 30–38). New York, NY: Rowman & Littlefield.

Larson, D. B., & Larson, S. S. (2003). Spirituality's potential relevance to physical and emotional health: A brief review of quantitative research. *Journal of Psychology and Theology, 31*(1), 37–51.

McCall, L. (2005). The complexity of intersectionality. *Signs, 30*, 1771–1800.

McFarlane, J., Hughes, R. B., Nosek, M. A., Groff, J. Y., Swedlend, N., & Dolan Mullen, P. (2001). Abuse assessment screen-disability (AAS-D): Measuring frequency, type, and perpetrator of abuse toward women with physical disabilities. *Journal of Women's Health & Gender-Based Medicine, 10*, 861–866.

Mitchell, D., Jr., Simmons, C. Y., & Greyerbiehl, L. A. (2014). *Intersectionality & higher education: Theory, research, & praxis*. New York, NY: Peter Lang.

Nagel, J. (2003). *Race, ethnicity, and sexuality: Intimate intersections, forbidden frontiers*. New York, NY: Oxford University Press.

National Center for Education Statistics. (2015). *Fast facts: Students with disabilities*. Retrieved from http://nces.ed.gov/fastfacts/display.asp?id=60

Phelan, S. (1994). *Getting specific: Postmodern lesbian politics*. Minneapolis: University of Minnesota Press.

Phipps, A. (2009). Rape and respectability: Ideas about sexual violence and social class. *Sociology, 43*, 669–685.

Phipps, A. (2010). Violent and victimized bodies: Sexual violence policy in England and Wales. *Critical Social Policy, 30*, 359–383.

Razack, S. (1994). From consent to responsibility, from pity to respect: Subtexts in cases of sexual violence involving girls and women with developmental disabilities. *Law & Social Inquiry, 19*, 891–922.

Reinharz, S. (1992). *Feminist methods in social research.* New York, NY: Oxford University Press.

Rhedding-Jones, J. (2002). An undoing of documents and other texts: Towards a critical multiculturalism in early childhood education. *Contemporary Issues in Early Childhood, 3*(1), 90–116.

Richie, B. (1996). *Compelled to crime: The gender entrapment of battered Black women.* New York, NY: Routledge.

Richie, B. (2000). A Black feminist reflection on the antiviolence movement. *Signs, 25*, 1133–1137.

Rose, V. M. (1977). Rape as a social problem: A byproduct of the feminist movement. *Social Problems, 25*(1), 75–89.

Smith, D. L. (2008). Disability, gender and intimate partner violence: Relationships from the behavioral risk factor surveillance system. *Sexuality and Disability, 26*(1), 15–28.

Smith, L., Foley, P. F., & Chaney, M. P. (2008). Addressing classism, ableism, and heterosexism in counselor education. *Journal of Counseling & Development, 86*, 303–309.

Sokoloff, N. J., & Dupont, I. (2005). Domestic violence at the intersections of race, class, and gender: Challenges and contributions to understanding violence against marginalized women in diverse communities. *Violence Against Women, 11*, 38–64.

Stotzer, R. L. (2009). Violence against transgender people: A review of United States data. *Aggression and Violent Behavior, 14*, 170–179.

Student profile. (2013). Retrieved from http://www.stonybrook.edu/commcms/irpe/fall.html

Tevis, T., & Griffen, J. (2014). Absent voices: Intersectionality and college students with physical disabilities. *Journal of Progressive Policy & Practice, 2*, 239–254.

Thapar-Bjorkert, S., & Morgan, K. J. (2010). "But sometimes I think . . . they put themselves in the situation": Exploring blame and responsibility in interpersonal violence. *Violence Against Women, 16*, 32–59.

Tjaden, P. G., & Thoennes, N. (2006). *Extent, nature, and consequences of rape victimization: Findings from the National Violence Against Women Survey.* Washington, DC: U.S. Department of Justice.

UC is best top-ranked university at enrolling low-income students, study says. (2004). Retrieved from www.ucmerced.edu/news/2004/uc-best-top-ranked-university-enrolling-low-income-students-study-says

UC Merced. (2015). *Fast facts.* Retrieved from www.ucmerced.edu/fast-facts

U.S. Department of Justice. (2015). *FY 2012 OVW grant awards by program.* Retrieved from www.ovw.usdoj.gov/fy2012-grant-program.htm#2

Villalpando, O. (2003). Self-segregation or self-reservation? A critical race theory and Latina/o critical theory analysis of a student of Chicana/o college students. *International Journal of Qualitative Studies in Education, 16*, 619–646.

Watlington, C. G., & Murphy, C. M. (2006). The roles of religion and spirituality among African American survivors of domestic violence. *Journal of Clinical Psychology, 62*, 837–857.

West, T. (1999). *Wounds of the spirit: Black women, violence, and resistance ethics.* New York: New York University Press.

Wooten, S. C. (2015). Heterosexist discourses: How feminist theory shaped campus sexual violence policy. In S. C. Wooten & R. W. Mitchell (Eds.), *The crisis of campus sexual violence: Critical perspectives on prevention and response* (pp. 33–51). New York, NY: Routledge.

Wooten, S. C., & Mitchell, R. W. (Eds.). (2015). *The crisis of campus sexual violence: Critical perspectives on prevention and response.* New York, NY: Routledge.

The sample for this study includes the following:

Institution	State	Sexual Misconduct Policies
Samford University	Alabama	Title IX Sexual Misconduct Policy (2012–13)
Humboldt State University	California	Policy Against Sexual Harassment and Sexual Assault (2005)
University of California, Merced	California	Sexual Harassment Policy (2006) and Protocol (2012)
Gallaudet University	District of Columbia (DC)	Sexual Misconduct Policy (2013–14)
Joliet Junior College	Illinois	Title IX Policy on Sexual Harassment and Assault (2012)
Loyola University Chicago	Illinois	Sexual Misconduct Policy (n.d.)
Wheaton College	Illinois	Sexual Assault Policy (n.d.)
Clark University	Massachusetts	Sexual Violence Policy (n.d.)
College of St. Scholastica	Minnesota	Sexual Assault and Violence Policy (n.d.)
University of Mississippi	Mississippi	Sexual Misconduct Policy (2012–13)
University of Montana	Montana	Policy on Discrimination, Harassment, Sexual Misconduct, Stalking, and Retaliation (2013)
Stony Brook University	New York	Sexual Harassment Policy (2008)
North Carolina Central University	North Carolina	Sexual Violence Policy

(Continues)

(Continued)

Institution	State	Sexual Misconduct Policies
University of North Carolina at Chapel Hill	North Carolina	Policy on Prohibited Harassment, Including Sexual Misconduct and Discrimination (2013)
Minot State University	North Dakota	Policy on Harassment (2008)
Ohio University	Ohio	Sexual Misconduct Policy (2012)
Bucknell University	Pennsylvania	Sexual Misconduct and Relationship Violence Policy (2013–14)
University of Tennessee at Martin	Tennessee	Sexual Misconduct (n.d.)
North Central Texas College	Texas	Student Welfare Policy on Freedom From Discrimination, Harassment, and Retaliation Policy (2013)
Old Dominion University	Virginia	Sexual Misconduct Policy (2011)
Virginia State University	Virginia	Sexual Misconduct Policy (2009)
Fairmont State University	West Virginia	Policy on Sexual Assault (n.d.); Consolidated Student Code of Conduct (2013)

Note. From "FY 2012 OVW Grant Awards by Program," by U.S. Department of Justice, 2015, www.ovw .usdoj.gov/fy2012-grant-program.htm#2

CONCLUSION

History, Identity, and Power-Conscious Strategies for Addressing Sexual Violence on College Campuses

Chris Linder and Jessica C. Harris

As we wrap up writing and editing this text, sexual violence continues to command attention from educators, policymakers, and activists. Newspaper articles, blogs, social media, scholarship, and conference sessions remain focused on sexual violence on college campuses. Some authors, activists, and scholars are seemingly more aware of the complexities of sexual violence and have attempted to center the voices of students often at the margins of the conversation (e.g., Badejo, 2016; Odem, 2016; Wanjuki, 2016). Unfortunately, the majority of scholarship, media, and policy continues to focus on one type of survivor: stereotypically attractive, white cisgender heterosexual college women at elite institutions.

In fact, as we continued to review emerging scholarship about sexual violence while editing this book, we observed how this literature seemed to become increasingly problematic as more researchers attempted to delve into scholarship about sexual violence. For instance, some scholars focused on "personal safety" (Zugazaga, Werner, Clifford, Weaver, & Ware, 2016, p. 33) as a sexual assault prevention tactic, which reinforces a myth that sexual violence is committed by strangers and that potential victims can reduce their risk through safety precautions. Additionally, some scholarship still examines experiences of minoritized groups from a deficit perspective. Curran, Monahan, Samp, Coles, DiClemente, and Sales (2016) used a "social skills deficit hypothesis" to examine the link between "mental health problems and sexual risk for African American women" (p. 1). This research places blame on the individual rather than historical and societal systems of domination.

We also acknowledge that some scholarship over the past year has critically advanced knowledge concerning sexual violence on campus. Littleton and Dodd (2016) accounted for the societal and cultural influences on the differing rape scripts of white college women and African American college women. Additionally, Hipp, Bellis, Goodnight, Brennan, Swartout, and Cook (2015) used feminist theory to explore perpetrators' damaging justifications of sexual violence. Finally, Patterson (2016) centered on queer and trans* resilience related to sexual violence.

In an attempt to counter the majoritarian narrative, often upheld by deficit and ahistorical extant literature, the contributors to this volume highlight ways historically minoritized populations have experienced sexual violence and the ways these populations have been systematically ignored in sexual violence prevention, awareness, and response efforts on college campuses. In Chapter 4 Marine examines how prevention and response programs failed to consider the experiences of trans* students in programming and policies, highlighting the importance of gender-conscious policies and programs in sexual violence education and response. Williams's Chapter 7 examines the ways Deaf and hard-of-hearing students experience high rates of sexual violence, yet few college and university education and response programs provide resources specific to Deaf and hard-of-hearing students or any students with disabilities. Harris examines in Chapter 2 how ahistoricism contributes to a lack of understanding of the ways racism intersects with sexual violence to influence women of color's experiences with sexual violence, resulting in ineffective prevention and response.

Several contributors also examined the assumptions embedded in sexual violence work on college campuses. In Chapter 11 Iverson discusses how policies related to sexual violence largely ignore power and identity-related issues in sexual violence. Most campus sexual violence policies fail to consider the role of power and privilege in their policies, resulting in ineffective sexual violence responses. Similarly, Hong illustrates in Chapter 1 how addressing sexual violence as an individual, rather than a systemic issue, results in ineffective prevention and response because educators and administrators deal with the symptoms rather than the roots of sexual violence. In Chapter 3 Linder examines the role of racism in the history of sexual violence activism, highlighting ways Black women have engaged in intersectional activism since the late 1800s related to sexual violence.

Palacios and Aguilar's Chapter 10 addresses the importance of distinguishing among prevention, awareness, and response related to sexual violence policy and education. Prevention requires educators and policymakers to address potential perpetrators because only perpetrators of sexual violence can stop it from happening. Awareness refers to activities related to education and consciousness-raising among students, a form of risk reduction but not prevention. Response efforts often refer to the activities that happen after the occurrence of sexual violence. College and university administrators spend the vast amount of their time related to sexual violence on response because legislators, lawsuits, and student activists largely spend their time and energy on the institution's response as well (Mangan, 2016). We believe this is a misdirected approach to addressing sexual violence on campus, as spending significant amounts of time and energy on responding to sexual violence after it happens takes away from the important work of preventing assault.

Finally, contributors describe significant gaps in our knowledge about students' experiences with sexual violence. Tillapaugh's Chapter 5 on men who survived sexual assault in college is one of the first studies to examine this population. Although some previous scholarship examines men's experiences with childhood sexual violence, very little scholarship addresses adult or college men's experiences with sexual assault. Similarly, Garvey, Hitchins, and McDonald's Chapter 8 on queer-spectrum students' experiences with sexual violence illustrates the complexities of research and assessment related to sexual violence. When researchers and educators do not ask accurate or complete questions, they end up with incomplete and inaccurate answers. When researchers ignore queer-spectrum students, men, trans* students, students with disabilities, students of color, and students from additional minoritized populations because of small sample sizes, these populations are rendered invisible. By centering the experiences of students relegated to the margins, we aimed to provide readers with a more nuanced understanding of sexual violence on college campuses. We acknowledge that there are additional perspectives and populations not represented in this book, yet we also believe that the scholarship presented here is a continuation of the conversation, not the end.

The populations discussed in this book are not mutually exclusive, although we recognize that the outline of this book may reinforce the understanding that they are. In other words, because one chapter is dedicated to women of color, one to trans* students, and one to Deaf and hard-of-hearing students, we risk essentializing the experiences and identities of these groups. We made a conscious decision to structure the book in this manner because we believed it was important to center one population at a time to help readers understand some of the unique experiences of students in and between those populations. In moving forward, we ask the readers to use these identity-specific chapters in an intersecting manner. How might Chapters 7 and 8 inform one another to analyze the intersections of being a Deaf woman of color? We in no way assert that these chapters should provide an additive approach to intersectionality, as that is the antithesis of the theory of intersectionality (Crenshaw, 1991). Instead, this book and its chapters must begin a necessary conversation that accounts for the intersections of multiple identities in sexual violence on college campuses.

We conclude by sharing our reflections and the lessons we learned through the process of editing the book. In our narratives, we focus on the importance of challenging ahistoricism and power-evasive, identity-neutral approaches to sexual violence. We also explore issues of reactive prevention education, including the conflation of sexual violence prevention and response. In closing, we offer recommendations for educators to consider the role of intersectionality in their work and encourage a power-conscious, historic, and identity-centered approach for the prevention of, awareness of, and response to sexual violence.

Reflections and Lessons Learned

In an effort to generate ideas for the final chapter, each of us reflected on the following question: What have I learned from editing this book? We then came together to discuss our reflections. We offer those reflections here in the spirit of transparency, in nonacademic, first-person language, to reflect the personal nature of reflecting on this work. After reflecting on our observations as editors, we highlight directions for future research and strategies for practice.

Jessica

I have learned an immense amount while editing this book, but I have *unlearned* even more in this editing process. In moving forward with addressing, eradicating, preventing, and responding to sexual violence I urge all of us—educators, students, survivors—activists, to unlearn just as much, if not more, than we attempt to learn about these issues.

From this process, I gained understanding about the power of collaboration, through which I have attempted to unlearn the individualistic tendencies I have been socialized in. Since starting this book, I observed a wide chasm between faculty and practitioners on the issue of sexual violence on the college campus. Similarly, there exist disconnects between scholarly theorizing and practitioner-oriented work concerning sexual violence in higher education. As a faculty member, I can theorize all I want on sexual violence, but my jargon-filled theorizing does not necessarily filter into practice and action on campus. Furthermore, practitioners take action on the college campus to eradicate sexual violence, but their work may not be guided by theories, or theorizing, on the issue. What is the point in researching and theorizing if it is not applicable to or useful for practice, which is often where the tangible change occurs?

Editing this volume allowed me to see firsthand how positive change on the college campus concerning sexual violence and other inequities will have a higher chance of occurring when faculty and practitioners work together. Chris and I used what we *learned* from faculty members' chapters to support *unlearning* in practitioner-based chapters, and vice versa. For instance, Susan Marine pointed out that women-only or men-only prevention programs almost always reinforce a gender binary. We used her assertions to shift language and implications in other chapters that encouraged women-only or men-only programming. Using one chapter author's knowledge to shift language and recommendations in other chapters is just one small example of how faculty and practitioners can work together to eradicate sexual violence and intersecting systems of oppression.

Collaboration is often, if not always, arbitrarily cited as the answer to campus issues, but it is not often actualized. There are many reasons for the lack of collaboration between campus constituents: lack of time, isolated departments and offices, and professional hierarchies, to name a few. Additionally, the impetus for collaboration is often placed on practitioners, not faculty. This edited volume has taught me to unlearn the individualistic barriers, such as working in isolation or offering recommendations without reaching out to others for advice and feedback, that I have been socialized to believe and exist in as a faculty member. I urge faculty to reach out to and collaborate with practitioners at their institutions to jointly explore approaches to and the destabilization of sexual violence on campus. I believe it is still important to theorize about sexual violence, but faculty should ensure that this theorizing helps and influences practice.

Editing this book also contextualized the ways white supremacy, patriarchy, and other systems of domination are ingrained and embedded on the college campus to maintain the prevalence of sexual violence. Both Chris and I observed that several of the contributors, myself included, perpetuated the same dominant ideologies we aimed to break down through the writing and editing of this book. For instance, one chapter was about race, but only through a monoracial understanding of racial identity. Another contributor suggested gender-specific and separate programming for men students and women students, a recommendation that perpetuates a gender binary. I do not state this to shame our colleagues and contributors; instead, I relay this information to acknowledge that scholars, practitioners, students, community members—all of us—have unlearning to do. We exist in a colonial society and work and learn in a colonially based education system (Patton,

2015). Our minds are colonized, even when we strive to believe otherwise. We must acknowledge this colonization and unlearn the continual, often tacit, lessons of the colonizer if we are to have any chance at eradicating sexual violence (which is grounded in colonization).

Chris

Through the process of editing this book, I reflected on how knowledge is created through scholarship among experts. I set up Google and library database alerts of scholarly material about sexual violence and sexual assault on college campuses. As I reviewed the articles from the alerts, I was troubled to see that most scholarship approaches sexual violence from an ahistoric, identity-neutral, victim-responsible perspective. Many scholars assume that sexual violence is perpetrated by male strangers toward female victims. These uninterrogated assumptions by researchers lead to poor scholarship. If we are not even asking good questions to address sexual violence, how can we get helpful answers? How can we shift the ways we ask questions so that we can find different answers? How can we shift deciding on who is expert on this topic?

I also reflected on my own role in determining who gets to be an expert and what gets to be knowledge throughout editing this book. As the contributors sent us their chapters, Jessica and I edited them. As we made suggestions for clarity and pushed authors to be bolder, I frequently felt that something crucial was missing. And as we kept moving forward, I realized, as Jessica stated, we are colonizers and colonized. Even with permission to be bold and innovative and suggest new approaches to address sexual violence, all of us minimized our voices, used oppressor language, and named and subscribed to current best practices in our work. We limited our thinking based on how we have been socialized to believe that we must fit in a system. We do not even know what it would look like or feel like to work outside a system.

For some of us, we cannot consider new ways to respond to sexual violence because we are in crisis mode. When I have survivor after survivor sitting across from me, I don't have the time or energy to be innovative or creative. I only have time to take care of the person sitting across from me and attempt to take care of myself in the process. I am striving to support that survivor in navigating the poor systems we have, and I have little energy left to attempt to interrupt those systems. For example, in a session at a conference this spring, a person asked us our recommendations for working with police who "don't get it" (sexual violence). My immediate response was, "Don't work with them! Our current system of policing is racist, homophobic, transphobic, and sexist . . . all of the roots of sexual violence." And I also know that is not realistic. That person, who works as a professional in residence life, doesn't have the option of not working with police. However, I hope this book provides us with an opportunity to start to ask what it might look like if we did things differently.

What would it mean if we didn't work with police? What would it mean if we listened to survivors, especially women of color survivors, when they tell us, "I don't want him to go to jail. I don't want to put him in the racist criminal justice system. I want him to stop raping people." How could we accomplish this? What if we didn't rely on police for our primary point of response and adjudication? What if we dismantled and challenged the notion created by white women that restorative justice was never appropriate for sexual or interpersonal violence? What if we got out of our own way, stopped professionalizing this field, and listened to survivors about how to respond and prevent sexual violence?

There are no better experts than the people who have survived sexual violence to help educators, policymakers, and scholars understand sexual violence. No research on blue lights, self-defense, self-esteem, prior victimization, or rape myth acceptance is going to tell us what we need to know. We must *listen* to survivors and to the advocates who support survivors. Advocates and educators on college campuses frequently have a deep understanding of the day-to-day experiences of survivors and a nuanced understanding of perpetration based on the patterns they learn about from survivors every day. The knowledge of these advocates is minimized because many of these practitioners do not have PhDs or other markers of knowledge generators in the academy, and we are doing a significant disservice to sexual violence prevention by overlooking the knowledge of survivors, educators, and advocates. Sometimes the people doing the most innovative, victim-centered, complex, and identity- and power-conscious sexual violence work do not see themselves as experts because we, the people with the power to determine who has the knowledge, have not acknowledged them for what they do.

Recommendations for Addressing Sexual Violence

In the sections that follow, we offer recommendations for addressing the challenges raised by the contributors to this book and raised by our own reflections. We foreground the utility of employing intersectionality as theory and praxis for addressing sexual violence on campuses. Additionally, we advocate for the importance of power, identity, and history-conscious strategies for addressing sexual violence and argue that educators must move beyond reactive prevention to proactive sexual violence prevention.

Using Intersectionality as Theory and Practice

Intersectionality theory must frame educators' approaches to sexual violence on college campuses. Intersectionality accounts for individuals' and groups' identity-specific experiences and foregrounds the social process and structures that shape these experiences (Crenshaw, 1989, 1991; Thornton-Dill & Zambrana, 2009). This theory not only highlights the differing experiences of sexual violence for individuals with intersecting identities but also focuses on and destabilizes macrolevel systems of oppression that influence sexual violence on college campuses.

On the microlevel, an intersectional approach centers the experiences and voices of students who exist outside dominant understandings of who are, or who can be, survivors of sexual violence. Accounting for the microlevel of intersectionality in sexual violence work includes enhanced understandings and programming on men students, trans* students, women of color students, and other populations that are not often included or represented in sexual violence scholarship and practice. Intersectionality theory also encourages educators to approach research and practice from an identity system, such as gender or students of color, rather than an individual identity group, such as men or women. This approach welcomes and may more fully account for students across identities rather than targeting and addressing one specific identity or one narrow population of students.

Intersectionality requires educators to move beyond a microlevel approach to multiple identities to examine and address interlocking systems of domination that contribute to the prevalence of sexual violence on college campuses. The macrolevel of intersectionality shows how institutions, including U.S. higher education, reproduce power structures (Crenshaw, 1989, 1991). Concerning sexual violence, educators must focus on institutions, not only in higher education but also those that influence higher education, that reproduce patriarchal, white supremacist, transphobic, heteronormative, and other ideologies that influence sexual violence on college campuses. For example, fraternities are institutions that support patriarchy; whiteness; hetereonormativity; transphobia; and, ultimately, cisgender white male dominance and power (see Cabrera, 2012; Harper & Hurtado, 2007). These systems and institutions, not alcohol, hormones, or the way women dress, influence individual fraternity men's feelings of privilege, power, and entitlement to violate and own others' bodies.

On the macrolevel, intersectionality theory also allows an exploration of how "discourses of resistance (e.g., feminism and antiracism) could themselves function as sites that produced and legitimized marginalization" (Carbado, Crenshaw, Mays, & Tomlinson, 2013, p. 304). Anita Badejo (2016) offers an example of how competing discourses of resistance work to silence individuals with multiple marginalized identities. In her article, Badejo detailed how Black women students at Spelman College, an all-women's historically Black college, were silenced when they attempted to report or speak out about sexual violence perpetrated by Black men at Morehouse College, an all-men's historically Black college and Spelman's brother school. Badejo and the Black women described in the article explored how antiracist discourse and concern for Black men at Morehouse trumped the discourses and needs of Black women. "Respectability politics and expectations that Black women stand in solidarity with Black men in the quest for racial justice make the conversations surrounding gender and sexual violence particularly fraught" (para. 6). In this example, antiracist discourse obscures the intersections of race and gender, racism and sexism, in the Black community. Moreover, because Black women are not accounted for in feminist discourse, which focuses on white womanhood, Black women at Spelman are "theoretically erased" (Crenshaw, 1989, p. 139). This erasure (re)contributes to the invisibility of Black women in sexual violence policies, procedures, and programs that aim to keep campus communities safe and equitable. Unfortunately, if these policies, procedures, and programs do not account for or represent Black women, then Black women are not protected by or given a voice through these mechanisms.

An intersectional approach focuses on how and why individuals with multiple marginalized identities fall into a chasm and are not often represented in and by sexual violence prevention efforts and discourse on college campuses. For example, community agencies and national nonprofit organizations should train advocates who work with survivors and campus judicial officers to understand the intersections of identities and how they may influence women of color's choices over reporting their experiences with sexual violence. Educational programs should center students' experiences with multiple forms of oppression, raising awareness about the unique ways trans* people, gay men, or Deaf and hard-of-hearing students navigate experiences with oppression related to sexual violence. Educators may also organize support and community-building groups for specific populations to discuss their experiences with oppression. A support group specifically for women of color survivors of sexual violence may be a space to address and validate the ways women of color who are assaulted by men of color may feel torn about how to effectively move forward and advocate for themselves without further marginalizing or contributing racist perceptions of men of color. These identity-conscious approaches to addressing sexual violence may also create opportunities for a more historic approach to sexual violence prevention and response.

Historic and Power- and Identity-Conscious Approaches to Sexual Violence

We work in a colonially grounded education system and live in a nation grounded in colonization (Patton, 2015; Wilder, 2013). Delving even deeper into this discomforting narrative, the United States was founded on the rape, violation, and terrorization of indigenous women's bodies (Smith, 2005). These acts of terror supported the implementation of a patriarchal and white-dominated society. A white patriarchal society flourished while white slave masters raped Black women in an effort to terrorize the Black community, assert ownership over Black bodies, and produce more slaves (for free), which enhanced the economic prospects of the individual white masters and the collective white nation (Freedman, 2013; Hunter, 2005; Smith, 2005). These are only two examples of the counterhistories that surface when we explore and expose less comforting, but perhaps truer, majoritarian stories of sexual violence.

Grounding sexual violence in history is not an attempt to sensationalize the act. Instead, we urge all educators to work toward a better understanding of the embedded histories of sexual violence and to use this understanding to inform their work on campus. Understanding history is important because history continues to construct and influence the macrolevel systems of domination that influence microlevel experiences with sexual violence on campus (see Chapter 2). For instance, as described in the previous section, Spelman students were silenced by "respectability politics and expectations that Black women stand in solidarity with Black men" (Badejo, 2016, para. 6). These macrolevel systems, respectability and solidarity, are embedded in the history and long-standing expectations of the Black community and continue to influence Black women's experiences with sexual violence (Badejo, 2016; Collins, 2005; White, 2001; for more on respectability politics, see Chapter 6).

An ahistoric approach not only covers up the historical influences on identity-specific experiences but also glosses over the root causes of sexual violence. If educators do not consider the roots of sexual violence, the chances of eradicating this form of violence are compromised. Ahistoricism contributes to perspectives that position sexual violence as a new phenomenon. Media, scholars, and institutional actors perpetuate this ahistoricism, asserting that sexual violence is an "epidemic" (Durney, Shepardson, & Carey, 2015, p. 678) or something new affecting college communities because it is unique and uncommon, yet upsetting. Negating the history of sexual violence obstructs our ability to see how sexual violence is intertwined in the foundation of many U.S. institutions, compromising educators' ability to root out this endemic act of terrorization. Sexual violence is not new; it is not a wave or an epidemic that is here today and gone tomorrow. Exploring the history of sexual violence allows us to expose how this act of violence was always and continues to be about power, dominance, privilege, and colonization.

Identity- and power-neutral approaches build on ahistoricism to contribute to ineffective strategies for addressing sexual violence. Educators frequently strive to develop inclusive programs that meet the needs of and highlight the experiences of all students. Completely inclusive programming is nearly impossible. No program can meet the needs of all students or represent all students' experiences. There is no one-size-fits-all approach to addressing sexual violence. When educators and policymakers strive to create a policy or program that incorporates all students, we fail.

Iverson explores this failure in Chapter 11, citing the identity-neutral policies and practices that fail to address power, privilege, and identity-specific experiences. Instead of creating programs designed for all students at once, we advocate for educators to consider explicitly addressing multiple forms of identity in their work and consider developing programs that focus on specific populations. For example, instead of tokenizing and adding one man or one person of color to a program or poster, why not create an entire program dedicated to examining gender identity and sexual orientation as it relates to sexual violence? Identity-specific programming results in centering a particular population rather than adding it on in educational programs. Focusing on a particular population does not take away from understanding the broad issues of sexual violence; in fact, it contributes to better understanding of sexual violence. When students and educators are aware of the multiple ways people experience sexual violence, they will likely become more informed on their own experiences as well. Identity-specific programming also provides educators with the ability to create programs focused on cisgender heterosexual white women who do, in fact, experience assault in unique ways that are frequently portrayed as the norm. By naming issues unique to specific populations, we create opportunities to name and describe ways that dominant groups' experiences are not the norm yet are still important to consider. Once educators account for history, and challenge ahistoricism, this knowledge can be used to get at the root systems of sexual violence. A historic, power-centered, and identity-conscious approach to sexual violence changes our approaches to research and practice, which, hopefully, changes the prevalence of sexual violence on campus.

Proactive Prevention and Reactive Prevention

Sexual violence awareness, prevention, and response are frequently conflated in higher education. In the current climate of urgency and fear, educators and administrators spend a significant amount of resources on response to sexual violence after it happens. Although culturally appropriate, power-conscious, survivor-centered response is of importance, it is not the same as prevention and should not be framed as such. Some argue that effective response is prevention because perpetrators of sexual violence will be deterred from committing sexual violence; we contend we are a long way from that reality. Furthermore, focusing on addressing sexual violence after it happens is not prevention. Prevention focuses on intervening with potential perpetrators, who are the only people who can end sexual violence. However, we take this argument one step further. We argue that we must shift the unilateral focus from preventing and responding to sexual violence to eradicating sexual violence altogether. We must spend more energy on *proactive* prevention instead of *reactive* prevention. The aim of prevention should be to eradicate the root causes of sexual violence and the act of sexual violence, rather than focus on how to respond when sexual violence occurs. Additionally, intersectionality and the history of sexual violence should inform this proactive stance on prevention. When historical and contemporary interlocking systems of domination are accounted for in proactive prevention, we may be better equipped to dismantle the root causes that lead to the continuation of sexual violence on college campuses.

Proactive prevention focuses on addressing the culture around sexual violence, all of the pieces of oppression that contribute to the existence of sexual violence. Specifically, by addressing oppression as the root of sexual violence, along with all other forms of oppression, we will eradicate sexual violence rather than need to prevent it. Reactive prevention is what we currently do. Right now we function as though sexual violence is always going to exist, as though the realities of our culture are such that it will never cease to exist and this is how we must function. Sexual violence prevention programming on college campuses frequently centers on programs to raise awareness among potential victims of sexual violence to reduce their risks of being victimized or on bystander intervention programs, designed to teach people how to intervene in potential sexual assault situations, rather than address a culture of violence and oppression. As Hong states in Chapter 1, bystander intervention programs "are important to a comprehensive, ongoing campaign to end sexual violence, [but] they are insufficient and do not adequately address the root causes of sexual violence" (p. 30, this volume).

Over the past few decades, educators have engaged in bystander intervention programs designed to educate college students about the dynamics of sexual violence and to help give them skills and strategies to interrupt potential sexual violence behavior. Although this strategy does attempt to address sexual violence by addressing potential perpetrators rather than potential victims, it still presents challenges. Because people still have significant misinterpretations of sexual violence, including who the victims and perpetrators are, bystander intervention has proven ineffective. No study has shown a decrease in sexual violence after educators have instituted a bystander intervention program on a campus (McMahon, 2015). The socialization, misinformation, and entitlement of perpetrators are much stronger than a bystander intervention program can address. When college students subscribe to the myths that white women are most likely to be targeted as victims of sexual violence and that most sexual violence is perpetrated by strangers or men of color, they are not intervening in the right moments. As long as our culture continues to center, praise, and idealize wealthy white college men, believing they would never commit sexual violence, college students will also believe this myth and fail to intervene in situations where an entitled wealthy white man attempts to sexually assault his peer. Students will not intervene in these situations because they have not been socialized to believe that this is what sexual assault violence looks like. They have been socialized to protect wealthy white men because they are the ones with power in our culture, and they need to stay close to people with power so that they can get some of that power.

Additionally, bystander intervention programs generally promote gender-segregated spaces. Bystander intervention programs often focus on men as potential perpetrators and women as potential victims (of men perpetrators). This fails to consider the ways nonbinary people and men are targeted as victims and the agency women have in preventing sexual violence. By setting up a culture in which women need men to protect them from sexual violence by intervening in potential sexual violence situations, we continue to perpetuate problems of patriarchy, genderism, and the myth of who is worth saving (e.g., white women) in U.S. culture.

What if educational programs centered on the realities of historically marginalized communities, helping people better understand the relationship between sexual violence and systems of oppression such as colonization, racism, genderism, and homophobia? What if people understood that sexual violence keeps happening because we, as a culture, protect the most privileged people in society and fail to hold them accountable for sexual violence? What if systems held privileged perpetrators accountable? What would it look like if rich white cisgender heterosexual men were held responsible for sexual violence in the same (or better) ways that men of color, poor men, and queer men were held accountable for sexual violence?

Addressing sexual violence from a proactive prevention perspective rather than a reactive prevention perspective requires educators to acquire and integrate an understanding of the intersecting roots of oppression in their work. Examining the roots of oppression requires time, energy, and an open mind on the part of all involved.

Complicating Recommendations

As we conclude this book, we recognize the recommendations provided here may seem lofty, theoretical, and impractical; they are certainly not easy to implement. We have had list after list after list of checkbox recommendations from numerous reports over the past 50 years and rates of sexual violence have not budged. We contend that no checkbox solutions will work; sexual violence is much more complex than can be addressed overnight or with a to-do list. Educators must consider the deep, complex, historical issues associated with sexual violence in our communities and address them in very specific and unique ways depending on their campus contexts, the student populations on their campuses, and the resources available to them. Educators, policymakers, students, and other key stakeholders must have a better understanding of the roots of sexual violence to truly eradicate it from college campuses.

We also acknowledge the theoretical nature of our work. A significant number of our contributors are faculty members with active research agendas focused on sexual violence and equity. However, many of these faculty members also have years of experience working as administrators and student affairs educators in higher education, many specifically with survivors of sexual violence. We are cognizant of the challenges of the day-to-day realities of putting strategies like the ones examined here into practice. It is not easy, especially in the urgency of supporting survivors of sexual violence. However, we must try. We need to push against the boundaries of what we know and how we think about sexual violence on college campuses. By pushing against the boundaries, we may make progress or see new ideas we had not yet considered.

In response to those who find our recommendations theoretical, we ask, for whom? Although these ideas may seem theoretical to some, to many, they are daily, lived experiences of oppression and marginalization. Theory exists to explain, name, and address human experiences (hooks, 1994). If these ideas seem too theoretical or impractical to you, we ask you to consider why. Are they impractical or theoretical because they are not your own experiences? What does that mean in the context of engaging in sexual violence work? What might you do to better understand and work with experiences different from your own?

References

Badejo, A. (2016, January 21). *What happens when women at historically Black colleges report their assaults.* Retrieved from www.buzzfeed.com/anitabadejo/where-is-that-narrative#.jlLeN4605

Cabrera, N. L. (2012). Exposing whiteness in higher education: White male college students minimizing racism, claiming victimization, and recreating White supremacy. *Race Ethnicity and Education, 17*(1), 1–26.

Carbado, D. W., Crenshaw, K. W., Mays, V. M., & Tomlinson, B. (2013). Intersectionality: Mapping the movements of a theory. *Du Bois Review, 10*, 303–312.

Collins, P. H. (2005). *Black sexual politics: African Americans, gender, and the new racism.* New York, NY: Routledge.

Crenshaw, K. (1989). Demarginalizing the intersection of race and sex: A Black feminist critique of antidiscrimination doctrine, feminist theory, and antiracist politics. *University of Chicago Legal Forum, 1*, 139–167.

Crenshaw, K. (1991). Mapping the margins: Intersectionality, identity politics and violence against women of color. *Stanford Law Review, 43*, 1241–1299.

Curran, T. M., Monahan, J. L., Samp, J. A., Coles, V. B., DiClemente, R. J., & Sales, J. (2016). Sexual risk among African American women: Psychological factors and the mediating role of social skills. *Communication Quarterly.* Advance online publication. doi:10.1080/01463373.2015.1132241

Freedman, E. B. (2013). *Redefining rape: Sexual violence in the era of suffrage and segregation.* Cambridge, MA: Harvard University Press.

Harper, S. R., & Hurtado, S. (2007). Nine themes in campus racial climates and implications for institutional transformation. *New Directions for Student Services, 120*, 7–24.

Hipp, T. N., Bellis, A. L., Goodnight, B. L., Brennan, C. L., Swartout, K. M., & Cook, S. L. (2015). Justifying sexual assault: Anonymous perpetrators speak out online. *Psychology of Violence.* Advance online publication. doi:10.1037/a0039998

hooks, b. (1994). *Teaching to transgress: Education as the practice of freedom.* New York, NY: Routledge.

Hunter, M. L. (2005). *Race, gender, and the politics of skin tone.* New York, NY: Routledge.

Littleton, H. L., & Dodd, J. C. (2016). Violent attacks and damaged victims: An exploration of the rape scripts of European American and African American U.S. college women. *Violence Against Women.* Advance online publication. doi:10.1177/1077801216631438

Mangan, K. (2016, February 8). A closer look at 7 common requirements in resolved federal sex-assault inquiries. *The Chronicle of Higher Education.* Retrieved from www.chronicle.com/article/A-Closer-Look-at-7-Common/235220

McMahon, S. (2015). Call for research on bystander intervention to prevent sexual violence: The role of campus environments. *American Journal of Community Psychology, 55*, 472–489.

Odem, J. (2016, March 23). *To Black men who have survived sexual assault: We have to speak up.* Retrieved from www.theroot.com/articles/culture/2016/03/to_black_men_who_have_survived_sexual_assault_we_have_to_speak_up.2.html

Patterson, J. (2016). *Queering sexual violence: Radical voices from within the antiviolence movement.* Riverdale, NY: Riverdale Avenue Books.

Patton, L. D. (2015). Disrupting postsecondary prose: Toward a critical race theory of higher education. *Urban Education, 51*(3), 1–28.

Smith, A. (2005). *Conquest: Sexual violence and American Indian genocide.* Cambridge, MA: South End Press.

Thornton-Dill, B., & Zambrana, R. E. (2009). Critical thinking about inequality: An emerging lens. In B. Thornton-Dill & R. E. Zambrana (Eds.), *Emerging intersections: Race, class, and gender in theory, policy, and practice* (pp. 1–21). New Brunswick, NJ: Rutgers University Press.

Wanjuki, W. (2016, March 14). *What it's really like to be a survivor in the public eye.* Retrieved from www.theestablishment.co/2016/03/14/what-its-really-like-being-a-survivor-in-the-public-eye-lady-gaga-oscars

White, E. F. (2001). *Dark continent of our bodies: Black feminism & politics of respectability.* Philadelphia, PA: Temple University Press.

Wilder, C. S. (2013). *Ebony and ivy: Race, slavery, and the troubled history of America's universities.* New York, NY: Bloomsbury.

Zugazaga, C., Werner, D., Clifford, J. E., Weaver, G. S., & Ware, A. (2016). Increasing personal safety on campus: Implementation of a new personal security system on a university campus. *College Student Affairs Journal, 34*(1), 33–47.

EDITORS AND CONTRIBUTORS

Karla L. Aguilar graduated with her master's degree in social work from the University of Southern California, concentrating in community organization, planning, and administration. Her passion for prevention of and intervention in sexual and other interpersonal-based violence has led her to organize and implement several on-campus programs, policies, and training events that have examined the impact of violence through the lenses of gender, race, advocacy, and social justice. She has served as a community case manager, and a sexual assault advocate, and currently she is Project S.A.F.E.'s survivor advocate and program manager, where she oversees prevention and intervention education, services, and outreach. Aguilar is certified in domestic violence intervention and in her free time volunteers as a certified sexual assault counselor/advocate at Peace Over Violence, a rape crisis and domestic violence agency in the Los Angeles metro area.

Jason C. Garvey is assistant professor of higher education and student affairs at the University of Vermont. He received his PhD in college student personnel administration from the University of Maryland with a certificate in measurement, statistics, and evaluation. Garvey's research examines student affairs and college classroom contexts with a focus on assessing and quantifying student experiences, with particular attention to people with marginalized sexual and gender identities. Prior to his faculty appointment, Garvey worked in student services in a variety of functional areas, including lesbian, gay, bisexual, transgender, and queer student advocacy; student affairs research and assessment; academic advising; and undergraduate research.

Jessica C. Harris is assistant professor of higher education and organizational change at the University of California, Los Angeles. Her research explores interlocking systems of domination that influence the experiences of people of color in higher education. Harris's recent research topics center on multiraciality within higher education, women of color and sexual violence at historically white institutions, and critical race theory in education. Her research endeavors are political choices informed by her personal experiences. Prior to becoming a faculty member, Jessica worked with race-oriented student services and housing and residential education at three different college campuses.

Jessi Hitchins is founding director of the Gender and Sexuality Resource Center at University of Nebraska Omaha. She is also a doctoral candidate at the University of Alabama in the Department of Social and Cultural Studies in the College of Education. She holds graduate certificates in qualitative research and women's studies, a master's degree in college student personnel administration, and a bachelor's degree in social science secondary education. She has nearly a decade of practitioner experience in higher education and community outreach through various roles in women, gender, sexuality/LGBTQIA+, and victim/survivor advocacy centers; reproductive justice health work; and multicultural offices.

Luoluo Hong, a campus rape survivor, is now vice president for student affairs and enrollment management and Title IX coordinator at San Francisco State University. She has worked toward sexual violence prevention since 1990 and in higher education leadership since 1992, including as dean of students at University of Wisconsin–Madison, dean of student affairs at the west campus of Arizona State University, and vice chancellor for student affairs at the University of Hawaii at Hilo. In her free time, Hong can occasionally be found masquerading as a Level 100 human warlock in World of Warcraft. She resides with two rambunctious felines: Phoenix and Comet.

Susan V. Iverson is professor of higher education leadership at Manhattanville College. Iverson's research interests focus on equity and diversity, status of women in higher education, feminist pedagogy, and the role of policy (e.g., sexual violence) in shaping perceptions and culture. She has two coedited volumes: *Feminist Community Engagement: Achieving Praxis* (Palgrave Macmillan, 2014) and *Reconstructing Policy Analysis in Higher Education: Feminist Poststructural Perspectives* (Routledge, 2010). Prior to becoming a faculty member, Iverson worked in student affairs administration for more than 10 years. Iverson earned her doctorate in higher educational leadership with a concentration in women's studies from the University of Maine.

Chris Linder is assistant professor of college student affairs administration and an affiliate faculty member with the Institute for Women's Studies at the University of Georgia. Prior to becoming a faculty member, Linder served as the director of a campus-based women's center, where she dedicated a significant portion of her career to supporting survivors of sexual violence. Linder's research centers on creating and maintaining equitable campus environments, with a specific focus on race and gender. In her recent work, Linder has focused on sexual violence on college campuses in the United States, including the role of campus activists in elevating sexual violence to the national agenda and examining the intersection of racism and sexual violence in historical and contemporary contexts.

Susan B. Marine is assistant professor and program director of the higher education graduate program at Merrimack College. Active in the movement to end sexual violence on college campuses she has served as a victim advocate, prevention educator, and policy consultant to numerous universities and community agencies for the past two decades. Her research interests include feminist praxis in the academy and the advancement of lesbian, gay, bisexual, transgender, and queer student visibility and agency. She is the author of *Stonewall's Legacy: Bisexual, Gay, Lesbian and Transgender Students in Higher Education* (Jossey-Bass, 2011).

Elizabeth McDonald is currently a residence life coordinator with University Student Housing at Texas Tech University. She received her master's degree in higher education administration from the University of Alabama in 2015, where her mentors included Jason C. Garvey and Jessi Hitchins, also contributors to this volume. She also holds a bachelor's degree in history from the University of South Alabama. McDonald's background is in housing and residence life, gender and women's resources, and fraternity and sorority life. She is originally from Alabama.

LaVerne McQuiller Williams is chair and professor of criminal justice at the Rochester Institute of Technology. She earned her PhD in sociology from the University of Buffalo, her JD from Albany Law School, and her MS in criminal justice from Buffalo State College. Her research centers on intimate partner violence among underrepresented populations, human trafficking, and restorative justice.

Jess S. Myers is director of the Women's Center at the University of Maryland, Baltimore County (UMBC). She received her master's degree in student affairs and higher education with a certificate in women's studies from Colorado State University in 2010. Jess has 10 years of experience working in higher education and has spent the past several years dedicated to advocating for and supporting women and marginalized student groups. Her current research focuses on campus-based sexual assault activism.

Naddia Cherre Palacios has 10 years' experience in sexual violence prevention, equity, and diversity work. She has developed programs on issues of identity, access, gender, social justice, and sexual violence intervention. Naddia earned a BA in Latin American studies from San Diego State University, an MEd in postsecondary administration and student affairs from the

University of Southern California, and is a trained sexual assault and domestic violence counselor and advocate. She is currently director and advocate for campus advocacy, resources, and education at the University of California Riverside. She resides in Southern California with her partner, Ramon, and children, Santiago and Isabella.

Ciera V. Scott is staff psychologist at George Mason University Counseling and Psychological Services in Fairfax, Virginia. Scott earned her PhD in counseling psychology from the University of Georgia. Her professional interests include trauma in minority populations; specifically sexual assault, interpersonal and relationship violence, and childhood maltreatment. Scott is passionate about conducting outreach with historically marginalized and oppressed populations. In her clinical work, she integrates cognitive-behavioral and interpersonal therapeutic approaches through a multicultural and feminist lens.

Anneliese A. Singh is associate dean of diversity and equity in the College of Education at the University of Georgia. She is a past president of the Association of Lesbian, Gay, Bisexual, and Transgender Issues in Counseling, where her initiatives included the development of counseling competencies for working with transgender clients in counseling; supporting queer people of color; and ensuring safe schools for lesbian, gay, bisexual, queer, and questioning youth. Singh has been honored with more than 11 national awards for her work in community building. She also founded the Trans Resilience Project to translate findings from her more than 10 years of research on the resilience that transgender people develop to navigate societal oppression. She actively works on being a better ally to transgender people and developing empowering spaces for people of color who have survived sexual abuse and has worked on initiatives to end child sexual abuse in South Asian/Indian communities. She is a Sikh American and passionately believes in and strives to live by the ideals of Martin Luther King Jr.'s beloved community as well as Audre Lorde's statement, "Without community, there is no liberation."

Daniel Tillapaugh is an assistant professor of counselor education in the Graduate School of Education at California Lutheran University. Prior to becoming a full-time faculty member, he worked as a student affairs administrator for 10 years. His research interests revolve around intersectionality and college student development; lesbian, gay, bisexual, transgender, and queer issues in higher education; and college men and masculinities and leadership development and education. Dan is passionate about engaging in research that makes a difference in students' lives. He served as chair for the Coalition on Men and Masculinities for ACPA–College Student Educators International.

Wagatwe Wanjuki is a feminist activist, writer, speaker, and digital strategist best known for her work as a national campus anti-violence advocate. She's a founder of the antirape organization Survivors Eradicating Rape Culture and is a founding co-organizer of Know Your IX's ED ACT NOW campaign. Her writing and work has been featured in outlets including MSNBC, *The Establishment, ESSENCE magazine, and the New York Times.*

career to have a baby. Excellent bibliography and list of disciplinary and other extra-university resources for change make this book an invaluable resource for all faculty or students looking for insight into strategies for real inclusivity. Highly recommended."—*Choice*

Sty/us

22883 Quicksilver Drive
Sterling, VA 20166-2102   Subscribe to our e-mail alerts: www.Styluspub.com

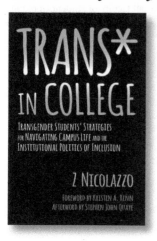

Trans* in College
Transgender Students' Strategies for Navigating Campus Life and the Institutional Politics of Inclusion
Z Nicolazzo
Foreword by Kristen A. Renn
Afterword by Stephen John Quaye

"*Trans* in College* is a beautifully written, rigorous, and masterful insight into the lives of nine trans* collegians at City University [a pseudonym] and how postsecondary educators can do better to support the education, resilience practices, and life chances for trans* collegians. Through the use of critical theoretical frameworks and methodologies that begin from the experiences and needs of the participants, Nicolazzo also demonstrates new possibilities for both the doing and the reporting of research in higher education. As a scholar, I look forward to sharing this book with future graduate students as an example of how we can proliferate possibilities through and for scholarship. As a trans* parent of a trans* child, I am unspeakably grateful to the nine trans* collegians who have collaborated with Nicolazzo to create together this beautiful reflection of us."—**Dafina-Lazarus Stewart**, *Higher Education and Student Affairs, Bowling Green State University*

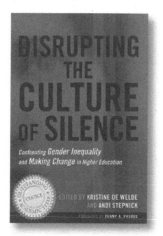

Disrupting the Culture of Silence
Confronting Gender Inequality and Making Change in Higher Education
Edited by Kristine De Welde and Andi Stepnick
Foreword by Penny A. Pasque

"Engagingly written and rich in formal data and telling anecdote, this sociologically smart collection will be an important tool for graduate students and faculty confronting what remains a male-biased system of higher education. The editors draw on their own interviews with women in many academic disciplines and enlist other researchers and activists to provide a rich and deep look at gendered experiences in academia today. Commendably, the editors give strong representation to women of color, disabled women, and lesbians in defining how 'women' experience (and overcome) diverse challenges. Variation among disciplines and between institutions is also highlighted. The beauty of the volume emerges most in its telling details: e.g., the problematic idea that 'just say no' to service work is a feasible organizational strategy; the value in changing policy rather than seeking *ad hoc* accommodations; the self-contradictory advice about when in an academic

(Continues on previous page)